Modern Poetry in Translation
New Series / No.18

European Voices

Edited by Daniel Weissbort

Published by
KING'S COLLEGE LONDON
University of London
Strand, London WC2R 2LS

Modern Poetry in Translation
No. 18, New Series
© Modern Poetry in Translation 2001
ISBN 0-9533824-4-3
ISSN 0969-3572
Typeset by Wendy Pank
Printed and bound in Great Britain by Short Run Press, Exeter

Editor:
Daniel Weissbort

Manuscripts, with copies of the original texts, should be sent to the Editor and cannot be returned unless accompanied by a self-addressed and stamped envelope or by international reply coupons. Wherever possible, translators should obtain copyright clearance. Submission on 3.5" disk (preferably Macintosh formatted, in MSWord or RTF) is welcomed.

Advisory Editors:
Michael Hamburger, Tomislav Longinović, Arvind Krishna Mehrotra, Norma Rinsler, Douglas Robinson, Anthony Rudolf
Managing Editor: Norma Rinsler

Subscription Rates: (two issues, surface mail)
UK and EC   £20.00   post free
Overseas   £24.00 / US$36.00 post free

Sterling or US dollars *payable to King's College London*
Send to:
MPT, The School of Humanities,
King's College London,
Strand,
London WC2R 2LS

Represented in UK by Signature Book Representation
Sunhouse, 2 Little Peter Street, Manchester M15 4PS
Distributed by Littlehampton Book Services
tel 01903 828800, fax 01903 828801.

Contents

5 **To the Reader** / Daniel Weissbort

European Voices

7 **Apollinaire** / tr. Martin Bennett
9 **Bernardo Atxaga** / tr. Amaia Gabantxo
15 **Yves Bonnefoy** / tr. Michael Edwards
17 **Volker Braun** / tr. David Constantine
25 **Camões** / tr. William Baer
27 **Cavafy** / tr. David Black
30 **Paul Celan** / tr. Michael Hamburger
36 **William Cliff** / tr. James Kirkup
42 **MM Dizdar** / tr. Natalija Boni
46 **Johanna Ekström** / tr. Sarah Death
49 **HM Enzensberger** / tr. Richard Dove
50 **Gerhard Fritsch** / tr. William Stone and Anthony Vivis
53 **Goethe** / tr. Ken Cockburn and by Tessa Ransford
57 **Heine** / tr. WD Jackson
72 **Hédi Kaddour** / tr. Marilyn Hacker
74 **Uwe Kolbe** / tr. Michael Hamburger
77 **Reiner Kunze** / tr. Robin Fulton
80 **H Leyvik** / tr. Richard Fein
83 **Antonio Machado** / tr. Paul Burns and Salvadore Ortiz Carboneres
87 **Mallarmé and Verlaine** / tr. James Kirkup
92 **Claire Malroux** / tr. Marilyn Hacker
95 **Mayakovsky** / tr. Augustus Young
100 **Eugenio Montale** / tr. Andrew Fitzsimons
107 **Henrik Nordbrandt** / tr. Robin Fulton
111 **Boris Pasternak** / tr. Angela Livingstone
121 **Cesare Pavese** / tr. Martin Bennett
124 **Cesare Pavese** / tr. Marco Sonzogni and David Wheatley
127 **Halina Poświatowska** / tr. Anna Gąienica-Byrcyn
131 **Pushkin** / tr. Stanley Mitchell
147 **Pushkin** / tr. Timothy Ades
148 **Salvatore Quasimodo** / tr. Marco Sonzogni and Gerald Dawe
152 **Jacques Réda** / tr. Jennie Feldman
154 **Umberto Saba** / tr. Simon Carnell and by Robert Chandler
157 **Egon Schiele** / tr. Will Stone and Anthony Vivis
159 **Antun Branko Simic** / tr. Courtney Angela Brkic
161 **Paul Snoek** / tr. Kendall Dunkelberg
165 **Luís Amorim de Sousa** / tr. by the poet and by Marc Widershier and Alberto de Lacerda

169 **Alain Suied** / tr. Steve Light
172 **Jesper Svenbro** / tr. John Matthias, Lars-Håkan Svensson and Göran Printz-Påhlson
178 **Lőrinc Szabó** / tr. George Held and Katherine Mayer
180 **Jan Twardowski** / tr. Sarah Lawson and Małgorzata Koraszewska, and by Ryszard Reisner
183 **Giuseppi Ungaretti** / tr. Andrew Fitzsimons, by Stuart Flynn and by Andrew Frisardi
187 **Mihai Ursachi** / Adam Sorkin with Ileana Orlich, Georgiana Farnoaga and Doru Motz
192 **Liliana Ursu** / Michael Naydan, Tess Gallagher and the poet
196 **Paul Valéry** / James Kirkup
199 **Aleksandr Wat** / Frank L Vigoda
220 **Mehmet Yashin** / Taner Baybars
224 **Andrea Zanzotto** / Andrew Fitzsimons

Plus
225 **Ten lyrics from the Greek Anthology** / John Wareham
228 **Three Polish Poets** / Ryszard Reisner
232 **Three Russian Poets** / Steven Capus

Featured translator:
236 **Peter Viereck** by Daniel Weissbort

Review article:
259 **Jonathan Wilcox**
Beowulf: A New Translation by Seamus Heaney
Beowulf: A New Verse Translation by RM Liuzza

Review:
274 **Marianna Spanak**
The Free Besieged and other poems by Dionysios Solomos

276 **Books Received**

To The Reader

After "Mother Tongues", "European Voices". *MPT* seems to have become a little myopic perhaps! But as a New York friend of mine told me, the great Yiddish fiction writer Isaac Bashevis Singer once advised her: Never go anywhere! Of course, Singer himself had left Poland, thank goodness, but once ensconced in New York, he rarely travelled further than Long Island. The biggest adventures are to be had at home, since our present selves rather than projected ones are engaged. The Mother Tongues issue taught us residents at *MPT* a great deal, and the readings in Sheffield, Oxford, Cambridge and London, organized with such flare by our publicist Sian Williams, made it clear how worth while the venture had been. Not only were we given a glimpse of the great range of literatures in England, but also these writings were placed in the context of the whole rather than, as so often hitherto, appearing as local manifestations.

"European Voices" makes no attempt to represent the poetries of Europe today – how could it? – but gathers material that has come to us over a period of a year or so. Some 17 languages are represented, of Eastern, Central, Western, Southern and Northern Europe. On display are translations ranging from Classical Greek (from the Greek Anthology) to quite recent poetry, as well as re-translations of major European poets (Goethe, Verlaine, Pasternak, Montale . . .). The proper business of magazines, I think, is to be as eclectic as is consistent with the tastes of the editors, to showcase work in progress and to encourage experimental work. With *MPT* this would include new translations of the much translated, since we have always interpreted "Modern" as referring to the translations rather than to the source texts themselves. Magazines also often try to provide something of a platform for those writers they wish to keep in the public eye, as for instance, in our case, with James Kirkup, an astonishingly versatile and adventurous translator (his work was featured in *MPT* 11, summer 1997). Kirkup continues not only to translate major poets, like Verlaine and Mallarmé, but also to introduce new talents, discovered by him on his travels. Such dedication to the larger life of literature is, we believe, to be celebrated.

In the same spirit, the present issue contains a feature on the American poet, teacher, historian, translator Peter Viereck. Like Kirkup, in his eighties, Viereck too has always lived in that larger world of literature. The actual location of the writer is less important than a continuing commitment to language as such. Joseph Brodsky, who was a close friend of Viereck, once remarked that wherever he was, Leningrad, New York, South Hadley, Mass., the gesture he made as he reached for a dictionary was the same. Which is not to say, of course, that one is indifferent to one's surroundings or that one accepts with equanimity exile or marginalisation of whatever sort.

A friend of mine remarked to me that the trouble with *MPT* was that it contained too much material, that the mixture was simply too rich! This may be so. I suspect that the reason for this tendency to produce an embarras de choix goes back to our early days, when we were more or less on our own in the field. We didn't know how long we would last, and certainly had no thought of lasting for close on forty years! Ted Hughes had wanted the magazine to be, as he put it: "an airport for incoming translations". We were its somewhat delirious air-traffic controllers, but the flights magically sorted themselves out, without collisions! So, we got as much into print as we could each time we were able to produce an issue. In any case, there seemed no end of worthwhile material. Somehow the cornucopia seemed inexhaustible (I suppose that is the nature of cornucopias!). Probably this was because, as we advanced into these virgin territories, more and more was revealed and, along with it, a number of dedicated lone translators who'd been there long before us, of course. As a member of the Poetry International Committee of the early 70s, I remember being shocked when it was suggested that by now we had invited all the best foreign poets and there was no one left to invite; if we continued, we'd have to ask them all again!

So, is there, in fact, too much in each issue? The danger, I suppose, is that with such a wealth of material competing for attention, many items might simply go unnoticed. I don't believe this. At least, I myself am always coming across items in old issues of magazines that I missed first time round. Either they were too softly spoken for me at the time, or I just wasn't ready for them. But once in print, at least, a poem has a chance of being noticed.

Anyway, we will keep up the barrage for as long as we can! As I survey the contents of the present issue I am once more struck by the eclecticism of the "translation scene". So many people, often working in isolation or at least unaware of each other's activities; I hope that the magazine also helps to spread a sense of common endeavour. The destructive polarities of today make ours just as much an "age of anxiety". Meanwhile, translators labour on. America used to be spoken of as a melting pot. But Europe, too, is a melting pot. At least translators make it seem so. The eternal question for them is how to celebrate diversity while facilitating "intertraffic" between languages and cultures. It is no exaggeration to say, though, that the body lives only while its blood circulates.

Daniel Weissbort

Apollinaire
France

Translated by Martin Bennett

Martin Bennett *translates from French and Italian, and contributed translations of poems by Primo Levi, Pasolini, Pavese, Quasimodo and Ungaretti to* MPT *15* (Contemporary Italian Poets).

Five poems from **Le Bestiaire**

Caterpillar

Work leads to wealth and getting.
Let us poor poets also try:
A caterpillar by fretting, fretting,
Becomes the rich butterfly.

Serpent

Beauty, that's what you prefer:
Ah, the women that feature
On your hit-list: Cleopatra,
Eve, Eurydice, others to whom I'll not refer,
Though I still know three or four.

Mouse

Beautiful days, o mouse of time,
So you nibble my life away.
God, I'll soon be twenty-nine,
Nothing to show but regrets and joy.

Elephant

An elephant has got its ivory
But I also have a treasury
In my mouth ... Words precious
As the grandest tusks ...

Peacock

Raising a wheel in the air
With its otherwise drooping tail
Makes this bird lovelier still,
Though it uncovers its derrière.

Bernardo Atxaga
Spain (Basque language)

Translated by Amaia Gabantxo

Bernardo Atxaga, *born in 1951, is well known in Spain, where he is considered one of the most innovative of European writers. His poems were published in several collections in Basque, and collected in a bilingual Basque/Spanish edition,* Poemas & híbridos *(reprinted four times, most recently in 1990). His novels, originally written in Basque, have been translated by Margaret Jull Costa from his own Spanish versions; the latest to be published (Harvill, 1999) is* The Lone Woman. *The poems here date from the late seventies and early eighties, and have been translated directly from Basque.*

Amaia Gabantxo, *born in the Basque country in 1973, holds an MA in Literary Translation from the University of East Anglia, and is currently editing and translating an anthology of Basque literature, including work by writers in the three languages of the Basque country: Basque, Spanish and French. She writes: 'As far as I am aware, there have been no previous attempts to translate literature written in Basque directly into English ... this is precisely the gap I try to fill'.*

The Tale of the Hedgehog

In his nest of dry leaves the hedgehog has woken
his mind so suddenly filled with all the words he knows.
Counting the verbs, more or less, they come to twenty-seven.

Later he thinks: The winter is over,
I am a hedgehog, Up fly two eagles, high up,
Snail, Worm, Insect, Spider, Frog,
which ponds or holes are you hiding in?
There is the river, This is my kingdom, I am hungry.

And he repeats: This is my kingdom, I am hungry,
Snail, Worm, Insect, Spider, Frog,
which ponds or holes are you hiding in?

However he remains still like a dry leaf, too,
because it is but midday and an old law
forbids him sun, sky and eagles.

But night comes, gone are the eagles; and the hedgehog,
Snail, Worm, Insect, Spider, Frog,
disregards the river and undertakes the steepness of the mountain,
as sure of his spines as a warrior
in Sparta or Corinth could have been of his shield;
and suddenly, he crosses the boundary
between the meadow and the new road
with a single step that takes him right into my and your time.
And given that his universal vocabulary has not been renewed
in the last seven thousand years,
he neither understands our car lights,
nor realises his forthcoming death.

Bizitzak (Life)

Life knows only
thorny extremes.
When not Jungle
Desert.
It dreams no more.

And so, this September of
Red Ferns,
wants only
Snow,
and Wolf,
aims at being bare,
frozen Immensity.

And Sun dreams
of Light pure and sharp,
blinding memory
of Bees.

While Night
remembers fondly
that first moment
of only night.

And so
Never, Never,
or,

Always, Always,
loudly beats my Heart.
Measuring,
against those two words, unfortunately,
all desires.

Four Snowfalls

The first time the snow arrived early in the morning, and the flakes came to rest on the ground slowly, so slowly, like butterflies, or rather, like butterflies that had fallen asleep, and the old woman who used to take care of us back then looked out of the kitchen window and they'll say there is no God, she laughed in delight, and that delighted laughter arose from her profound faith, like fire from embers. And then, like a conductor cueing an orchestra, she raised her hand to the top of her apron and began the silence that was quietly so quietly covering everything, and then we too, my brother, my sister, all three of us, never leaving the window, or quite the opposite, moving even closer to the window, fell silent like moles, birds, wild boars and mountain tigers, silent like the madman always screaming, silent like the delivery boy always whistling, and even the angels stopped playing their trumpets, and the bell-ringers released the bell-ropes, and in the gypsy camp too the violin and drum were returned to their cases, and the school emptied, and the carpenter's too, and the butcher's, and in the end everything, but everything was left empty, still and quiet, our town, province, country, France, Sweden, and Asia, and the planets, Venus, Mars, Jupiter, Pluto, everything, but everything was left empty, still and quiet until the end of the movement. And when it finished, the old woman that used to take care of us repeated again and they'll say there is no God pointing at the snowflakes like butterflies, and at that very moment two dogs began barking and pirouetting in the snow, and the church bell ringing, and the madman screaming, and the delivery boy whistled his tune over and over, and the gypsies danced, and the school teacher also danced, and the carpenter went to the baker's for bread, and the baker went to the carpenter's for a plank of wood, and our town, our province, our country and all the other countries, our planet and all the other planets, all those places awoke from their stupor and returned to their everyday lives, and we too, my brother, my sister, all three of us, put our coats on and went out, to slide on the sledge, or play with the dogs, or dance with the teacher.

Twenty years later, the snow appeared on the upper pane of the window, and a woman got out of bed completely naked and, oh look, she said, it is snowing after all, the weather man on TV was right, and at that exact moment the snow seemed to flicker around her hair, or so it appeared at least, the flakes creating an aura that turned her into one of those queens in an astrology magazine, and, oh, how white everything is, she sighed, that mountain in front of us looks like whipped cream. I pushed the sheets and covers aside and looked out of the window too, and realised the sky looked leaden, and that for once the chatterbox had got it completely right and that we would have snow for a few days or perhaps a week. We're a bit isolated in this cabin, I said. Fantastic, she answered. Come, come here, I said, come to bed so we don't get cold, how beautiful the snow is, how beautiful winter, how beautiful you are with your two little mounds that look like whipped cream.

Twenty years later, the snow arrived all of a sudden, with daybreak once again, and before I realised the roof of the car and the windows were covered in snow, and the temperature inside was steadily dropping. Moments later, as I reached a slope I'd never noticed before, my wheels started to skid and I ended up on the side of the road trapped in the midst of a white tornado. I switched the radio on. Don't go out on the roads, said the reporter, don't go out on the roads without making the necessary telephone enquiries first, or better still, stay calmly at home listening to our programme. I switched the radio off. Opened the window a few centimetres and looked out. Not a thing in sight, not even a lorry. I was alone. As in a dream, I felt everything in my life began to fade away. My wife, my children, my job, my opinions, everything seemed foreign to me. I tried to make the windscreen-wipers work, but to no avail. The snow had almost covered the car. It began snowing even more heavily, the snowflakes were now grey, as if made of ash. I switched the radio on. Don't go out, said the reporter right then, take my advice, don't go out on the roads all morning. I swore to myself that if I didn't die of the cold I'd find that radio reporter and hit him over the head with a bottle. It seemed a very sensible idea to me: in the event of having to reorganise my life, the wisest starting point I could possibly hope for.

Twenty years later, the snow was two metres high and we were unable to get out of the old-folks home for three days; in the end, bored with doing nothing, I took my walking stick and out I went. The sky was blue, the air cleaner than ever and I slapped my thighs standing in front of a patch of dirty snow that hadn't melted, very soon afterwards I broke my leg when I slipped on a frozen puddle on the pavement and fell over one of those concrete flower pots decorating the doorway. Thankfully, they took me to hospital, or perhaps I should more accurately say they took me to the hospital where they gave me a room all for myself, thankfully, and not sharing with someone else, like in the old-folks home. So, are you getting very bored? asks the nurse every now and then. Not at all, I answer. This room has a very nice view, adds the nurse, you can see the whole city from here. Yes you're right, I say, and stare out of the window until she leaves me alone again. This window for me is the same window in the kitchen of the house where my brother, my sister, all three of us, were born. It is snowing again, and the flakes of snow, looking like butterflies that have fallen asleep, come to rest ever so slowly, and the old woman that takes care of us looks out of the kitchen window and they'll say there is no God, she laughs in delight, and that delighted laughter arises from her profound faith, like fire from embers. And then, like a conductor cueing an orchestra, she raises her hand to the top of her apron and begins the silence that is quietly so quietly covering everything, and then we too, my brother, my sister, all three of us, never leaving the window, or quite the opposite, moving even closer to the window, fall silent like moles, birds, wild boars and mountain tigers, silent like the madman always screaming, silent like the delivery boy always whistling, and even the angels stop playing their trumpets, and the bell-ringers release the bell-ropes, and in the gypsy camp too the violin and drum are returned to their cases, and the school is emptied, and the carpenter's too, and the butcher's, and in the end everything, but everything is left empty, still and quiet, our town, province, country, France, Sweden, and Asia, and the planets, Venus, Mars, Jupiter, Pluto, everything, but everything is left empty, still and quiet . How's that leg doing? I hear all of a sudden. It's the doctor who's looking after me. She's wearing a white coat. Same as usual, I reply, same as usual.

Translating 'Bizitzak' ('Life')

Amaia Gabantxo *writes:* The translation of this poem took some chiselling away of initial translation choices that were too elaborate. In the original Atxaga inhabits the nature of things, an inside outsider. He recollects the thoughts of natures different from his own effortlessly, and reflects on them with ease. 'Bizitzak' opens rather harshly: *'Bizitzak ez du etsitzen / ezpada muga latzetan; / ezpadu Ohianarekin egiten amets, egiten du Desertuarekin'* ('Life will only hold on/ to the harshest of frontiers/ when it doesn't dream of the Jungle/ it dreams of the desert'). It is through the abundance of 'ch' sounds that he achieves this effect. In terms of sound it is a very powerful opening, containing the echo of an important statement.

In my translation I try to maintain that strangeness and sparseness; thus my opening stanza becomes *'Life knows only thorny extremes. / When not Jungle / Desert. / It dreams no more'*. I made up for the lack of harsh sounds with the inclusion of the idea of 'thorny extremes', which I thought was harshly juxtaposed and strange-sounding. The line 'It dreams no more' closes the stanza with a gravitas similar to that of the original text.

In stanzas two, three and four, the poet enumerates his innermost wishes, wishes for the absolute, for September, the Sun, the Night. In stanza five, he confesses to the dogmatism of his heart, which will only accept an 'all or nothing at all' view of life.

As in the hedgehog poem, in 'Bizitzak' Atxaga makes a recipient and ally of Nature. There is a lack of control as to what the poet's own nature is in these two poems. The sparse words, aligned precariously along the page, reflect that instability in the English version. Like September, Sun and Night, the poet wishes for an extreme version of himself, and it is his misfortune that he will not be happy with less.

But it is his own heartbeat that determines this condition.

There is a beautiful achievement in cadence, particularly in the first three lines of the last stanza, for *'egundo ez'* ('never') and *'beti beti'* ('always') evoke the beating of the heart. When coupled with the verb *'esan+ka'* (*'esan'* means 'to say', the suffix *'ka'* implies infinite repetition, and it would be something like 'says and says and says . . .') and placed next to *'Bihotza'* (heart), the image of a heart beating 'never, never' – 'always, always' – 'never, never' – 'always, always' ad infinitum is emphasised. So my solution to this beautiful but problematic image was to reproduce this repetition, literally, in the English poem.

Atxaga uses capitals for all the nouns that people this poem, thus subverting their meaning, their position in the poem; perhaps calling for a more intimate understanding of them: 'Desert' as the essence of the desert? 'Jungle' as the essence of the jungle? The use of capitals implies these are *their names*. This contributes to the sensory tangibility of the poem, to its ability to transcend the page; and thus, at a subconscious level, those capitals become heartbeats.

Yves Bonnefoy
France

Translated by Michael Edwards

Yves Bonnefoy *is widely regarded as France's greatest living poet.* His Hier Régnant Desert, *translated by Anthony Rudolf as* Yesterday's Wilderness Kingdom, *was published by MPT Books in 2000, and his work was featured in MPT 1, the first volume of the New Series.*
    Michael Edwards *studied at Cambridge and is currently holder of the European Chair at the Collège de France in Paris. He has published several collections of poetry, books of literary criticism (including* Towards a Christian Poetics, Poetry and Possibility, Of Making Many Books *– all from Macmillan) and art criticism (*Raymond Mason, Thames and Hudson*).*

Snow, first of the winter, early this morning.
Ochre and green take refuge under the trees.

Another fall, towards midday.
All that survives
Of colour
Is pine needles also falling more thickly at times than the snow.

Then, towards evening,
The flail of the light stops moving.
Shadows and dreams have the same weight.

A soft wind
Writes with its toe a word outside of the world.

The Mirror

Yesterday clouds
Were still passing
On the dark wall of the room.
But the mirror now is blank.

Snowing
        untangles from the sky.

The Plough

Five o'clock. Snowing still. I hear voices
At the front of the world.

A ploughshare, sharp
Like the backward moon,
Shines, and then
Is muffled by night in a fold of the snow.

And now the child
Possesses the whole house. He moves
From window to window. He presses his hand
Against the pane. He sees
Drops form where he ceases to push
The mist outwards to a falling sky.

Summer still

I move through the snow, with closed eyes,
And yet the light knows how to pass
Through porous eyelids, and I see
That in my words there is also snow,
Swirling, massing, drifting apart.

Snow,
A letter one comes across, unfolds,
And the ink has faded, and over the signs
The clumsiness of mind is plain to see,
For merely confusing their lucid shadows.

And one tries to read, but one cannot make out
Who it is in memory that gives heed to us,
Except that summer is here still,
And that one sees
Under the flakes, the leaves, and warmth
Rising like mist from the hidden ground.

Volker Braun
Germany

Translated by David Constantine

Volker Braun *was born in 1939 in Dresden. He worked as a labourer between school and university, then studied philosophy at Leipzig. He was both dramatist and director at the Berliner Ensemble (with Helene Weigel) and at the Deutsches Theater in Berlin. Author of numerous plays, and of volumes of fiction, poetry and essays, he has won many prizes, most recently the prestigious Georg-Büchner-Preis, in 2000.*

David Constantine *was born in 1944 in Salford. He has published several volumes of poetry, and translations of Hölderlin, Goethe and Kleist. Until October 2000 he was Fellow in German at the Queen's College, Oxford.*

Art

She dances on the graves, with grace
With her rogue memory. WE KNOW
WE CAN'T HOLD ON TO ANYTHING. She
Calls up the croaked, the forgotten, them
With their knives and demands. Love
Gone out, anger gone cold, the wasted times. What
Is the thought that we are mortal set against
THE GREAT IN VAIN? She dares to think it
Underground where everything lives. How
Is it possible that things the way they are
Are dancing?

After the Massacre of Illusions

Guevara under the runway with his hands
Hacked off, he doesn't "work i' the earth" any more so now
The ideas are buried
Out come the bones
State funeral FOR FEAR OF RESURRECTION
O Sacred Head Sore Wounded Marketing
FOLLOW YOUR FINE PHRASES
TO THE POINT OF THEIR INCARNATION
Valery Chodemchuk, covered up

In the sarcophagus of the reactor, can wait
How long will the earth endure us
And what shall we call freedom

[1996]

Volker Braun's note: 'FOLLOW YOUR FINE PHRASES' is said by
Deputy Mercier to his fellow prisoners in Act III of Büchner's
Dantons Tod. Danton replies: 'Nowadays they do everything
in human flesh . . . They will use my body too.'

Oysters
(For Alain Lance)

It isn't often I live really, you
For hours now in my kitchen have been opening
The immigrant (with many papers) oysters and
With a hurting hand in a plastic apron

Singing. Take the Wolfs, all they can think
Of nowadays is eating, which they do,
Like everything they do, in depth. They're human beings.
And I, with a lot of lemon, I anaesthetize

The naked little creatures then my palate
And swallow glumly. You meanwhile, with gusto and
Disgust, have slurped two dozen of these
Small cunts of the sea. Well then, I say

Let life melt in the mouth, a life
Between appetite and loathing, yes.

[1973]

Volker Braun's notes: Importing living creatures into the GDR
involved a great deal of paperwork (l. 3). The Wolfs are
Christa and Gerhard Wolf (l. 5).

The Magma in the Heart of the Tuareg

With a German passport landing at Agadir
In the winter sun: a change of identity
Slaves are watching me and thieves
Prowling about my feet, who am I
A nomad in the 4-star hotel, room with a view of the sea
I can choose my season
LEISURE IS EPIDEMIC even in the gear
Of a tourist I'm on the dole and hanging around
In the last-minute lands LIFELONG
The throw-away man, only COCA COLA needs me
The tea-drinkers of Marrakesh have still to be converted
To the global gods, and I
No longer driven to find the place and the solving word
I belong to all the useless peoples.

[1996]

Volker Braun's note: The penultimate line derives from Rimbaud's *Illuminations* ('Vagabonds').

Lagerfeld

Rome: an open city A laager
Down the catwalk troop the fashions
Of the millennium, bulletproof vests
For copulation Two gladiators
Are fighting for the job, long practised
In the tricks of throttling, they win applause
That's what they went to school for HIM OR ME
The stink of fear In his empire
Lagerfeld is making a dream come true A PACK
OF WOMEN THE PICK OF BEAUTY
The winter collection for the wars in Dacia
Has made him rich IT IS ENOUGH TO TURN YOUR STOMACH
They are bearing my ideas, these are summer clothes
To the spoilt world A festival of beauty
Helena Christensen in evening wear Meanwhile
The two craftsmen have not let go
One is Commodus, the wild son
Of a cool father, the mother's indiscretion
When he croaks the throne stands empty

And Septimius Severus the African
Will march with the XIVth from the wilderness of Vienna
Against the capital POOR ROME A barbarian
Emperor On his heels the rest of the world
Lagerfeld doesn't watch He has a problem
He can make them more beautiful but not better
More and more beautiful Outfit of the brute beasts
RICH AND POOR A divided clientele
ATROCIOUS Paying and thieving
I enjoy undivided attention But
He knows what's going on, he isn't blind
The fifteen-year-old killer from Springfield
A MOUNTAIN OF CORPSES IN THE HIGHSCHOOL CAFETERIA
He has learned to lend a hand
He is in custody now in paper clothes
Another fashion From America Gangs of children
Are combing North Rhein-Westphalia trainees
Looking for food at Hertie's and Woolworth's
A light-fingered tribe from the future
In the employment exchanges carrion
Is waiting to be recycled It will wait a long time
Those in work are waiting on machines
The others are waiting to be allowed to wait on something
Legions While the world turns black
As Africa VIOLENCE MUST NOT ONLY BE THREATENED
IT MUST ALSO BE USED The Foreign Office
Inwardly grinning states its position
On Bosnia We'll show you what work is
A machine with limbs sexually neutral
The mannequin for tomorrow's work
AT THE END OF THE DAY YOU ARE JUST ANOTHER PRODUCT
Thinking is, precisely, what I try to avoid
Day after day the covering of paper with print
Custody, to prevent the suicide of the species
I don't read it, I don't watch
A theatre full of equanimity
THE ONLY PLACE I FEEL AT EASE
DESPAIR Kleist on the edge
At Stimming's Inn MY ONE TRIUMPHANT CONCERN
TO FIND A DEEP ENOUGH ABYSS he lends a hand
Two dots near Potsdam Waiting for nothing
That's the drama: there is no action
We know otherwise and refrain from action No
We can do no other The dress

Fits like a second skin NOWADAYS THEY DO EVERYTHING
IN HUMAN FLESH Goes on and on
Look at Commodus, a death off the peg /
Lagerfeld or Serenity He
Doesn't love the beauties he can have His heart
Seeks beauty everywhere Beauty
Is a son of the gutter, has previous convictions
See here, his description, black skin
I enjoy the luxury of having been expelled
An idiot in the third millennium A citizen of the world
Helena Christensen leaves the catwalk
Why should I become fashionable
In the throwaway society
The arena full of the last screams Ideas
Rome's last era, unseriousness
Now watch the finale ME OR ME
Greetings, barbarians

[1998]

6.5.1996

I overslept in the Art Hotel, it was raining
Cats and dogs into the Elbe, no breakfast
But a hungry look at the walls
Penck, offspring of no class in particular, has painted himself a museum
Hunting scenes for cavedwellers ART OF THE WEST or
THE MATCHSTICK MEN OF PLANNING, the taxi
Got stuck in the traffic on the Dimitroff the Augustus Bridge
Nothing functioned while my mother died
I went on foot, rounding a piledriver
A tool that Antaeus a land speculator
From Libya with his subcontracted workers
The city was torn up like after the air-raids
Baroque rubble, you can stroll in the foundations
And look for the error, in the Chancellory
A dumb pushing and shoving, static artists
They hold out whatever the government
Adam Schreier Güttler Hoppe and Braun
GO AND SEE HIS HIGHNESS WHEN
HE ASKS YOU TO, AND ONLY THEN
King Kurt the Early Riser
Summoned the still sleepy Academy

To a morning roll-call, my tiredness
Has a more complicated origin, I yawn
From more epochs, my mockery is a late vintage
From the slopes of my consciousness
In the place of my instant dismissal
We printed FRÖSI sing and be joyful
Four colours offset TRUE, IF THE CHILDREN
WERE ALWAYS CHILDREN my wideawake brother
Confirmed my political immaturity
The second went over the border without a licence
One of five, that was only realistic
I carried a suitcase for the daughter of a musician
She wanted to study music without politics
Wide awake to the station after a night of love
In the land of Hanns Eisler, a struggler in vain
Against STUPIDITY IN MUSIC
On the way home I became a poet in Germany
Among the stubblefields under a starry sky
A muddy path under my feet, or sand at least
On the corridors of power, my gentleness
Was hard won in the cement factory SOCIALISM the question
Abiding no answer or, as it might be, the answer
Abiding no questions, now in Moscow
The Synod has met to discuss the question
CAN THE APOCALYPSE HAPPEN IN ONE COUNTRY?
And the joke has worn thin, gone bust as it seems
Goldmann, my feet are going to sleep
On the parquet floor, we were awake too long
Too awake with waiting for the morning
Until it dawned on us that the morning had been and gone
I was drinking champagne in the Saxon Academy
While my mother was dying, I saw her yesterday
Life in her wasted body, pain
Was twisting her into her last shape, for a moment
She had lost her courage and was tired
A chance to MAKE HER COMFORTABLE, she lay
With her head back and in puzzlement /
Rage she was lifting her arm with the tube stuck in it
And felt at her face and the oxygen mask
Not knowing we were there / not being able to move, today
We find her removed to the cellar, hard by
The door, her chin bound up, her head
Little as a mummy's, a scrap of gauze on her eye
Still lying, and her cheeks are cold
I've got another thirty years to live

I'm sitting at a table with my dead father
It's barley-soup, the soldier spoons it up
His gun on his shoulder, the soup tastes salty
From the tears that in secret over the stove
Have been mixed in, or twenty
If I don't get tired, fed artificially
By the times I live in EAST WEST
A MIXTURE says Penck BELOW ABOVE
Speedy deliveries in red and black acrylic
No a separation IN AND OUT
LIFE AND DEATH, when will the poet
Be born, AFTER YEARS OF DEFEAT
AND GREAT UNHAPPINESS WHEN THE SLAVES BREATHE AGAIN
AND THE IMAGES AWAKE AT THE STUPENDOUS VISION.

[1996]

Volker Braun's notes: King Kurt is Kurt Biedenkopf, *Ministerpräsident* of Saxony. 'TRUE, IF THE CHILDREN . . . ' is from Brecht's poem 'Die Jugend im Dritten Reich' (the lines continue 'Then we could go on telling them fairy stories'). 'When will the poet be born . . . ' derives from Diderot's *Dissertation sur le poème dramatique* (1758).

from **West Shore**

V

Breakfast, 'Waiter, the traffic menu, please'

They crouch on the flats like comical birds
    Claws out downwards
        Plastic bags like black
    Craws, swags, the grubbers for mussels
In La Tranche-sur-Mer. Lonely lascivious work
Of poets,
    for a crude meal.
                What does
The End of History
        Count in this everyday silt
Where above is below and death life.
  . . . And he used the time pondering
    The paradox
        That we enjoy being hit

      'Pokes in the ribs . . . gratefully accepted.'
         In a woman's face
So he reads, opens what can be opened
    The mouth, the eyes, he reads
        More in a woman's face.
Boiling water. They slurp the mussels
      One night after another
    Stunned with lemon
And again I hoped of the things
   I encounter
     As a chosen one
        To show myself worthy.

VI

A midday without an address, fleeing the wind and sick
   For sun you stray
      Out of this gulf of politics
            ('given back
To life') into the flowering steppes. Would you
    (Or anyone for you) ever
Have dreamed it? Like a girl
   Your soul, wandering the mudflats, freed
       From the petrol pumps
You can sense the equal buoyancy of the land masses
    On the pulsing core of the earth. *Change of subject.*
       Cannibalism among the galaxies
          You can say you are there. The plate tectonics
Of history ('like a rear-end collision')
   And the supercontinent
     Pangaea arises
         COCA COLA out of the ocean.
Now you have everything (that you don't need), relax

The change of the seasons sixty times
   Thrice the change of an era
You won't do it for less;
                take
       Things as they're not any longer
With cold respect: not a passer-by . . .
                     en passant.

[1992]

Luís de Camões
Portugal

Translated by William Baer

Luís de Camões *(1524/5-1580) is generally considered the greatest writer in Portuguese history. The author of the last great Western epic poem,* O Lusiadas, *about the monumental voyage of Vasco da Gama around the Cape of Good Hope to the Orient in 1497, Camões was also one of the earliest sonneteers, often compared to Petrarch, Dante, and Shakespeare (whom he predated).*

William Baer, *a former Fulbright Professor in Coimbra, Portugal, is currently editor of the US poetry journal,* The Formalist. *His first collection,* The Unfortunates, *was published by New Odyssey Press and received the 1997 TS Eliot Poetry Prize. He has also edited two books for the University Press of Mississippi:* Conversations with Derek Walcott *(1996) and* Elia Kazan: Interview *(2000).*

Exile

Here in this Babylon, that's festering
forth as much evil as the rest of the earth;
here where true Love deprecates his worth,
as his powerful mother pollutes everything;
here where evil is refined and good is cursed,
and tyranny, not honour, has its way;
here where the Monarchy, in disarray,
blindly attempts to mislead God, and worse;
here in this labyrinth, where Royalty,
willingly, chooses to succumb
before the Gates of Greed and Infamy;
here in this murky chaos and delirium,
I carry out my tragic destiny,
but never will I forget you, Jerusalem!

Sepulchre

Who lies in this great sepulchre? Who
reclines at rest beneath this glorious shield?
No one. All things decay, and all things yield,
but once, he achieved all that a man could do.
Was he a king? He did what a king does best;

he studied the arts of justice, peace, and wars,
and soundly vanquished the encroaching Moors:
may the Earth now lightly dust his final rest.
So is it Alexander? No, no such thing:
he strove to "nourish," not to subjugate.
Is it Hadrian, once "King of Everyone"?
No, he chose God's laws, not the depths of hate.
Then is it Numa? No, it's a Portuguese King:
John the Third, and second to none.

Jacob

For seven years, the shepherd Jacob slaved
for the father of beautiful Rachel, working not for the man,
but only for her, knowing ever since he began
that she alone was the only reward he craved.
His days, dreaming of the wedding that lay ahead,
passed by, content to see her from time to time,
until her father plotted his duplicitous crime,
by placing Leah in Jacob's marriage bed.
Learning the cruel deception, Jacob, in tears,
had lost the one he loved, as if, somehow,
he hadn't truly earned the proper wife.
But he starts all over again, for seven more years,
saying, "If life wasn't so short, beginning right now,
I serve even longer for Rachel, the love of my life."

Cavafy
Greece

Translated by D M Black

*Poems by **C P Cavafy** (1863-1933) appeared in MPT 13, where the translators – David Ricks, Avi Sharon and George Kalogeris – simply stated that he "needs no introduction".*
   ***D M Black**'s translations from Goethe appeared in MPT 13 and 16.*

A Half-hour

I never had you and no doubt I never
will. A few words, an approach
like at the bar two days ago – nothing more. For me,
I must admit, I'm sorry. But we others,
the Art's adepts, by force of concentration, can create
fleetingly, sometimes, a pleasure
that impresses one by being almost concrete.
Thus, in the bar, two days ago, with alcohol
helping me greatly in its kindly fashion,
that half-hour was for me profoundly erotic.
It seemed to me you understood, and deliberately
you lingered just a little. Now, what was there
was something very necessary, for, with all
possible fantasy and the magic of alcohol,
I had to see your lips as well,
I had to have your body near.

Desires

They are like beautiful bodies that age has not touched
and which one lays gently with tears in a magnificent tomb
with roses at their head, and at their feet jasmine –
they are like such bodies, these desires which now are quenched
without ever having asserted themselves, without ever having
        were it but one
single night of pleasure or one enchanted dawn.

Insomnia

(Note: the soul in this poem is referred to as 'she'.)

My soul is, in the heart of night,
disturbed, defeated. It's outside,
outside of her her life goes on.

She waits for the unlikely dawn.
And I, within her, or beside,
wake, and am worried, and am worn.

The Walls

Without regard, without shame, without mercy,
tall, thick walls have ringed me round.

And here I am, apprenticed to despair,
dreaming only of a destiny that would consume my thought.

I had so much to do outside:
how was I not aware of these walls that were being constructed?

But no noise from the builders reached me, not a sound.
Very quietly, they have walled me out of the world.

We owe an apology to D M Black, whose translation of Goethe's 'Anacreon's Grave' unaccountably appeared as quasi-prose in MPT 16. He writes: 'Elegiac couplets are particularly difficult to write in English, and I was rather pleased with these!' – adding that 'an acute reader would be able to construct the lineation for himself' although the line-breaks were 'in confusion'. So are we, and hereby make amends.

[NR]

Anacreon's Grave

Here where the roses bloom, where vines intertwine with the laurel,
    Here where the turtledoves call, here where the cricket shrills,
To what grave have we come, that every God has delighted
    Thus to festoon with life? – here Anacreon lies.
Spring, and summer, and fall enchanted the fortunate poet;
    Now from winter the earth keeps him secure in the end.

Paul Celan
Romania (German language)

Translated by Michael Hamburger

Michael Hamburger, *the most respected of translators from German, has contributed many translations to MPT. His last book of poems,* Intersections, *was published in 2000 by Anvil Press. Anvil will be reprinting his book of translations from Peter Huchel in 2001, and a limited edition reprint of his memoir,* Philip Larkin: a Retrospect, *is forthcoming later this year from Enitharmon Press.*

Michael Hamburger *writes:* These poems, translated later than those in the Anvil Press and Penguin selections, belong to different phases of Celan's life and work, and were intended to fill gaps in my earlier selection for a slightly enlarged edition due in the USA. The first poem is a very early one, the others belong to Celan's middle period and that of his last years. 'IN THE GREAT listening' originated in a visit of Celan's to Berlin and refers to sights seen there just before Christmas, the former Hotel Eden from which the revolutionaries Karl Liebknecht and Rosa Luxemburg were escorted to be shot, and the building in which the 1944 conspirators against Hitler were hanged on meathooks.

Your Hair above the Sea

Your hair too hovers above the sea with the golden juniper.
Together with it turns white, but I dye it stone-blue:
that city's colour where last I was dragged to the south . . .
With ropes they bound me and knotted a sail to each one
and spat at me from their misty mouths and sang out:
"O come over the sea!"
But I as a dinghy painted my pinions purple
and wheezed a breeze for myself and before they slept sailed away.
Now it is red I should dye them, your locks, but I like them stone-blue:
O eyes of the city where, felled, I was dragged to the south:
with the golden juniper now your hair too hovers above the sea.

*

VOICELESS, ABOVE, the
travellers, vulture and star.

Below, after everything, we,
ten in number, the sad folk. Time,
how could it not, has
an hour even for us, here
in the sand city.

(Tell of the well, tell
of the well-shaft, well-wheel, of
well cisterns – tell.

Count and recount, the clock,
even that, runs down.

Water: what
a word. We're wise to you, life.)

The stranger, uninvited, from where,
the guest.
His dripping clothes.
His dripping eye.

(Tell me of wells, of –
Count and recount.
Water: what
a word.)

His clothes-and-eye, like us
he's filled with night, he betokens
insight, he counts now,
as we do, to ten
and no further.

Above, the
travellers
remain
inaudible.

The Vintagers
For Nani and Klaus Demus

They autumn the wine of their eyes,
they press all the wept, this too:
so night will have it,

that night they lean against, wall,
so the stone demands,
that stone over which their crutch talks away
into the answer's silence –
their crutch that once,
once only in autumn,
when the year swells to death, as a bunch of grapes,
that once only speaks through the dumbness, down
into the shaft of the merely thought.

They autumn, they press the wine,
they press time as they press their eyes,
they press the trickles in, the wept,
in the sun's grave they prepare
with hands made strong by night:
so that a mouth will thirst for it, later –
a late mouth, resembling theirs:
skewed towards blind things and maimed –
a mouth to which drink foams up from the depth while
the sky descends to the waxen sea,
to gleam from afar as a candle stump
when at last the lip moistens.

Argumentum e Silentio
For René Char

Chained up
between gold and oblivion:
the night.
Both reached out for it.
Both let it be.

Lay,
you also now lay down that which seeks
to rise dawning beside the days:
the word overflown by stars,
drenched by the seas.

To each the word.
To each the word that sang for that one
when the pack attacked from behind –
To each the word that sang for that one and froze.

You, the night,
the overflown by stars, the sea-drenched.
You the won by silence
whose blood did not clot when the poison fang
pierced the syllables.

You the word won by silence.

Against those others who soon,
whored about by the bloodsucker ears,
climb time and eras too,
it bears witness at the last,
at the last, when chains only sound,
bears witness to her who lies there
between gold and oblivion,
sister to both from the outset –

For where
but with her does it dawn, tell me,
who in the river zone of her tears
shows the seed to submerging suns
again and ever again.

*

IN THE GREAT listening you lie,
flaked over, all bushed up.

Go to the Spree, to the Havel,
go to the butchers' meat-hooks,
to the red apple stooks
from Sweden –

Then comes the table with gifts,
it curves round an Eden –

The man is a sieve now, the woman,
that sow, does a belly-flop,
for herself, for no one, for everyone.

The Landwehr Canal will not roar.
Nothing
    comes to a stop.

*

ON BOTH HANDS, yonder
where stars grew for me, far
from all skies, near
all skies:
How
one's awake there! How
the world opens up for us, right
through our middle!

You are,
where your eye is, you are
above, are
below, I
find my way out.

Oh this meandering empty
hospitable middle. Separate,
I grow yours, you
grow mine, loosed
from each other, we see
right through:

the
same
has lost
us, the
same
has forgotten
us, the
same
has — us.

*

BLACK,
like memory's wound,
my eyes root for you
in the crown land bitten
bright by the heart teeth,
our bed even now:

through this shaft you must come –
you come.

In the seed-
sense
the sea stars you forth, inmostly, for ever.

The name-giving ends here,
on to you I throw my fate.

*

ETERNITIES I have
died away from,
a letter touches
your fingers, un-
injured still,
the radiant brow
comes leaping in
and beds itself
in fragrances, rustlings.

*

WAYS IN THE SHADOW-ROCKSLIDE
of your hand.

From the four-finger furrow
I root out for myself the
petrified blessing.

William Cliff
Belgium (French language)

Translated by James Kirkup

William Cliff, *fourth child of a family of nine, was born in 1940 in Belgium, near the French border. He studied philosophy and literature at the University of Louvain and began teaching, but gradually gave it up to devote himself to writing and world travel. His work was discovered by Raymond Queneau, who introduced him to Gallimard.* Homo Sum *(1973) at once established his sexual orientation and his poetic reputation. Four more collections were followed by* Conrad Detrez, *a sequence of verses dedicated to the memory of his friend the novelist Detrez, who died of Aids (Le Dilettante, 1990). More recent works from Gallimard are* Fête Nationale *(1992) and* Journal d'un Innocent *(1996); his* Autobiographie *appeared in 1993 (La Différence). He has also published a volume of translations of poems by the Yugoslav poet Brane Mozetic (*Obsession*; Aleph/Editions Pastre, 1991), and his latest work is* L'État Belge *(La Table Ronde, 2000).*

James Kirkup *has been a frequent contributor to* MPT *and was the featured translator in* MPT *11.*

from **America** *(1983)*

Montevideo

It's a good feeling to find yourself in a city
far far away and for the first time
and where you don't understand
a single blessed word of what they're talking about
and to sit down on a stone feeling all alone and at a loss
and to stay there for hours just watching the way
the stinking waters of a port come and slap against the stone
on which your carcase has humbly taken seat and
to think think think for hours on end until
the day slips by on the flowing tide like
that dead fish floating among those dog-ends
dead leaves spat-out pips slowly being drifted out to sea

and behind you the roar of traffic passing and fishermen
after sitting there for ages dangling a hook
in front of fish gorging on filth until at last fed-up
they've packed it in with their rods and balls of twine

and gone on their way to anyone willing to listen to them

and still to keep sitting there watching a wave
forever covering the same rock then uncovering it for you again
you begin to realize that evening is washing over this city
where no one knows you or cares what becomes of you
as you sit there all alone in the deepening darkness
without even a bed where you might lie down and sleep

then one by one the stars as they come out give you shots
of the pleasure you feel in letting yourself go into death
with the fear of seeing once more the wreck of yourself
coming and begging you to drag it through the streets from door
to door until you find it a place to lay its bag of bones

with twilight the harbour's stale stink grows stronger
aaarrgh! the dead fish comes washing in again the gulls
dig their beaks into their prey then fly back up I get to
my feet and stagger off towards the bugs of yet another bed

I became the object . . .

I became the object of an old man's lust
he was toting his corporation among the grasses of the dunes
where he kept darting his dirty old man's eyes at my sprawling body

while I was trying to assume an air of insulting indifference
to get him to piss off and leave me to my own devices
but all the time that bay window of his kept looming up

and his advanced age his moustache and the prerogative of
that loathsome belly that he nursed like a dead foetus
licensed him to keep looking me over with the bulging eye of authority

I ran down to the sea hoping that meanwhile the old shit
would slope off somewhere else to get his rocks off
but from afar lo and behold his breadbasket bobbing after me

back in the sand dunes I gather up my things
and go and lie down as far as possible from the monstrosity
but the wobbling paunch comes heaving alongside me again

then the old fruit starts making obscene gestures at me
and suddenly I boil with rage I want to punch his face in
stamp on his guts and smash his dentures

then plunging a long knife into that shuddering udder
scatter to the winds his rancid liver and lights
to feed the filthy maw of ocean's scavengers

from **L'État Belge** *(2000)*

Ballade of Boys from Days Gone By

Tell me, where now is noble Alcibiades
he who once drove wild with love Plato, Socrates
Aristotle and all those other great philosophers?
tell me, where is his brother in the lists of love
he for whom Shakespeare created many a verse?
and where now are the lads whom Michael Angelo
found so beautiful he made them into statues
bent to his will in attitudes of tortured slaves?
where are they now, all those nameless adolescents?
Their beauty endured for only one brief summer

Where now is the divinest boy Antinoüs
whose image was immortalised by Yourcenar
bringing back to life the Emperor Hadrian?
he was swept away from the riverbanks of Nile
for in order to preserve the flower of his youth
he had dared to challenge dying's dread arcana
men are still bewailing his miserable fate
while Hadrian, consumed by grieving at his loss
tried to console himself with thousands of his busts –
his beauty endured for only one brief summer

Where now are the darling sons of the Renaissance
whose long limbs were revealingly moulded under
form-fitting hose? and where are those page boys who once
made Henry the Third faint clean away with rapture?
and all those gold-embroidered equerries are they
not dead? I am afraid that their delicious flesh
is now compounded with the worm-infested clay
despite the pleasures they may have enjoyed on earth
their beauty endured for only one brief summer

O all you fine young lads from those days long gone by
will you ever listen when tears are being shed
by one who faces now the plunge into the depths
of that dark trap where you are eaten by the worms?
He, too, once believed he would escape that fate – but
his beauty lasted only for one brief summer

Eggs and Greens

in the olden times the women set off for the market
my grandmother used to tell me carrying a basket
majestically upon the topknots of their heads
they swung their hips as they went their long skirts
with their trains had trailed in pig shit
and now were raking up the droppings of the town
whose pavements they were tramping on their way
to sell their eggs and greens they'd brought in from their barns

but if they were taken by a need to "do it" what to do?
they'd put one foot down off the pavement and there and then
without losing anything of their majestic calm
they would do it in the gutter after slightly lifting up
their trailing skirts so that they would not get
too clarted up then going on their way
still full of dignity they went with swaying hips
proceeding with their baskets on the topknots of their heads
the glorious country women who in her girlhood days
came down on foot into the towns to sell
the eggs and greens they'd brought in from their barns
my grandmother used to tell me in the olden times

today I'd like to see those women
who pissed in public without feeling shame
who made a living simply from selling of their wares
borne in a basket on the topknots of their noble heads
while behind them their bustling trains
swept up the rubbish of the farms or dog dirt
of city streets but time goes by and all our appetites
today are glutted with inferior stuff
sealed in cellophane and the putrid smell of which
only gets worse year in year out and
further ever further off those great working dames
who once proceeded proudly with their baskets for to sell
their eggs and greens they'd brought in from their barns

Two-Stroke

the clapped-out two-stroke drove
its rubbers over sharp-edged gravel
(beer had turned us both to sad-sack idiots)
we were negotiating a track
that died away among the brambles
the wrecks of rusted barbed-wire fences
the moon lit with a sinister gleam
a water-tower penis erecting against the sky
the monstrousness of its great concrete knob
the engine finally extinguished its complaints
a carcase barely blacker than
the black of time on fields and trees
we were buck naked skin to skin upon the springs
of the bone-shaker I was talking into your mouth
and my words all gluey with your spit
struggled hard and suffered having to lie

the two-stroke wasn't comfortable
it creaked and squealed beneath our weight
suddenly day broke through the crevasses
in the clouds and then we went home knackered
to bed down again on their ordinary rack
the atrocious solitudes of our flesh

Courage!

you the old who go hobbling on who mumble
complaints about the bad state of your health
you old women who lament the lack of males
so few men to be seen now in the markets
you the aged sad shadows human horrors of the flesh
owls dead ugly and all moulting you old men
I prefer you a hundred times more than all these braggarts
who bore us stiff with their decorous parades
those fat cats with their patter songs of pelf and penis
those small-screen crooks those TV channel high-ups
they no longer put it over you the old
you've seen worse things than that and if they've
left you on the shelf your abject being all the same is one
great mute gob of spit shot right between the eyes

bravo the old you're well within your rights when you
persist like crabs in occupying
the entire length and breadth of pavements bravo the old
shamelessly showing up in café restaurants
with your ugly phizzogs yes you the old ones
hang on there everywhere show them up those pension-packers
stupidly clinging to the rungs of their careers
go everywhere and show them what you are
that they may behold the outcome of their miserable triumphs
and then because of having turned blind eyes on your distress
they'll soon have nothing better to do than come and join you
at your beer-swilling old folks evenings where you dance

you admirable old living rags and tatters
caricatures coldly demonstrating the end of human nature
courage! keep on disfiguring with your masks
the wretched landscape where our "happy few" go through their antics

Mak Mehmedalija Dizdar
Bosnia and Herzegovina

Translated by Natalija Bonić

Mak Mehmedalija Dizdar *(1917-1971) was born in Stolac, Herzegovina and attended grammar school in Sarajevo. At fifteen, he had already won the "Cvijeta Zuzoric" literary prize. At eighteen, he began working as a journalist, and in 1936 published his first collection of poems,* Vidovopoljska noć *(Vidovopolje Night), heavily censured for its socialist ideas. During the Second World War, Dizdar fought in Tito's Resistance. Unable to capture him, the fascist police arrested his mother and sister who subsequently died in the Jasenovac concentration camp. After the war, he worked as a journalist and literary editor until 1958, when he devoted himself solely to writing, publishing* The Swimmer *(1954),* The Return *(1958),* The Cruelty of a Circle *(1960),* Knees for Madonna *(1963),* Miniatures *(1965),* Islands *(1966), and* The Stone Sleeper *(1966).*

A small selection of Dizdar's poems appeared in MPT *17 (1973), translated by the late Anne Pennington.*

Natalija Bonić *was born in Tuzla, Bosnia and Herzegovina, in 1966. Two years later the family moved to Australia, where she lived until 1975. Back in Yugoslavia, in 1985 she studied English Language and Literature, and Philosophy, at the University of Split. She moved to Belgium in 1991 and in 1993 received an MA in Philosophy from the Catholic University of Louvain, where she is now in the Doctoral programme.*

Roads

You have decided I am not to be and no matter what
You advance towards me And in a rush
Laughing and weeping
You sweep
And crush
All that's ahead of you.

You have decided to destroy me no matter what
Yet you fail to find
The right road
To me

For
You know the forged and beaten roads
And no other

(In fact they are small and barren
Though to you
So vain and mighty
They seem
Laborious
And Long)

You know but those roads
That lead
From the heart
And
The eye

But that is not all

There are roads that stretch out
With no trace of traffic
With no timetable
Nor deadline

You think your passage to wretched me
Is well secured and tight
It
Leads
From either left
Or
Right

You fool yourself repeatedly I'm to be reached
By some such routes
From south
Or
North

But that is not all

The plague
Seeks always
Cleverly my eyes
Beneath the waving wind-stroked ryes
From earthy roots where darkness jells

Yet from the never measured heights
From up above

The chest
Most vigorously
Can
Be pressed
By anguish

But that is not all

You do not know the laws of cleft
Between the luminous
And the dark

But that is not all

For you know least that in your self
The battles are most sore
That in your ownmost
Being
Are the proper wars

You know not then that you're the least
Amid my
Many
Mounting
Evils

You do not know with whom
You're dealing
You know nothing of my map of roads

You do not know that the road from you to me
Is not the same as the road
From me
To you

You know nothing of my riches
Hidden to your mighty eyes
(You do not know that to me
Far more
Than you think
Fate
Has bequeathed
And
Granted)

You have decided to destroy me no matter what
But you fail to find the right road
To me

(I understand:
You are a man in one space and time
That lives but now and here
And knows nothing of the boundless
Space of time
In which I am
Present
From distant yesterday
To distant tomorrow
Thinking
Of you

But that is not all)

Inscription of Time

Long since have I lain
And long am I to
Lie

Long
That grass has my bones
Long
That worms have my meat
Long
That I gained many names
Long
That I forgot my own name

Long since have I lain
And long am I to
Lie

On the tombstone of a certain Stipko Radosalić in the cemetery of Premilovo Polje near Ljubinja there is a carving of a new moon: the boat that would eventually carry him to the real, eternal life. The couplet "Long since have I lain and long am I to lie" is the epitaph on Stipko's tomb.

Johanna Ekström
Sweden

Translated by Sarah Death

Johanna Ekström *(born 1970) is a writer and visual artist who lives and works in Stockholm. Her installations, collaborative and solo, involve a wide variety of media including sculpture, photography, film and dance. Her published volumes are:* Skiffer *(Slate, 1993),* Vitöga *(White of the Eye, 1994)* Rachels hus *(Rachel's House, 1995, with one section inspired by "Ghost", Rachel Whiteread's cast of an empty house),* gå förlorad *(getting lost, 1998). In prose she has published* Fiktiva dagboken *(Fictional Diary, 1997) and* Vad vet jag om hållfasthet *(What Do I know of Stability, 2000). One of the stories from the latter has been published in English, together with a longer biographical article, in* Swedish Book Review *(200:1).*

Sarah Death *is a freelance translator, reviewer and literary historian and Honorary Research Fellow in the Department of Scandinavian Studies at University College London. She specialises in translating modern Swedish literature and the work of Swedish women writers from various periods, and has been working with Johanna Ekström for a number of years.*

The poems below are from getting lost *and a new, as yet unpublished collection (provisionally entitled* En annan åder, *Another Vein) and were translated for the author to perform at international arts festivals in Portugal and the United States in spring 2001.*

from **getting lost**

I screamed for you
in nights as deaf
as silent films
Black lips
and jumpy sequences
A sharp lack scratched the lens
I am selling my loss
as one sells a horse
Producing a bundle
from the inside pocket by my heart
Take the money and run!

*

You say I am as sad
as a self-fulfilling prophecy

You know this country
But I know the names
For example Bougainvillea
What does that mean?
That I can express things with my eyes
seems to count for nothing

from **Another Vein**

Carrier, sinner
Felon, source of infections
all words I have forgotten and forget
Listlessness and shiver
shivering spaces
eyes
Not even the dreams
I am swimming in a royal blue
swimming pool and
someone screams:
Murderer, murderer
"This is a security announcement"

And I know that there is
no forgiveness and
there is no mercy
It is far too shallow to dive

*

Someone is watching as we make love
Silent as the globe
on the bedroom floor
a buoy in our ocean
In my so terrifying, rocking
"I know
that I can't speak"
An eye
as old as I
from the Palau Trench
Someone who remembers me
in my childhood room with the nightlight
shining greeny-blue
The world that held out against the world

the ticking in the pipes
the dark forest
Planet of the Apes

  *

The humming of the computer
a wheeling gull over the park
My beloved is coming
I stretch myself into
a landing ground
Turn on the lights
the deep-sea blue ones
along my hips

Hans Magnus Enzensberger
Germany

Translated by Richard Dove

MPT 16 – German and French Poetry – *included translations by Michael Hamburger of poems by Hans Magnus Enzensberger, and a review article on Enzensberger and his translators by Richard Dove, who has sent us the following postscript:*

Several months after the review had been completed, Enzensberger once again took his readers by surprise, publishing a 78-poem collection whose subtitle strikes a calculatedly jarring note in the Age of Anything Goes: *Leichter als Luft. Moralische Gedichte* (*Lighter than Air. Moral Poems*; Suhrkamp, 1999). It is to be hoped that Michael Hamburger will provide us with a complete English equivalent – *ghasels* and all. As an appetizer, and as a belated birthday greeting to Enzensberger, a stopgap version of the last poem in the book follows.

The Great Goddess (Die Grosse Göttin)

She mends things, mends things,
bent above her smashed darning-egg,
one end of the thread between her lips.
She mends day and night.
No end of new ladders, new holes.

At times she nods off,
for a moment only,
a century.
With a start she wakes up
and mends things, mends things.

How small she's become,
small, blind and lined!
She feels for the holes
in the world with her thimble
and mends things, mends things.

Gerhard Fritsch

Translated by William Stone and Anthony Vivis

Gerhard Fritsch *(1924-1969) lived in Vienna, where he worked as a librarian and later as the editor of important Austrian literary journals (*Wort in der Zeit, Literatur und Kritik*) and anthologies (*Finale und Auftakt, Aufforderung zum Misstrauen*). His first poems appeared in 1947 in a newspaper, and his first book of poems in 1951. Three books of poems appeared in the Fifties, and he also published two novels:* Moos auf den Steinen *(1956) and* Fasching *(1967). A selection from* Der Geisterkrug *(1958), translated by Gitta Holroyd-Reece, with a foreword by Harry Zohn, was published by the Menard Press in 1978 under the title* Between Evening and Night.

Will Stone, *born in 1966, is a poet and translator living in Suffolk. He studied for an MA in Literary Translation at the University of East Anglia. His translation of 'El Desdichado', the opening sonnet of Nerval's* Les Chimères, *appeared in MPT 11, and the whole sequence was published by The Menard Press in 1999. His translations of Trakl appeared in MPT 16. He has published several pamphlets of poetry and an essay concerning the fall and rise of songwriter/poet Nick Drake.* Shadow Symposium, *his latest collection of poems, is forthcoming from Ambros Press.*

Anthony Vivis *became a freelance writer in 1983 after working for the RSC and the BBC. Sixty of his translations have been performed, including plays by Büchner, Fassbinder, Goethe and Hauptmann, and he has published translations from Ausländer (with Jean Boase-Beier) and Kirsch (with Wendy Mulford).*

Self Portrait

I now see a head, huge and strange
There in the mirror, and a leaden gaze
Passing through me into the unknown . . .
And someone says: But that's you.
I know it's me. But does that mean
The features are less hidden, less distant,
The lines clearer and more familiar?
Dusk rains down over everything
About the eye sockets, mouth and chin,
No day is reflected – oh everywhere
Is dusk, into which the first star
Has not yet sent its light, for godless
Is my earth, dumb and wavering

And this face is a pond, grey and still
And far from the last houses;
Few pass by it, and if they do
Then often the image is not reflected.
For what it holds, falls in on itself, falling
And falling in its depth, where perhaps
The soul blossoms gently in its dreams
And waits
Yet the pond remains unsure.

November

The field earth breathes mist
Into the weak light of afternoon.
Red leaves on the cemetery wall
Drip tears into the yellow clay,
Which envelops your peaceful walk
Along every pathway into the empty land.
For hours the rain's been falling,
It runs down and robs time
From your smarting senses
As wilted leaves from black branches.
You walk and dream;
You walk past farms and huts
In which the first lamps are burning
And out as far as you into the unknown
A soft laugh beckons.
But you remain alone;
At best, a stray dog
Follows after you awhile in the darkness,
Until you suddenly drive him off
Away from your colossal loneliness.

October

The final
Bitter flowers
On the embankment
Snap silently
In the sickle wind.
Sooty and thistle-crowned
Lies the ballast

Across the sleepers.
Painfully
Smile the stones:
All is well.

Shadows

Shadows
Slowly wandering down
From the western woods,
Relentless surf of night,
Wave attack of silence furrow to furrow;
The meadows succumb, the herds
Drift home, before them
The fields conform
And even the beat of the threshing
Gradually ebbs away, for even that
Is overcome by the great poppy flood
Of sleep.

The morning
Was overhung
With mist and smoke.
The earth reeked of open graves,
They are waiting for the year.

Johann Wolfgang von Goethe

Translated by Ken Cockburn and by Tessa Ransford

Ken Cockburn *was born in Kirkcaldy in 1960, and studied French and German at Aberdeen University. He currently works as Fieldworker and Assistant Director at the Scottish Poetry Library in Edinburgh. A collection of poems,* Souvenirs and Homelands, *was published in 1998, and he recently edited, with Alec Finley,* The Order of things: Scottish sound, pattern and concrete poems *(pocketbooks, 2001). His other translations include work by Tankred Dorst and Swiss poet Ernst Ramseier.*

Tessa Ransford's *translations from Rilke appeared in* MPT *16 (German and French Poetry).*

from **Venetian Epigrams** (1790)

35

What, in the scheme of things, is one man's life? Yet thousands
    might discuss a person – what they did, and how.
Poems are even less; yet thousands might enjoy them,
    thousands denounce them. My friend, let life, and your poems, flow!

37

How, carved by the artist's hand, the delicate figure,
    soft and boneless, swims like an invertebrate!
Limbs, and joints, are everything, and everything is
    pleasing, in proportion, a strict-tempo dance.
People I've seen, and animals, birds as well as fishes,
    curious worm-like things, a vast and marvellous world;
yet I'm astounded by the marvel that's you, Bettina,
    being all of these at once – and an angel to boot.

46

Writing's a pleasant trade, I do though find it expensive:
    as these pages pile up, so does my overdraft.

50

All those preachy apostles of freedom, I never could bear them:
    all in the end they're after is running the show themselves.
If you'd free the masses, risk everything, and serve them.
    Level of danger entailed, what do you think? Just try!

52

Every prophet should be crucified at thirty;
    once he's known the world's deceit, he'll just turn bad.

55

"Of course we're in the right, we have to betray the masses.
    Look at how they carry on, so banal, so crude."
Crude and banal, OK, but only because you've betrayed them;
    treat them well and, believe me, they'll be straight and true.

56

Autocrats will mint, on thinly silvered copper,
    their imposing features; selling the people short.
Chancers will mint the spirit's likeness on lies and garbage:
    lacking critical tools, you'd think it heaven on earth.

80

Say there's a lad, and the road to his girl is less than straightforward,
    give him this book: it offers both consolation, and charms.
Should one day a lass await her lover, it's this book
    she should have too, though once he arrives, she can throw it away.

89

Words have failed me, and you're put out? I mean, why? You hardly
    register my gentle sighing, my eloquent gaze.
Knows your lips' encrypted password, a single goddess;

only Aurora, the day she stirs you awake in my bed.
Then indeed I'd hymn the early gods with praises,
    just as Memnon's statue once voiced sweet mysteries.

105

Out with the Lord's remains! out with God's remains!
    yelled an unhappy creature, blind with hysterical rage
when, to display the sacred relics on Maundy Thursday,
    a shifty figure appeared on the platform in St Mark's.
Lass, how are these splinters of God supposed to help you?
    Better the healing atoms of the Lampsacus sage.

112

Politicians, priests and pundits have us hoodwinked,
    yet, en masse, we worship them, this gang of three.
Sadly there's little these days, in terms of honest discussion,
    which the media, the state and the god-squad don't debase.

122

Undiscerning, Nauger burned the works of Martial.
    Pedant! – You'd chuck the silver just because it's not gold?

123

Horace didn't want more: one can, he found, want less with
    greater credit, not that one receives even that.

149

Everyone keeps telling me, child, of your deceptions:
    oh, deceive and deceive and deceive me, all you like.

    [KC]

Nature and Art

Nature and Art appearing disparate
Are found as one beneath our very eyes;
No incongruity to my surprise,
For each seems equally to fascinate.

This requires supreme, sustained endeavour,
Devotion to our craft, unceasing practice
With heart and mind; then only may we witness
Nature kindle again as free as ever.

Nothing is built, created, without Laws;
Nor is perfection reached without restriction;
And fullest grace demands most discipline.

We must contain ourselves to win applause;
The Master is discerned within constriction;
And visions are in vain without design.

   [TR]

Heinrich Heine
Germany

Translated with a commentary by WD Jackson

WD Jackson *writes:* In 1843 Heinrich Heine – who had been living in Paris for over a decade – revisited his native Germany, where he spent altogether about two months. On his return he wrote the 2056 lines of *Deutschland – Ein Wintermärchen*. At the end of this poem he acknowledges Aristophanes as his master, but there is a lot more to *Deutschland* than social comment or political satire, and like many of Heine's works – together with his life and opinions in general – it resists easy categorization. Heine had moved to Paris in 1831, inspired by the July Revolution, which deposed Charles X, the last Bourbon king, and placed the citizen-king Louis-Philippe on the throne. The complexities of Heine's politics present, as JL Sammons expresses it, "a rather knotty problem of interpretation ... Towards Louis-Philippe Heine could be very critical, but also very sympathetic, and he seems to have become increasingly sympathetic as the 1840s went on. In Heine's iconology king and poet were spiritual brothers, and this attitude informed much of his ironic view of the citizen-king. 'Kings, like great poets,' he wrote with a straight face, 'cannot defend themselves and must bear lies circulated about them in silent patience'" (*Heinrich Heine – A Modern Biography*, 1979). Heine, however, defended himself – usually by some form of attack – on every imaginable occasion. In 1834 he met the almost illiterate 19-year-old French shop assistant, Crescence Eugénie Mirat, who was later to become his wife. A further reason for staying in Paris was that his work had been banned along with that of other liberals by the German authorities – and while in Germany he was in some danger of being arrested. Apart from another trip to Germany in 1844, Heine was to spend the remainder of his life in Paris, where he died in 1856.

Of the following poems, the first is a more or less literal translation. "Hoffmann von F", who is mentioned in it, is Hoffmann von Fallersleben, who was dismissed from his Breslau professorship in 1842 for his ironically titled *Unpolitical Songs*. Hoffmann became a kind of 19th-century beatnik poet, travelling about from inn to inn with his guitar and his popular songs, which Heine disliked intensely, regarding them as symptomatic of the beginning of the end of high art – one of the prices the world would have to pay for the rise of democracy. The second poem, 'Liverpool Revisited – A Winter's Tale', is developed from the first and also from other sections of *Deutschland – Ein Wintermärchen*, incorporating in addition translations and adaptations of 'Das ist der alte Märchenwald', 'Abschied von Paris' (or 'Adieu à Paris') and 'Karl I'.

The latter part of the poem alludes as well to Heine's 'The Slave Ship', published in *MPT* 8. Van de Smissen is the ship's doctor and van Koek its supercargo. Heine spent some time in England in 1827 but did not, as far as I know, travel to Liverpool, although his father had once had business contacts there and Harry Heine himself (he became 'Heinrich' only on his conversion to Protestantism in 1825) had been named after a Liverpool merchant called 'Mr Harry'. In any case, for those unfamiliar with Liverpool's topography, which comes into the poem, the Anglican and Roman Catholic cathedrals stand at either end of Hope Street and the pub, The Philharmonic, is about halfway between them. A "jigger" is a back entry. As for Maggie May, she is treated here as a kind of tutelary deity of the city, much as Heine treats 'Hammonia' as the goddess of Hamburg in some of the most amusing – and scatological – sections of *Deutschland* (XXIII-XXVI).

In *MPT* 5 Daniel Weissbort wrote: 'For many translators, it seems, a threshold has been crossed, an era of self-consciousness entered, making it increasingly hard to limit oneself exclusively or unreflectively to the work in hand.' With this in mind, even a fairly loose imitation – which is partly what 'Liverpool Revisited' consists of – is a form of variation or commentary on its original(s) which may actually be going only a step or two further than what we usually think of as translation. The tension between what a writer actually wrote and what he *could* have written is in any case a frequently enough productive one in all but the most literal of translators' minds. Furthermore, this particular imitation is intended, directly and indirectly, as a meditation as well on the question of "Why translate?" Over the threshold, perhaps – but not out of the garden.

Finally, one or two notes on the subject of slavery – developed from 'The Slave-Ship' – in 'Liverpool Revisited'. As is well known, Liverpool grew to dominate trade not only in Britain but in Europe during the 18th century: "Almost every man in Liverpool is a merchant ... The attractive African meteor has so dazzled their ideas, that almost every order of people is interested in a Guinea cargo. Many of the small vessels are fitted out by attornies, drapers, ropers, grocers, tallow-chandlers, barbers, taylors &c" (J Wallace, *History of Liverpool*, 1795). The enormous profits derived from the slave-trade were invested in numerous enterprises, including banking, and Heywoods Bank, which is mentioned in the poem, was one of the earliest banks to be founded in Liverpool – in 1773. This bank was taken over by the Bank of Liverpool in 1883, which later became part of Martins Bank and more recently part of Barclays.

Variations on Heine (*from* **Then and Now**)

Deutschland. Ein Wintermärchen (ll. 1-48, 77-120)

November it was. And the cloudy skies
Grew daily more down-hearted;
The wind tore at the leaves on the trees;
And off for home I started.

And as I came to German soil
My heart seemed to be drumming
Harder and faster. In fact I think
The tears had started coming.

And when I heard my native tongue
I felt so strange for a minute
I thought my blissfully bleeding heart
Would spill all that was in it.

A girl was singing to a harp.
She sang with warm emotion
And tuneless voice, but I felt played
Upon by her devotion.

She sang of love and the pain of love,
Self-sacrifice, re-union
Above the clouds in that better world
Of unsuffering communion.

She sang of this earthly vale of tears,
Of the joys we cannot capture,
Of the life to come where the soul shall feast
In eternal radiant rapture.

She sang the old Forbearance Song,
The Lullaby of Later,
Which keeps the whining lumpen poor
From turning agitator.

I know the method, I know the text,
And I know the likes of the author;
I know that they secretly tipple wine
While openly preaching water.

A new song, a better song,
Companions, I shall write you!
And here and now on earth we'll build
A heaven to requite you.

We want our happiness here and now
On earth: we don't want hunger.
Let lazy bellies squander the thrift
Of hard-working hands no longer!

For human kind down here below
The bread we produce is ample –
And roses and myrtles, beauty and lust,
And garden peas, for example.

Yes, garden peas for everyone!
Come pile up the pods on the barrows.
And leave the heavenly pastures to
God's angels and the sparrows.

*

And while the maiden twittered and played
And panted after election,
The Prussian Customs Police undid
My bags for an inspection:

They poked their nose into trousers and shirts
And hankies, and fumbled for hidden
Laces and knick-knacks. And for books
Whose Knowledge was Forbidden.

O blockheads! poking in my bags
Where you won't find a dickey,
Confiscating the contraband
Of the mind 's a bit more tricky!

There I have needlework finer than
Any of Brussels or Mechlin,
And once I've got my needles out
You won't hear yourselves for heckling.

And I carry knick-knacks in my head,
Jewels to crown and enthrone one,

The holy gems of a future God,
Of the great, as yet Unknown One.

And in my head there are many books.
Or, more plainly stated,
My head's a singing nest of the sort
You'd like to see confiscated.

Believe me, in Satan's reading room
There can't be books more stinging:
They're twice as dicey as Hoffmann von F.'s
Unpolitical singing!

– A fellow-traveller starts to praise
But somehow in me arouses
Even more distrust of the Prussian State's
Long chain of customs-houses.

"This customs-union," he explains,
"Will characterize our nation –
Will help our divided Fatherland
To full Unification.

"It regulates each outward
Or material undertaking;
Whereas our spiritual unity
Is of the Censor's making.

"He regulates each inward
Aberrance, guiding sinners.
A United Germany we need –
Without us and within us."

Liverpool Revisited – A Winter's Tale

November it was. And the cloudy skies
Grew daily more down-hearted;
The wind tore at the leaves on the trees;
And off for home I started.

And as my plane flew gently on
I fell asleep. The thrumming
And thrusting of huge engines must
Have felt like spring was coming . . .

Anyway, May-time – Märchenwald –
And the moon's marvellous gleaming –
The limetree blossoms' sensual scent –
And whatever else I was dreaming –

Bewitched my senses. On and on
I floated, listening – aptly –
To 'songs of love and the pain of love':
To a nightingale, singing raptly –

Singing of love and the pain of love,
Of lovers' tears and laughter –
Sadly rejoicing – with happy sobs;
Forgotten dreams trailed after . . .

And I behind them . . . On I went
Through a clearing, like a plateau,
Till I came at last to the gables and towers
Of an almighty château.

The windows were shuttered. Silence reigned,
As if the woods were grieving;
The stillness of death itself was there.
All life had left. I was leaving,

When I saw at the gate the torso and claws
Of a Sphinx, and felt it summon
My terrified heart – with the shining eyes
And breasts of a beautiful woman.

A woman whose neck and face and eyes
Were glowing with bliss beyond measure,
While the curve and smile of her silent lips
Promised immoderate pleasure.

The nightingale sang sweet and low –
I simply couldn't resist it,
But took that lovely face in my hands
And gently, fatally, kissed it.

The marble statue came to life;
The stone itself was moaning:
She drank my kisses' passionate heat,
Thirsting and panting and groaning.

She almost drank my breath away –
Till at last, unable to bear it,
She pressed my body close, while her claws
Started to stroke and tear it.

O delightful torment, blissful pain!
What agony! What lust! What excess of it!
While her lips softly caressed my skin,
Her claws made a dreadful mess of it.

The nightingale sang, "O beautiful Sphinx!
O Love! Why this strange mixture
Of bliss and mortal agony?
I just don't get the picture.

"O beautiful Sphinx! Please solve for me
This marvellous riddle. For many a
Lover has asked. And I've racked my brains
Already for several millennia."

*

We were taxiing along on British ground
When I woke to hear the hostess
Thank us for flying with BA –
Most other airlines cost less.

And though everyone speaks bad English now,
I still felt strange for a minute
At Customs. My blissfully bleeding heart
Had started to spill what was in it,

When they poked their nose into trousers and shirts
And tissues, fumbling for hidden
Substances, pornographic mags
With the bits and bobs forbidden –

In England. But why me? I'd've thought,
Now I'm not far off fifty,
I'd little left of whatever inspires
In a policeman the thought, "He's shifty"!

From Manchester Airport a scenic ride
Through blackened dilapidation –

Past dreaming spires (Shell, ICI) –
Transports me to Lime Street Station.

Visiting one's parents can't have changed
A lot since the young took to living
Abroad: the latter suffer from guilt,
The former from forgiving.

Along that scenic route I read
My favourite poet's narration
Of what happened on one such trip. I give
A word-for-word translation.

– But, first of all, some verses scrapped
From the original opening passage
Of 'Deutschland', known as 'Adieu à Paris',
Which encapsulates their message:

Goodbye for now, o you merry French!
My amusing brothers and sisters!
I and my homesick heart will be back
Before you've as much as missed us.

Pour moi, I miss black bread and kraut,
And spas for taking the waters,
And German rudeness, officials and sheep,
And preachers' blonde young daughters.

Also I miss my mother a lot:
I frankly and freely admit it.
It's all of thirteen years since I paid
The poor old thing a visit.

Adieu, my wife, my lovely wife:
Anxiety – impatience – and anguish
You can't imagine – drive me to leave
You here to wilt and languish.

I'll be back, in good health, by the end of the year.
And, don't worry, we'll find a solution.
I'll bring you presents. We'll even make
A New Year's Resolution.

*

Deutschland. Ein Wintermärchen. Caput XX

From Harburg I travelled about an hour
To Hamburg. As if to charm me,
The stars looked down from the evening sky.
The breeze was blithe and balmy.

And as I came to my mother's, you
Could have knocked her down with a feather:
She wept and wailed, "My child, my boy!"
And clapped her hands together.

"My dearest child! It's thirteen years
At least since I last saw you!
You must be starving. Tell me what
I can put in the oven for you.

"I've a nice piece of fish and a fine roast goose,
And oranges as well to follow."
"So give me the fish and the fine roast goose,
And oranges as well to follow."

And as I ate with gusto and zest,
My mother, pleased and perky,
Asked questions about this and questions about that,
Some of them tricky, or quirky:

"My dearest child! and are you well
Looked after in foreign places?
Does your wife darn your socks and shirts?
Does she give herself airs and graces?"

"O mother dear, the fish is good,
But I'd better not talk while I eat it.
It's easy to swallow a fish-bone, you see.
Now don't let me have to repeat it."

And as I was finishing off the fish,
The goose appeared on the table,
And my mother asked about this, about that,
As sweetly as she was able.

"My dearest child, between life in France
And at home there must be some difference;

We Germans are hardly the same as the French:
Tell me, have you a preference?"

"O mother dear, a German goose
Is among the finest courses
On any menu. But the French
Make better stuffing and sauces."

And as I was seeing off the goose,
The fruit took up its station.
The oranges tasted so cool and so sweet,
Beyond all expectation.

But again my mother smiled and began
Asking a lot of questions,
Among them one or two which made
Some pretty hairy suggestions:

"My child, now tell me where you stand
Politically. Which direction
Do you tend in now? Which party line
Do you still support with conviction?"

"O mother dear, the fruit is good.
And I don't want to hurt your feelings:
But no matter how sweet and cool the juice,
I think I'll leave the peelings."

*

After I'd sat in my parents' house
For an hour or two, I needed
To walk about the city and see
How English life proceeded.

And should I fail to mention here
Any paternal greeting,
That may well be because he said
Nothing much worth repeating:

The arrogance which we post-war kids
Had imbibed with our free education
Reduced his ignorant virile heart
To silent accusation.

We lumpen Brits have always preferred,
Of course, to mock our masters
Behind their backs. But, given the chance,
I wouldn't put much past us.

And a finer chance for sons to cut
Their dads down to size has rarely
Been state-supported since the time
King Oliver topped King Charley.

Which is why the telly served instead
Of filial communication;
Helped soothe the disappointment caused
By my evident lack of vocation –

At least, of any which made sense
Or money. For starters, a prissy
Do-gooder. But – worst news of all –
"A poet? The mug! The cissy!"

And as I mused on past events
I passed The Philharmonic –
Or, more exactly, stepped inside
For a double gin-and-tonic.

A beer-drinker, as befits my class
But not on planes – I'd already
Had at least two en route. When I left
The pub I felt fairly steady,

Until, that is, the fresh sea-air –
Or not so fresh, but no matter –
Hit me, befuddling my brains, and turned
My stride to a lurch and a totter.

Which way to go? My brainless feet,
Rejecting il Papa's authority
At one end of Hope Street, chose the Church
Of England's free-thinking minority –

And staggered towards it. On the way,
As I paused for a piss in a jigger,
A mocking voice asked sexily,
"Eh, you, does it get any bigger?"

She stood bare-shouldered and bare-kneed
In a dark back-entry doorway.
She pulled up her skirt – "Remember me?"
She laughed. "I do it your way."

No moon – no blossom – no Märchenwald –
But November – and Maggie May-time.
Yet I followed her up an alley which
I wouldn't have dared in the day-time.

And as we picked our way between
Dog-turds and stinking litter,
She mocked my style of life in a voice
Which was neither sweet nor bitter.

"You poets, you've always been the same:
You think the world owes you a living.
You're takers – all of you – full of crap
About love or God or giving [. . .]

"And to make matters worse you kick against
The pricks. If you really must suffer
By committing every sin in the book,
You might at least act a bit tougher!

"But minor poets like you are the pits –
Pretending you're Joyce, or Heine.
Though from Dublin to Paris to Munich I've had
You all up my vagina.

"As long as you pay, my heart's of gold.
If a client's too shattered to shag, he
Is welcome to cry or spill his milk
On Anna – Hammonia – Maggie.

"Or if he's too drunk – or too old – to perform,
Instead of parting my legs I'll
Impart my wisdom. As long as you pay.
On marriage, for instance, or 'exile' [. . .]

"You see those two identical doors?
They contain the past and the future
Of where we both come from. Abandon hope
Like a man. And let me be your teacher!"

I opened the coal-shed door on the left,
Ready to look and to listen –
And entered a bank, whose chief cashier
Was Mynheer van der Smissen.

I knew him at once from his blood-red warts.
"So it's you", he whispered darkly.
"Van Koek and I joined Heywoods Bank –
Now it's a bit of Barclays.

"It was cleaner and safer than life on board
Those ships. Though the tales were all whoppers –
Re violence – bad air – bad hygiene – 'the flux' –
Abolitionists told to stop us [. . .]

"We did what we could – for instance, to sowse
The women and children daily.
The men were packed below the deck,
Where the air did get pretty smelly.

"For at least a hundred years the trade
Was pursued here with true resolution,
Encouraging growth at the heart and hub
Of the Industrial Revolution.

"Everyone gained, including those
Who are now the least forgiving.
How can you blame a Christian soul
For making a prudent living? [. . .]

"The trade in slaves began to boom
As merchants achieved their freedom:
We made our fortunes only because
Free colonists grew to need them.

"And in this modern world we're free –
To eat – or to be eaten:
Son against father – each against all –
Minds sold – mouths bought – backs beaten –"

And with that he waved his arm at a door
On which 'van Koek' was written:
"The manager – needs a private place
To contemplate his shit in –

"To wheel and deal – to plan – and to plot
The fall of any rival:
Only the fittest – the lean and mean –
Are blessed with financial survival . . ."

I entered, expecting to find van Koek
At his desk again, reviewing
Investments in this and interest on that –
And totting up the profit ensuing –

But found instead the small dark hut
Of some labourer, some low-wage earner:
Beside the fire hung the blackened clothes
Of a coal-man – or charcoal-burner.

And in that simple hut in the woods
A lonely king sat sadly,
Rocking the charcoal-burner's child
And singing a lullaby badly:

"Rock-a-bye, baby, the cat's away,
The lambs from the sheep-cote come peeping –
But the mark of Cain is on your brow,
And you smile a grim smile while you're sleeping.

"Rock-a-bye, baby, the mice will play,
I know why that mark was set there.
You'll soon be a man and swing a great axe –
The oak-trees will shake when you get there.

"The charcoal-burners' ancient faith
Is gone, and their children no longer –
Rock-a-bye, baby – believe in the King
Or in God, who was once even stronger.

"When the cat's away, the mice will play.
In the end we shall both of us snuff it –
Rock-a-bye, baby – the King in this world
And God in his heaven above it.

"My courage fails, my heart is ill,
And day by day it's iller –
Rock-a-bye, baby – you oak-burner's boy,
You were born to be my killer.

"Your lullaby becomes my dirge –
My boy, I can feel you cropping
The hoary hair at the nape of my neck,
Before you begin your chopping.

"Rock-a-bye, baby, the mice will play –
As for my kingdom, you've won it:
The cat is dead – you've chopped off his head –
My boy, you've finally done it!

"Rock-a-bye, baby, the cat is dead,
The lambs from the sheep-cote come peeping:
My kingdom's gone – and my song is done.
Are you sleeping, my baby, still sleeping?"

He sang with tuneless voice, but I
Felt moved by his emotion –
And bowed my less than sober head,
Like a priest at his devotions.

Behind me a mocking voice miaowed
Sweetly – "Well, isn't that pretty?
Almost as nice as the famous hit
By Paul of this very city."

I looked again and saw that the King
Had become my father. He carried
His gory head beneath his arm.
The face looked sad and worried.

But when he caught sight of me he smiled,
And I felt so strange for a minute
I thought again that my bleeding heart
Would spill all that was in it [. . .]

   [Munich, 1991/1998]

Hédi Kaddour

Translated by Marilyn Hacker

Hédi Kaddour *was born in Tunisia in 1945, but has lived in France since childhood and considers himself entirely European. He has published three books of poems wth Gallimard:* La Fin des vendanges *(1989),* Jamais une ombre simple *(1994) and* Passage au Luxembourg *(2000), as well as three books with smaller publishers, and a collection of essays on modern French poets,* L'Emotion impossible *(Le Temps qu'il fait, 1994). He lives in Paris, teaches comparative and French literature, drama and creative writing at L'Ecole Normale Supérieure in Lyon, and writes a quarterly column on theatre for* La Nouvelle revue française. *Other poems of his, in Marilyn Hacker's translation, have appeared or will appear in* APR, The Paris Review, Poetry, Poetry International, PN Review, Prairie Schooner *and* Verse.

Marilyn Hacker *is the author of nine books, including* Presentation Piece *(National Book Award, 1975),* Winter Numbers *(Lambda Literary Award and* The Nation's *Lenore Marshall Award , 1995) and the verse novel,* Love, Death and the Changing of the Seasons. *Her most recent book is* Squares and Courtyards *(Norton, 2001). Her translation of Claire Malroux's* Soleil de Jadis *(A Long-Gone Sun) was published by the Sheep Meadow Press in 2000, and her translations of the poems of Vénus Khoury-Ghata by Oberlin College Press in 2001. She lives in New York and Paris and is director of the MA programme in creative writing at the City College of New York.*

Tigers' Gold
        J-L Borges

As for us, when we spill our coffee, we say
that we were clumsy and that it brings
good luck, we so much want the looks of others
to be the pit in which our doubts hurl themselves. But
no light! Without blackness, the eye
would have no light. *Where are the microphones?*
he began, in front of him, his glass, his cane
and the firemen's siren in the rue de Ecoles. Then,
very quickly: *the word* moon *has been walked over
by Shakespeare.* He stumbled over
his own words, but what followed
had battled for a long time on every continent
against the hours when poems are seized
like saucepans, by the ass; *Misfortune*

he said *is more fruitful than victory*
and *I delete the astonishing.* Here:
one afternoon an old blind man's voice
rose up, he spoke of memory to amnesiac
voyeurs and threw gold pieces in the sea.

Parc de la Cité

She was being kissed
By a blunderer, the August night's
Firmament poured its
Starry milk down on them the lawn
Was even warmer
Than their skin alongside
The hedge a spied voyeur
Fled she insisted on
Uncovering her breasts. Neither
Of them had ever
Had sex did they want
That mixture of fervour and
Waste it was in the fullness of
Youth that they left each other.

Arènes de Lutèce

There are only a few chairs
And the grass is damp
Beneath our buttocks when the Steinway's
Phrases rise, but the pianist
Tonight is a fox who will not
Need to make Schubert shriek.
High up between the notes the airplanes
Pass by, the tail end of their rumbling
Sometimes fills up the curve
Of a rest, while a little
Girl rolls down her slope of lawn
Right to the edge of the rostrum around which
We'll gather afterwards for champagne
And harmonies shattered by laughter.

Uwe Kolbe
Germany

Translated by Michael Hamburger

Uwe Kolbe *grew up in the GDR and has been marked by that experience and by the later problems of German reunification. He is held to be one of the best of the younger ex-GDR poets. His work is published by Suhrkamp.*

from **Bornholm II** *(1985)*

A beautiful poem

A bay and a chestnut make up the carthorse pair.
I don't see it often, my eyes keep turning
Inwards. I see so little, and next to
The man the child in the rug not at all.

The putting up, numberless, suffered daily:
The unrest of what's meant to be talking;
The gag, to reel in the city refuse;
A friend's proper distance from loved ones, from loving.

Each one of these gentlemen thinks he'll pay off
The debts another time, soon, and the children
Think that the kitten has thousands of lives
– And yet it is only seven that are free.

A bay and a chestnut make up the carthorse pair.
I can't jump on, but must grin and bear.

Leaf-fall Bornholm I

A warm German wind, a few
degrees under zero, mutely upright
the barriers between existence,
being and life. Language forest
in the squares of grey fences (anti-
rust paint, red, among varnishes).
Deeply vision digresses, mounts
trains that go north, to the sea

and beech woods of many-bayed islands,
screeches, murmurs, green haze.
I had seen it once. Now,
in the upwind, stale city leaf
of a fruit-tree, sooty branch,
yellow derived from blackness, moist,
pale my favourite shade, the aster's
mauve quite cold in fire, motionless.
The wind rises, away from the east
as a phenomenon, continental, lifts
the bright things, hold back still, ramified
a tint with no origin, like tones,
poetry on the birth of man:
over the rails, free of frost to-
wards the city, whistling yelling,
concaving outward where ice holds and
stinks and derides (Eternal Nature).
The leap over the fence that was,
hesitation of concrete white, cream cheese,
shadowless and antibabylonian
towering, light electric, the
brighter for so clearly despising
us. The bashed-in panes then
of the station where no train
halts (when bashed-in, whose
blood rose sparkling into his eyes
and throbbed in his temples: too
visible, too feeble, just from the body,
not enough height), but upwind,
vanishing. To the other side then
leaf falls on leaf in nutritious death,
the humus
of a West Berlin allotment garden.

from **Nicht Wirklich Platonisch** *(1995)*

Never now anywhere

On the bridge they'll stay, detained,
each one in the other's arms,
kissing, and their eyes, wide-open,
up into the moon they'll stare.

Yes, they'll have a father, mother,
have forgotten both.
Are so young and yet so heavy,
all their turning circular.

To the heavens and the street lamps
love and their escape they'll swear.
But the lights, the streets stay silent,
nothing but the wind moves there.

From the bridge they will not stir,
not for parents but in vain,
only to themselves belonging
never now go anywhere.

from **Vineta** *(1998)*

You are still there?

You are still there,
    and did I see you in the graveyard?
You are still there
    and watch the same films again?
You are still there,
    take the same train and ask?
You are still there,
    can see the border clearly under the bridge?
You are still there,
    learn and share with the children?
You are still there,
    witnesses swear to it, do you hear?
You are still there,
    didn't you laugh with this stranger?
You are still there,
    with your father's mask on the wall?
You are still there,
    your mirror, look at it,
        isn't that a window?

Reiner Kunze
Germany

Translated by Robin Fulton

Reiner Kunze, *born in 1933, became well known as one of the voices trying to maintain poetic and human freedom in the restraints of life in the then DDR, from which he moved to the then BRD in 1977. His poems have been translated into over thirty languages and honoured by many major prizes.*

Robin Fulton, *born in Scotland in 1937, has lived in Norway since 1973. He has published poems and essays, and edited Robert Garioch's* Complete Poetical Works *(1983). His latest translations include Tomas Tranströmer,* New Collected Poems *(Bloodaxe, 1997) and* Five Swedish Poets *(Norvik Press, 1997). A revised and expanded selection from the Norwegian of Olav Hauge is forthcoming from Anvil Press Poetry. His translations of Werner Aspenström, Lennart Sjögren and Rose Ausländer appeared in MPT 5.*

Robin Fulton *writes:* ' . . . no doubt he'll go down in history as The Poet behind the Wall, but it would be a shame if people forgot him. His poems haven't crumbled like the wall.'

from **eines jeden einziges leben** *(1986)*

Departure

The guard swings the door shut in the silence

The signal stays at black

Further and further away the hand with the handkerchief,
the bird with only one wing

from **ein tag auf dieser erde** *(1998)*

The Little Church of St Peter's at Pyrawang

Count up to twelve it can
has never lost count

Remembers the number
by the number of apostles at supper
on the inside wall

And the belfry has four corners
the dome eight,
that makes
twelve for the day,
twelve for the night

So simple is it to know
to believe much harder

The little bell rings
as if the sexton
like a blacksmith hammered out Sunday

November

The heavens snow-black
and in the pond it starts
snowing upwards

Not a sound

As in us, when we turn grey

Going for a Walk, in all Seasons

Still arm in arm
we move away from each other

Until one winter day
on the sleeve of one of us
there will be only snow

Inland from Lisbon

On the stems of the alley trees
red letters
bark-rough

Indelible
as the revolution

The peasant though doesn't oil the axle
of his ox-cart: the squeaking keeps
wolf and devil at bay

Poetics
for Jakub Ekier

There are so many answers
yet we don't know how to ask questions

Poetry
is the poet's white stick

With it he touches things,
to recognise them

H Leyvik
Belorussia (Yiddish language)

Translated by Richard Fein

H Leyvik *is the pseudonym of Leyvik Halpern, who was born in Belorussia in 1886. Escaping from imprisonment in Siberia in 1912, he made his way to the United States, where he became a member of the Die Junge group. He is best known for his play,* The Golem *(1921). Leyvik died in 1962.*

Richard Fein *has published a* Selected Poems of Yankev Glatshteyn, *and his translations from the Yiddish of other poets have appeared in anthologies and in the four collections of his own poems, one of which,* Kafka's Ear, *won the Maurice English Award. His latest collection,* I Think of Our Lives: New and Selected Poems, *is forthcoming in 2001. Fein's memoir of Yiddish,* The Dance of Leah, *was published in New York and London (Cornwall Books).*

A Memory (I)

Once on *erev* Yom Kippur,
when I was around ten years old,
I went to my grandmother Reyzl
to receive her blessing.
A small, thin widow in her seventies,
a baker with shoulders sunken from work,
she suddenly said to me,
'Here my child is a real kosher strap,
like the one on *tephillin*; *
take it and, as the law says,
give me thirty-nine lashes.'
Surprised, frightened, I stared at her,
because I knew that lashings
were given in *shul* and only to a man.
A slight smile appeared on her lips,
as if to say, 'Don't be surprised, my child,
I've sinned and deserve to be whipped,
I'm steeped in sins.
What do you expect?
I mean, someone over seventy, how
could he not be steeped in sin?
Look, I'm up to my eyes in sin,
so, my dear child, take the strap
and give me thirty-nine lashes,

and when you've finished counting them off
I'll be able to give you my blessing
with a pure heart and, in addition
to the blessing, you'll have done a good deed.'
And before I knew it, my grandmother
got down on her knees, hunched up her shoulders,
and once again earnestly said to me, 'Go to it,
and give me thirty-nine lashes. I'm asking you.'
I did what my grandmother asked,
lifted the strap with my right hand
and brought it down on her back,
her small, bent and thin back, the strap
lightly hitting her, barely touching her clothes.
But my grandmother was annoyed, and grumbled,
'Don't spare me, whip me, the way a sinful Jew should be whipped.'
I felt my grandmother's wish
and whipped harder, and my grandmother began counting
with great pleasure, until she counted out
the full thirty-nine lashes.
Picking herself up from the ground,
filled with gratitude,
beaming, 'Ah, I feel better now',
she pressed me to her, caressed me,
and then placed her hands
on my head, spreading her fingers,
and each finger began to drip a warm prayer;
and sweet words, pure as olive oil,
tender words, like newly sprouted grass,
embraced both of my temples –
and as she went on, her prayer,
my shaking, and the flutter of my heart,
became calm, and calmer, and calmer.

* phylacteries

A Memory (II)

The rod my father used to beat
us with leaned between the oven
and the wall, warning – 'I might strike
at any time, a child better watch out.'

My father wasn't built like a hero,
the work of whipping was hard for him;
he scarcely counted out ten lashes
when he turned pale and cold.

Worn out, he'd sit on the bench,
hold his hand to his heart, grit his teeth,
and complain to the child he just whipped,
'See, you've made me sick, you thief!'

The beaten child stared at him,
unable to grasp the words, not knowing
what he did to deserve the whipping,
still baffled by the strange complaint.

Meanwhile, my mother ran to get a glass of water,
unloading her resentment through her tears:
'Why did you hit the child? He was quiet as a rabbit!'
My father couldn't hear a word of what she said.

My father had fainted on the bed,
drops of cold sweat on his white forehead:
and look – the whipped child is contrite,
and look – the whipped child revives the flogger.

Antonio Machado
Spain

Translated by Paul Burns and Salvador Ortiz Carboneres

Antonio Machado, *born in Seville in 1885, died in southern France in 1939, escaping from the Nationalist advance in the Spanish Civil War. He is increasingly recognized as one of the three or four greatest Spanish-language poets of the twentieth century. Machado's family moved to Madrid when he was eight, and at twenty-two he took a job teaching French in Soria, some hundred miles north-east of the capital. There he fell in love with the landscape and with his landlady's daughter, Leonor, whom he married two years later, when she was fifteen. She died of tuberculosis three years later, and his sense of the land and his loss marked all his subsequent poetry and gave Machado his distinctive voice – intimate, elegaic, at once detached and involved, most characteristically expressed in* Campos de Castilla (1917), *from which many of the poems here are taken. In later years his tone became more philosophical, meditating constantly on identity, and he invented the philosopher Juan de Mairena and his master Abel Martin in order to pursue his dialogues on appearances, illusions, personality, mystery, dreams and death.*

Paul Burns *is a publisher, an Oxford modern language scholar, and a lifelong part-time translator.*

Salvador Ortiz Carboneres *is Senior Spanish Language Tutor at the University of Warwick.*

These translations are from a group which received a commendation from the judges of the BCLA/BCLT Competition in 2000. The translators' bilingual edition, Antonio Machado: The Lands of Castile and Other Poems *is forthcoming in 2001 from Aris and Phillips.*

Portrait

My childhood is memories of a courtyard in Seville
and a sunlit garden with ripening lemons;
my youth, twenty years in the lands of Castile;
my story, some events I would rather not tell.
   In my dealings with women I've been no Don Juan
(I could never be bothered to dress for the part),
but I received the dart allotted me by Cupid
and have enjoyed all the comforts women bring.
   Through my veins flow drops of rebel blood,
but my verse rises from a calm, clear spring;

and, more than the learned, fashionable pious,
I am, in the true meaning of the word, good.

    I adore beauty, and in the modern fashion
I plucked the old roses from Ronsard's garden;
but I hate the excesses of modern cosmetics,
and I refuse to trill to the latest tune.

    I disdain the ballads of hollow tenors
and the chorus of crickets singing to the moon.
I pause to distinguish voices from echoes
and among all the voices listen to but one.

    Am I classical or romantic? Who knows? I wish
to bequeath my verse, as a captain leaves his sword,
famous for the virile hand that brandished it,
not valued for the forger's precious art.

    I talk to the man who always walks with me –
solitaries hope to talk to God one day.
My soliloquies are chats with this good friend
who taught me the secret of loving humankind.

    In the end, I owe you nothing; you owe me all I've written.
I bend to my work, and with my earnings I pay
for the clothes that cover me and the house I inhabit,
for the bread I live on and the bed in which I lie.

    And when the day for the last journey comes,
and the ship of no return is ready to set sail,
you will find me on board, travelling light,
practically naked, like the children of the sea.

On the banks of the Duero

It was mid-July and a beautiful day.
Alone, I climbed gullies in the rocky scree,
moving slowly, seeking folds of shade.
From time to time I paused to mop my brow
and find some respite for my heaving chest;
then hurried on, my body bending forward
and to my right, spent but supported
on my stick, like a shepherd on his crook.
So I climbed to the heights where great birds
of prey live, treading the strong-scented
highland herbs – rosemary, thyme, lavender and sage.
A fiery sun blazed down on the sour fields.
    A broad-winged vulture, in majestic flight,
lone in the sky, crossed the clear blue.

I could see, far off, a sharp mountain peak
and a rounded shoulder, like an embroidered shield,
and purple mounds rising from tawny earth –
scattered remnants of an ancient suit of armour –
the barren ranges where the Duero twists
to draw its crossbow curve
round Soria. Soria is a barbican
pointing to Aragon, with its tower in Castile.
I saw the horizon enclosed by dark hills
crowned with holm oaks and scrub;
naked rocks, some humble meadows
where merinos grazed and a kneeling bull
ruminated on grass; river banks thrusting
green poplars into the summer sun;
and silently, some far-off travellers,
so small – carters, horsemen, muleteers –
crossed the long bridge, while under the stone
arches the Duero's silvered waters
darkened.
        The Duero crosses the oaken heart
of Iberia and Castile.
        Sad and noble land,
land of high plateaus, of wilderness and rock,
of fields unploughed, no watercourse or grove;
of crumbling cities, of roads without inns,
and bewildered rustics with no dance or song
who still flow, leaving their dying hearths,
like your long rivers, Castile, to the sea.
   Wretched Castile, once the proud ruler,
wrapped in her rags, disdaining the unknown.
Does she sleep, wait, or dream? Does she recall
the blood spilt in fierce recourse to the sword?
Everything stirs, flows, wanders, turns or runs;
the seas change with the land and the observer's eyes.
Has she gone? Over her fields still roams the ghost
of a people who set their God above war.
   The once fertile mother of so many brave captains,
now barely a stepmother to indigent louts.
Once-generous Castile, long gone is the day
when Rodrigo of Vivar – El Cid – returned exulting
in his newly won fortune and wealth
to lay the groves of Valencia at the feet of Alfonso;
or when, after the deeds that proved your spirit,
you asked the court for the right to plunder

huge rivers of Indies; mother of soldiers,
warriors, champions, coming back laden
with silver and gold, to Spain, in proud galleons;
ravenous for their quarry, lions in the battle.

    Now philosophers nurtured on monastery gruel
listlessly gaze at the endless skies;
and if in their dreams they hear the far roar
of bustling merchants on the quays of the East,
they will not trouble even to ask what it is –
and now war has forced open the gates of your house.

    Wretched Castile, former proud ruler,
shrouded in tatters, despising the unknown.

    The sun is setting. A harmonious peal of bells
reaches my ears from the distant city –
time for the rosary for old women in black.
Two neat little weasels slip out from the rocks,
stare at me, flee, peer out once again –
so curious! The plain grows dark.
By the white road the inn door opens
on the sombre fields and the rock-strewn wastes.

Stéphane Mallarmé and Paul Verlaine

Translated by James Kirkup

James Kirkup *writes:* 'The problems posed by **Mallarmé**'s poetry are well-known to translators brave enough to attempt those perilous tests of language and form. [. . .] The greatest difficulty appears from the rhymes, which it is almost impossible to manage and still remain faithful to the original. [. . .] in producing these new versions . . . I have deliberately ignored the traps of rhyming. The poetic forms of the poems before **Igitur** are conventional sonnets, quatrains, alexandrines. So I have explored the possibilities of transforming those forms into something completely different in shape – the classical Japanese tanka, a verse of five lines of unrhymed 5,7,5,7,7 syllables – 31 in all. In previous experiments, I had discovered how suitable this form is when used in sequence to create narrative poems and extended lyrics. [. . .] I was astonished by the ease with which Mallarmé's intricate poetic style transfers into this alien form.'

Anguish

Tonight, I come not
conquering your body, O
beast of a nation's
sin: nor stirring in your hair's
impurities the sad storm

of incurable
ennui my kiss dispenses.
From your couch I crave
profound slumber without dreams,
hovering under nameless

mantlings, the remorse
that you, too, may taste, for all
your sable falsehoods –
you who of nothingness know
even more than all the dead.

For vice, devouring
natural nobility,
stamped me, like you, with
its sterility. – But while
your breast is stone, harbouring

a heart unscarred by
the dart of any crime, I
   flee – pale, defeated,
haunted by my shroud, in fear
of dying should I sleep alone.

Sonnet

   Virgin, vivacious,
beautifully present day —
   will it rend for us
with a beat of drunken wings
this hard lake beneath whose frost

   haunts the transparent
glacier of flights never flown?
   From days of old, one
swan recalls that it was he,
magnificent, without hope,

   who gave himself up
for not having sung the land
   of life, when sterile
winter glitters with ennui.
His long neck will shuffle off

   this blank agony –
space that a bird disavows
   but not the horror
of ground where plumage is trapped.
A phantom that his pure blaze

   assigns to this one
zone, lying immobilized
   in the chill dreaming
of his contempt, apparelled
in a fruitless exile – Swan.

Ultramarine

    Flesh, alas, is all
grief, and I've read every book.
    Fly away! Fly far
away from here! I sense now
the birds are drunk with foreign

    foam and foreign skies!
Nothing! not even ancient
    gardens reflected
in these eyes can now restrain
this heart deep-drenched in the sea.

    O nights! nor barren
radiance from my lamp upon
    the blank paper that
its blanknesses defend, nor
a young wife suckling her child.

    I shall put out to sea!
Steamship swinging her mastheads,
    weigh anchor toward
some more exotic landfall!
Ennui, made desolate

    by sad deceptions
still trusts the supreme adieu's
    fluttered handkerchiefs!
Perhaps these masts, inviting
tempests, are those that a wind

    inclines on shipwrecks —
lost, without masts, without masts
    nor fertile islets . . .
But O, my heart, lend ear to
those shanties the sailors sing!

Verlaine *is a perennial challenge to translators, and* **James Kirkup** *chose not to seek to reproduce the sonnet form that Verlaine constantly returns to, since it is 'just a convention, as is all form'. He also chose to avoid rhymes, not because they are too difficult to manage in English versions, but because tanka do not rhyme, and he prefers tanka to Verlaine's 'sweetly-chiming rhymes'. Verlaine, who wrote 'O qui dira les torts de la Rime!', may well have sympathised.*

Sentimental Stroll

The setting sun shot
its last rays, and the winds nursed
   pallid nenuphars,
giant nenuphars in reeds
sadly gleaming on dead calms.

   I was strolling, all
alone, perambulating
   my woes round the lake,
among sallows where a vague
mist evoked a vast, creamy

   phantom in despair
and weeping with the plaintive
   voices of the teal
calling to one another
amid clatterings of wings

   among the sallows
where I wandered all alone
   perambulating
my woes: the dense winding-sheet
of dark swallowed up the last

   rays of the setting
sun in its bloodless billows
   and the nenuphars,
among the reeds, the giant
nenuphars on their dead calms.

The Evening Star

The moon lies red
on fog-shrouded horizons;
   under bobbing mists
the plain falls in smoky sleep,
frogs cry in shivering reeds.

   Waterlilies close
their corollas; far poplars
   stand silhouetted,
stiff, close-set, uncertain ghosts;
fireflies seek the shrubberies;

   owls wake, soundlessly
labour black air with heavy
   pinions; the zenith
fills with their hooded lamps. – White,
Venus appears. – It is Night.

Song of Autumn
     (haiku)

   Long moans on autumn's
saxophone – wound my heart with
   languor's monotones

   Wan suffocations –
as hours creep – remembering
   days gone by – I weep –

   Borne on weary winds,
my grief – hither and thither –
   a withering leaf

Note: Because the English "violin" does not have the resonance of the French violon, *I have changed the instrument to a saxophone, invented by Adolphe Sax, who died in Paris in 1894, only two years before Paul Verlaine. [JK]*

Claire Malroux
France

Translated by Marilyn Hacker

Claire Malroux *is the author of seven books of poems, including* Soleil de jadis, *a poem-narrative of her childhood in south-western France just before and at the beginning of World War II. She is an acclaimed translator of English poetry, most notably of Emily Dickinson, and received the Grand Prix National de la Traduction in 1995.*

The Weight of the Day

the weight of the day
    slides like a sleeve
soiled or perhaps
not, from your shoulders

simply rubbed against the skin
the shoulders
    a bit more bent
from having carried
light's shadow for a while

you enter the night naked
memories run aground
    on a bank
between two currents
the stars float upside down

you don't know if
you'll wake up or where
when the owl's eyes
close, the watch kept
and the rat eaten

Night Breeze

Unexpectedly the windows open
Wide during the night. The rectangle
Swallows the bedroom, it's a different night where

Life turns inside out like a glove. A veined hand
Emerges, leaf of a negative
Hope on the phantom wall
Pointing towards what? The cliff of a lake
Sea-snows, lunar suns. A rough but tender
Tongue darts from it, paying no attention
To the guard-rails of speech.
Come unstuck, drawings, framed mirrors
The scribblings of the world
Slip from the walls docile and unafraid
Their fibres will be ripped.
A lamp gleams its star's hope in their wake
The sheets knot themselves for an escape
Exchange close body heat
For the sweet cold freedom of clouds.

Moons

While we, braced by our roots, grew old
The acacias had invaded
The sky of an aquatic garden
A whole network of riverbanks irrigating themselves
Trembling, eager to grope the unknown
No limit, it would seem, to their libido
(Beneath the forest's moss flows the torrent
Of birth, inaudible except to us
And naked flocks wander in the underbrush
Carrying out their amorous cycle)
A thrust in which passion has no
Place and the magpie chatters like a self-important God
Indentations, lips drawing away from lips
To breathe the maternal air, to climax, to murmur
(Consider these waves, leaves on a blind man's
Eyes, but for the poet, they are fertile
Moons falling into the trench of sky)

Storm

A bird the colour of almost-dawn poised
But floating spectrally above an emptiness
In the whiter emptiness of summer, beyond
This river, this city nonetheless familiar
The train-cars grip the curve as if
They would be uncoupled at the very moment
They ran into the ruins of a deserted
Town, Resafa with its gypsum ramparts
The tracks straying between two points in time
Or space with no visible distortion
The hereafter is the here-and-now seen differently
If you believe the omens in the blind spot
Where luck with no key, poetry lies in ambush

New Year

The man and the woman
behind him
their march shackled
in time

the distance between them
hardly less today
across marble-
glinted space

the sea with a pond's reflections
licking the dust
the sky split open
with inexplicable flights

blurred photograph
taken by a reporter
at the end of a long-ago
millennium

Mayakovsky
Russia

Translated by Augustus Young

Augustus Young *was born in Cork in 1943. He has published seven books of poetry, including* Lightning In Low Places *(University of Ulster, 1999). His translations from the Irish* (Danta Gradha, *Advent/Menard Press, 1975, 1980) and of Brecht's sonnets* (Adaptions, *Hardpressed Poetry, 1982) have been published widely.*

A Slap In The Face Of Translator Taste

Augustus Young writes: This free version of Mayakovsky's 'The Cloud In Pants' (1915) attempts to understand and present a Futurist poem for the new century.

Previous translations by Max Hayward and George Reavey (*The Bedbug and Selected Poetry*, Meridian Press, 1960) and Bob Perelman and Kathy Lewis (*Russian Poetry; The Modern Period*, University of Iowa Press, 1974) are out of print. Both tend towards literal renditions.

Reading Pasternak's *Safe Conduct* in the 1960s, I came across Mayakovsky for the first time. He leaped off the page into my imagination: 'The accumulating thunder of his voice'; 'A man for whom truth held an almost animal attraction'; 'Poetry that flows though history and its collaboration with real life'; 'The novelty of the age ran through his veins'; 'I was astonished by the gift he had for seeing the perfect frame for any landscape'.

'Cloud' anticipated Mayakovsky's suicide note by fifteen years. His last words are a coda to it: 'The love boat has crashed against the everyday. You and I, we are quits, and there is no point in listing mutual pains, sorrows and hurts.' Pasternak remarks: 'His drama needed the evil of mediocrity to highlight it', and he describes Andrei Beily listening to Mayakovsky reciting his poems 'entirely lost within himself, carried away on a joy which regrets nothing, because on the heights where it feels itself at home, only sacrifices exist and the eternal eagerness for these'. Pasternak's 'His dead body resembled the State' is an epitaph for the Revolution. This lumberjack's son from Georgia was already a totem in my mind.

In the mid-1970s Brian Coffey commissioned me to obtain a copy of the original on a visit to Leningrad. Subsequently, over several years, we delved into versions of 'Cloud' comparing them against the Russian topography. He regarded translation as the poet's way of understanding alien corn or foreign gold. That nothing came of our exploration may have been due to our mutual ignorance of Russian. But something was learned. Brian's epic poem 'Advent' derives structural and topographical effects from Mayakovsky. I came to realise, after conscientious efforts, that a literal translation of 'Cloud' could never do justice to its poetry. In 'The Cloud in Pants' Mayakovsky rarely says one thing when he can say another to compound or confound it. It is more than punning. As many things as possible are being communicated in order to create a public world of personal chaos. The intimate and the political coexist in a universe of multiplicities.

Last year, after an interval of fifteen years, I resumed my quest to adapt 'Cloud' into English. In the no man's land between arrogance and desperation, impatience took over. Largely monoglot and ignorant of scholarly trends, I threw caution to the wind and let fly. Within a week a draft was completed. My method (or madness) was blind as Braille. I traced the meaning and significance of the poem with clumsy hands, feeling for its shape and sharpnesses. Mayakovsky in life was clearly a great actor. I employed Method School techniques to enter his character, aspiring to more rather than less, inscaping into his personality through memoirs by people who knew him, a rich and varied field. I became his understudy, fumbling the lines on his night off.

But what about the original? Lila Brik, his great love, used to muse over the distinction between honest lying and dishonest lying. I went for the spirit rather than the letter, which is closer to the former, I think. Andrei Voznesensky wanted an explosion, not a monument, to commemorate Mayakovsky's 80th anniversary in 1984. I decided to detonate, believing the whole to be greater than the fragments. I have taken liberties with meanings and prosodic modes. Making the poem come alive demanded risks and wild guesses. To Mayakovsky arrogance and desperation were not vices. Adapting him in his own spirit struck me as a left-handed way of being faithful to him. I trust that the original has not been compromised by my presumption.

The spirit of Mayakovsky's poem is a ghost visiting a very different age. In this version I respond to 'Cloud' personally, rather than its historical context. Lila Brik in *Notebooks* records: 'Vladimir appeared at the Evening of Satire. The speaker maintained that in our conditions satire was unnecessary, that it was simpler to report things to the proper authority.' The proper authority for Mayakovsky is poetry. This is my report.

The Cloud in Pants: a tetraptych
IM Brian Coffey

Prologue

Your stuffy notions
sit on a spongy brain pan
like a puffed up timeserver
on a standing committee
that never stands
except on ceremony.

The ego lands!
And it is me.

Big shots,
I promise to embolise
your expense-account complacency
with a clot from the infarctions
of a broken heart,
and to sate
brash youthful
disregard when gangrene
sets in.

I won't wait
for grey hairs
and wordly cares
to soften my views.

I'll melt down
the chairman's iron bottom
with a poker, sizzling
spit.
    A direct hit,
disordering his points
with out-of-order
interventions.

I'll solder
his seat to the throne
of supreme deference –
a metal chamber pot

steaming with terms of reference,
previous minutes and what not.

I'll walk around the plush
boardroom shouting 'enough'
with the shrill ennui
of an impossible young man
of twenty-two.

I won't wait
for grey hairs
and worldly cares
to soften my views
('How would you behave
if you were in my shoes?')

    *

Sophisticates
play their love on a violin.
For yobbos a drum will do.
They like to bang.
             But who,
except me, can turn him-
self inside out into
a pair of lips
spitting out pips?

    *

You, upper echelons
of bemedalled bureaucrats,
learn this lesson –
the lisping party hack
in his Party hat
should know
that the doily
on a headrest
soils easily.

       Best
not to lie back
unless you want to trace
a negative Veronica

on the cambric – a blank
surface rather than a face.

Learn too not to blab your lips
like a cook finger-tipping
through a gourmet
manual –
        globs of saliva
will smudge the print.
(Isn't it
awful
what can go wrong between
the recipe and the dinner,
the Black Cap and the guillotine?)

   *

Let me pull
a grimace like the winner
of the Raw Meat Steak
competition.
           Or if you'd rather
I'll go all soggy
like a sunset
distempering night's shroud.
No longer a man with a mission,
something wet
and tender
– a cloud in pants.

           Forget this –
(the scene of the crime
is a beauty spot,
more often than not).
The idyllic does not exist.

I sing instead
men as crumpled hospital beds
and women as clichés.
The world of faeces.

Eugenio Montale
Italy

Translated by Andrew Fitzsimons

Eugenio Montale *(1896-1981) is among the most important of twentieth-century Italian poets, and was awarded the Nobel Prize for Literature in 1975. The 'Motetti' were written between 1933 and 1939, and published in 1939 as the central section of* Le Occasione, *his second book. Peter Robinson's very different version of these poems appeared in* MPT 8.

Andrew Fitzsimons *was born in Ireland, educated at Trinity College, Dublin, and is currently a lecturer at Tokyo University. His translation of Montale's* Diario Postumo *appeared in* MPT 15 (Contemporary Italian Poets).

Motets

You know this: I must lose you again and cannot.
I am like an old wound every movement,
every cry re-opens, even the salt spray
rising from the piers darkening Spring
at Sottoripa.

Town of ironworks and masts
dark and deep in the evening.
A long cold buzzing comes from the sea,
scraping like a nail on glass. I look for an unkept
promise, the pledge I had from you.
                And Hell is certain.

*

Many years, and one harder above a foreign
lake where sunsets dipped.
Then you came down from the mountains
to bring me back
Saint George and the Dragon.

If I could print them on the banner
of my furling heart . . . and descend for you
into a whirlpool of fidelity, immortal.

*

Frost on the windows. Always
together and yet always apart,
the infirm; and at the tables
long soliloquies about cards.

This was your exile. Now I think again
of mine, of the morning
when I heard over the rough terrain
the 'ballerina' bomb, dancing.

And they lasted a long time those nocturnal
Bengal lights: like at a festival.

A coarse wing brushed by, you touched your hand,
in vain, this was not your card.

*

Far away, yet I was with you when your father
entered the shade and left you his goodbye.
What did I know until then? That the pain
of *before* had saved me only for this:

you were unknown to me and need not have been: the pain
of today tells me so, as if time
had folded and brought me back Cumerlotti
or Anghébeni – among the exploding shells,
the screams, the panic of the squadrons.

*

Goodbyes, whistles in the dark, nods, winks, coughs
and hatches lowered. It's time. Maybe
the automatons are right. How they look
from the corridors, *enwalled*.
....
– Can you too feel it choke,
the again and again of the express, the merciless
beat of an endless carioca?

*

I had lost hope almost
of ever seeing you again;

and I asked myself if this thing which enclosed me,
cut me off from you, this screen of images
was a sign of death or some presence
come from the past, distorted and wavering,
a *you* dazzle:

(at Modena, through the arches
a servant in livery dragging
two jackals on a leash).

*

The black and white ups and downs of the
martins from the tele-
graph pole to the sea
don't comfort your sorrows on the pier
nor bring you back where you no longer are.

Already the elder's sap bastes
the upturned earth; the squall ends and begins and
ends. If this glimmer is a truce
your sweet threat consumes it.

*

Here is the sign; it shivers
on a wall that is turning to gold:
a lattice of palm fingers
burnt by the dazzle of the dawn.

The step that comes
so lightly from the hothouse
is not muffled by the snow, is again
your life, your blood in my veins.

*

The green lizard, if it darts
under the great whip
out of the stubble –

the sail, when it flaps
and sinks beyond the jut
of the rocks –

the cannon at noon
fainter than your heart
and the chronometer if
it counts without a sound –
....
what then? A flash of lightning
in vain can change us into something
rich and strange. You were made of different skin.

*

Why wait? The squirrel in the pine tree
beats its torchlike tail on the bark.
The half-moon sinks with one tip
shading into the sun. Day is done.

The lazy smoke is startled by a breath,
it musters itself to enclose you.
Nothing ends, or everything, if you, flashlightning,
leave the cloud.

*

The soul that releases
reels and rigadoons to each new
season of the street, feeds
on hidden passion, and finds it
at every corner more intense.

Your voice is this diffuse soul.
On wires, on wings, in the air, by accident; with

the blessings of the muse or of some device,
it comes in happy or sad. I speak of other things,
to others who don't know you and your design
is there and insists do re la sol sol . . .

*

I free your brow of the icicles
that formed as you crossed the high
clouds; you have feathers torn
by cyclones, you wake with a start.

Noon: the black shadow of the medlar tree
lengthens across the square, a gelid sun lingers
in the sky; and the other shadows nipping
into the alley do not know you are here.
*

The gondola that glides in a flash
of tar and poppies,
the insinuating song that rises
from the mass of rigging, the high doors
that close above you and the smiles of masks
that flee in swarms –

an evening in a thousand and my night
is deeper still! A dull rope writhing
in the water awakens me
layer by layer and I am one with that fisher
of eels so absorbed on the bank.

*

Is it pelting salt or hail? Laying waste
the bellflowers, scattering the cedrina.
An underwater chime comes nearer,
what you kindled in me, then fades away.

The pianola of the afflicted
is speeding through the scales, rising to the
spheres of ice . . . – it shines like you did
as Lakmé when you trilled through
the Aria of the Bells.

*

At dawn, when
of a sudden a train's
noise speaks to me
of trapped men racing
through a tunnel of stone
lit now and now
by sky, by water;

at dusk, when
the woodworm punching through
the writing-desk redoubles
its effort and the step
of the guard comes closer:
at dawn, at dusk, reprieves forever human
if you weave them together with your thread.

*

The flower that repeats
its forget-me-nots
from the cliff-edge
has no colours happier nor brighter
than the space thrown between me and you.

A metallic screech sets off, drawing us apart,
the dogged sun can do no more.
In the almost-seeable swelter the funicular
brings me back to where I was, and already it's dark.

*

The frog, first to try its chord again
from the pond that trenches into
jonquils and mists, to rustle the entwined
carobs where a heatless sun
is dousing its own light; slowly around the flowers
the coleopters' buzzing suggests
there's still a little juice; last sounds, the ungiving
life of the country. A breath
smoors the hour; a slate sky

prepares for an irruption of skeletal
horses, the sparks of hooves.

　　　*

Do not cut away, scissors, that face
that one and only from a memory slowly emptying.
Do not diminish that intent gaze
within my everlasting fog.

A cold descends . . . a hard scything blow.
And the wounded acacia shakes off
the husk of a cicada
into the first russets of November.

　　　*

The reed that sheds
slowly its red
flabellum in Spring;
the stonepath over the marsh, on the black
current overflown by dragonflies;
the panting dog come home
with a bundle in its mouth,

today there is nothing I can recognise;
but there where the reflection burns clearer
and the cloud descends, beyond her eyes
by now so distant, only two
strands of light that cross.
　　　　　　And time passes.

　　　*

. . . so be it. The sound of a cornet
answers the swarms in the oakgrove.
On a seashell where the evening sun settles
a painted volcano billows contentedly.

The coin encased in the lava
shines too on the table and holds down
these few pages. Life which had seemed
so vast lasts no longer than your handkerchief.

Henrik Nordbrandt
Denmark

Translated by Robin Fulton

Henrik Nordbrandt *(born 1945) has published over a score of poetry collections since the mid-1960s and has for long been regarded as one of Denmark's most original poets. He has spent much of his life outside Denmark, mostly in Turkey and Greece. His 1998 collection,* Drømmebroer (Dream-Bridges), *won the Nordic Council Literature Prize. A selection of his translations of Nordbrandt is forthcoming from Dedalus Press.*

My Grandfather's House

The storm makes the house tremble
but grandfather's old numbers
of *Popular Mechanics*
lie firmly in their place
dusty, faded and yellow
and full of pictures
of sensational mechanical things
out-of-date now for twenty years.
– If I opened the house doors
they'd fly off in every direction.

Instead I put my ear to the wall
where grandfather's rusty nails are resting
in timber that was already old
when he bought it.
And through the pauses in the storm
I hear him driving round the roads
in a big American car
whose engine sounds better and better
each time he stops
repairs it and starts it up again.

To de Nerval

My life too has become like a lobster
yes, a lobster
I take walks, on a lead,

because it doesn't bark
and it knows the secrets of the deeps.
I know who I am
because the lobster belongs to me
and the lobster knows it's a lobster
because I have it on a lead.
And I divide people
into four groups:
those who see only the lobster
those who pretend not to see it
those who call the lobster a dog
and those who look at me
as if they haven't seen the lobster at all.

Quicksilver

The strip of moonlight on the sea between two tall buildings
reminds me of quicksilver, that remarkable metal
that has fallen to earth from a colder world
where they use it to make images of their gods.
All that quicksilver they pour into thermometers, I thought:
it would surely fill a lake so huge no-one could see across it.
And wouldn't it really be better to use it like that
instead of wasting that beautiful metal on arses
– if we let the incurably ill saunter to and fro
on the surface of that lake in their hospital clothes
and some in wheelchairs, thin and shivering with fever
and each assisted by at least two nuns of the order
that has big white hats like full-rigged tea-clippers.
And even if this were their last outing
wouldn't they feel it to be a meaningful death
giving our life a meaning, we who would stand on the shore
following them with half-pitying, half-envious glances
when like Christ they walked out on the glittering lake, waving
their blood-stained handkerchiefs.

from **The Trembling of the Hand in November**

3
When the sun at last shines in November
it shines so powerfully
even the blind are startled
hearing the din of their shadows

4
A good land to die in, this:
a tent on an endless plain,
the tent open to the world's four corners.
You can't think further than wind and stars.

16
For God's sake don't settle down in a city!
Each city has its graveyard.
Build yourself a wooden house on a flat plateau
and ask your Lord for a nice stroke of lightning.

43
November is truly the month of darkness.
When the sun at last comes out
it's like a dictator's smile
when he praises the peacefulness of his country.

44
Beneath the November dark lies the land.
Beneath the land lie the dead.
As the land lies, some of them lack their heads
and in that respect resemble the land's rulers.

45
This skull was once born of a woman.
But its bearer has shaped it, as it is.
Through the empty eye-holes you can still see
the will that held it upright when the executioner's sword swung.

51
Him, sitting waiting for death, that's me.
Him, who can't believe in death, that's me.
Him, who has lived up till now, that's me.
Him, who can't believe that he has lived, that's me.

65
My words are fortuitous. Not symbols.
Yet now and then I recognise something
like the outline of a fish drawn on earth
in a Roman army camp in Britain.

The Address Book

I don't know where to turn:
half the names in my address book
are blocked off by an invisible cross
and the keys in my pockets belong to locks
which have long since been changed.

I have to share my feverish nights
with each of the houses I have lived in.
In the morning strangers carry me
home to no-man's-land.

I recharge myself like a magnet
that runs wild when darkness falls:
everything and everyone wants to cling to me
only to die when the current fades out.

My time is like the time we can read
on an inherited clock
and I don't dare buy a new one.

Boris Pasternak
Russia

Translated by Angela Livingstone

Boris Pasternak *(1890-1960), with Anna Akhmatova, Osip Mandelstam and Marina Tsvetaeva, is seen as among the greatest Russian poets of the Twentieth Century. He was awarded the Nobel Prize in 1958 but under extreme political pressure was forced to decline it.*

Angela Livingstone *taught literature, mainly Russian, at Essex University for thirty-one years. She has published a book on Lou Andreas-Salomé, three books on Pasternak, and two volumes of translated Tsvetaeva: one of these is* The Ratcatcher, A Lyrical Satire *(Angel Books, London, 1999), part of which first appeared in MPT 10. She is now mainly trying to write about the prose of Andrei Platonov, ten of whose stories she translated with Robert and Elizabeth Chandler (published by Harvill Press, 1999).*

Angela Livingstone *writes:* In each of these translations I have sought to reproduce or at least emulate the original's metre, and I have used rhyme wherever I could. In 'Snowstorm' my attempt to echo the original's sounds (e.g. the first line goes: 'V pos*a*de, kud*a* ni odn*a* nog*a*...') did not succeed (e.g. 'In the yard, in the archways of markets past...') so I substituted a pattern of equally frequent but quite different sounds ('In this ou*ter* quar*ter* where nev*er* a foo*t*..').

Five Poems of Admiration *(1926-31)*

To the Memory of Larisa Reisner

Now is the time, Larisa, to lament
That I'm not death, compared to death I'm nil.
I'd have found out what makes a living tale
Hold to the shards of days without cement.

How closely I examined the materials!
The winters tumbled in a heap, rains drenched,
And, wrapped up in their blankets, all the snowfalls
Held towns like tiny babies to their breast.

Glimpses of walkers in the toils of weather.
Carts creeping around a turn in the road.
Years sinking up to their throat in water,
And more years, damming up the ford, a flood.

While in the alembic nests were being woven
And life was bubbling stubbornly as ever,
And street-lamps cordoned off the various labours,
Lit up by words, lit up by stars and reason.

Now look – have any of us not been made
Of snowflakes and the secrecies of mist?
We've all been reared upon the loveliness
Of ruins – only you are beyond praise.

Wonderfully beaten into shape by battles,
You alone surged ahead, like charm, like shot.
Should life forget the meaning of enchantment
You're the unswerving answer, straight to the point.

You flew like smoke, you were a storm of grace.
One single moment in your living fire
And everything imperfect fell from favour,
Everything mediocre met disgrace.

Wander, then, heroine, into legend's depth.
That path won't tire your feet.
Spread like a loftiness above my thoughts.
In your great shadow, thought draws easier breath.

To Anna Akhmatova

It seems to me I'll pick out words that fit
Your nonpareil originality,
And if I get them wrong – so what?
I'll keep my errors, come what may.

I hear the murmuring speech of drenched roofs,
Silenced eclogues sunk in woodblock cobbles.
Manifest from the first lines, a town
Resounds and grows with every syllable.

Springtime around us, yet we can't go out.
Some miserly employer won't relent.
Hunched over her sewing, dawn burns,
Tear in her eyes from work by light of a lamp.

She'll breathe the smooth space of a great lake,
Speed to the water, fight her own flagging.
But nothing's profited from such excursions.
Canals smell of mould of mildewed packaging.

Dipping along them like an empty nutshell,
Hot wind flicks the lashes
Of stars and branches, street-lamps and land-marks
And bridge with seamstress gazing into distance.

The sharpness of an eye will often vary,
Images can be apt in various ways.
But a potion of the most dread potency
Is night's distance under a white night's gaze.

This is how I see your face, your look –
Not prompted by the pillar of salt you used,
Five years ago, to fasten onto verse
Your fear when looking back,

No, but beginning with your earliest books
And all their sharp-eyed grains of prose, your look
Makes everything that's in them pulse with truth –
The way a wire makes sparks.

To Marina Tsvetaeva

You're right to turn your pocket out
And say: go on, then, rummage round.
I don't care why the mist is dark.
Anything real is a morning in March.

Trees in soft coats of heavy cloth
Stand in a ground of gluey grey,
Though branches surely can't enjoy
Being in the thick of so much coverage.

The dew makes every tendril shiver,
It flows like fine merino fleece,
And flees and, like a hedgehog, quivers,
On its brow a dry sheaf.

I don't care whose the talking is
That floats from nowhere, overheard.
Anything real is a springtime yard
Muffled up with morning mist.

I don't care how the law's laid down
For styles of clothing in my time.
Anything real will be swept aside
Like dreams, the poet caulked up inside it.

He'll wreathe about in plumes and curls
And move like smoke
Out through a fateful age's holes
To another trackless cul-de-sac.

Pouring out smoke, he'll tear his way
From crowds of pancake-flattened fates,
And his heirs will say, as in talk of peat,
'So-and-so's epoch is alight.'

To the Meyerholds

Now the corridors' gutters have dried
And the roar has rolled back, to abate.
At the window, too late for the show,
The storm knits a stocking from flakes.

Lie in hiding backstage, in your lair.
Getting blackened in everyone's sight,
Like a fool I shall come to your door
At the interval, speechless and shy.

I shall see roofs and trees, I shall gaze
At where beauty spots whirl into space.
And from winter's behaviour – that traipse –
I'll learn how you play cat-and-mouse.

I shall say: that your pouts and your scowls
Almost shattered me, down in the stalls,
That the parcel got soaked, came unstrung,
But I'll bring you another one soon,

That on earth there's no rescue from thrall,
That my hands bring the foyer's applause,
And that these declarations are all
For you both, yet the best of them – hers.

How I love your disorder, your lope,
Avid grey in your shock of wild hair.
Well, if *you*'ve played your way into this,
Then you're right, it's the right way to play.

Once a certain archgifted director
Played so well to the young earth like that
That as spirit he moved on the waters,
Then rubbed at a rib he had snapped,

And pushed through into world from a random
Arrangement of planets and moon
To lead out an artiste by her trembling
Hand to her fateful début.

In that same unrepeatable play
As if breathing the odour of kohl,
You rubbed your whole self out – to take
On the make-up whose name is the soul.

(Chopin)

Chopin – again not seeking gain
but growing wings while on the wing –
alone is laying an exit path
from likelihood to truth.

Backyards, their picket fencing breached,
and tow-caulked huts –
two maples – at the third, abrupt,
the neighbourhood of Reitar Street.

All day these maples hear the children,
but when we light the lamps again,
and sew motifs on leaves like napkins,
they crumble in a fiery rain.

Then roaming, rounding, piercing – like
white pyramids, white bayonets,
over the street, in horse-chestnut tents,
music thunders at window height.

Bursting out of windows, Chopin
thunders, while below him, stirred
to straighten up the chestnuts' candles,
last century regards the stars.

Now how it pounds in his sonata –
swinging a massive pendulum –
with study sessions, clefs, departures,
dreams, and never death in them.

All over again? From underneath
acacias, to be crushed beneath
Parisian carriages? Stagger, race,
like life's own dangerous *diligence*?

And chase, peal, clang again, and flog
soft flesh to blood? Again
give birth to sobs, yet never cry –
only not die, not die?

One visit to the next – ride
by mailcoach in the damp of night,
overhearing graveyard tones
in wheels, foliage, bones?

At last — like a recoiling girl
who by a miracle stops the tide
of pesterers in the dark – you'll go still,
a grandpiano crucified?

*

So now a hundred years have gone
and in self-defence you brush white flowers,
and fling winged truth like stone
crashing onto common floors.

Again? – And, offering up to petals
the piano's resonant ceremony,
you fall, with all the nineteenth century,
onto these ancient cobbles.

Four Seasonal Poems (1913-22)

(February)

February. Get ink and weep!
Burst into sobs to write and write
of February, while thundering slush
burns like black spring.

For half a rouble hire a cab
and ride through chimes and the wheels' shriek
to where the drenching rain is black,
louder than tears or ink.

And where, like thousands of charred pears,
rooks will come tearing out of trees
straight into puddles, an avalanche,
dry grief to the ground of eyes.

Beneath it – blackening spots of thaw,
and all the wind is holed by shouts,
and poems – the randomer the truer –
take form, as sobs burst out.

Dream

I dreamed of autumn in the windows' half-light
and you among a joking crowd of friends
and, like a falcon that's got blood from the sky,
my heart began descending to your hand.

But time moved on, becoming deaf and old,
and, setting silver lace around the frames,
dawn from the garden overwhelmed the panes
with tear-drops of September, drops of blood.

But time moved on, becoming old. The ice-
frail sofa-silk began to crack and melt.
Suddenly you, so loud, stopped short, went quiet,
the dream fell silent, like the trace of a bell.

I woke. Daybreak was autumn-dark. The departing
wind – like rain that runs behind a cart
carrying straws – was carrying a line
of birch-trees running straight across the sky.

Snowstorm

In this outer quarter where never a foot
Stepped except for the foot of a blizzard
Or sibyl, steeped in a demon region,
Where snows are sleeping a sleep of the dead –

Stop, in this outer quarter where never
Foot ever stepped except for a sibyl's
Foot or a blizzard's, the wayward shard
Of a halter battered a dormer's glass.

No jot to be seen, and yet this very quarter
Could be a part of a borough, an area
Nearer the border (some wanderer, haunter
Of midnight, went shying from me with a shudder) –

Listen, in this far quarter where never
Foot ever stepped, there's no one but murderers.
Lipless and speechless, a spectre, an aspen
Leaf is your messenger, whiter than linen.

It knocked at all portals, it hurtled and tossed,
Peered round in a spiral of snow from the road . . .
'This is not the right city, it's not the right midnight,
And you, night's herald – you're utterly lost!'

But you whispered a purposeful message to me.
In this outer quarter where biped never . . .
I too am utterly lost . . . I'm a sort of . . .
'Not the right midnight and not the right city.'

Winter Morning

Air falls in little grey plaits and pleats.
Snow with its fugitive glances recalls:
'Time for bye-byes' – the whispers, the treacle,
While day falls behind the cradle.

Go out and you shiver all over, your skin
Stings, tingles: satchels, children,
And the street is laying itself down in the quiet
Pleats of a grey fishing-net.

All things were folded: the fox in the folktale
Who flung out fish from the truck,
The tree, shed, knitting-needles, mittens,
Wintry air, wonder-struck.

And later, by flower-pots, under the bird-cage,
Wasn't it arithmetic's pleating and plotting
That chilled the school-desk, from out in the open,
Blowing and snowing?

Your aching tooth would be treated, anointed.
But the doctor's eye had in it a madness,
Ruled and chequered, of schoolbags, snowballs,
Sums all sleepy scrawls.

Today that same purring and wintry folktale
Rustles like a snowstorm across my gazette,
To be thrown past the foam of manes and pavements
Like a grey fishing-net.

Tiny-windowed, ice-stuck, sleeved in fleece,
That same old eeriness of nestless birches
Rolls clothy night up, at dawn, over tea-cups.
Wintry air, wonderstruck.

Notes *(assisted by the notes of Pasternak and Polivanov in the volume mentioned below)*
The Russian poems can be found in Volume I of Boris Pasternak, *Sobranie sochinenii v piati tomakh*, edited by EB Pasternak and KM Polivanov (Moscow, 1989), on the following pages: 'Reisner' – 246; 'Akhmatova' – 227; 'Tsvetaeva' – 229; 'Meyerholds' – 230; (Chopin) – 406; (February) – 27; 'Dream' – 51; 'Snowstorm' – 176; 'Winter Morning' – 211.

'To the Memory of Larisa Reisner' (1926). Reisner (1895-1926) was a well-known revolutionary and writer. Pasternak met her in the winter of 1918 in a revolutionary sailors' barracks in Moscow ('I immediately realized that before me was an astonishing woman') and they talked about Rilke, on whom Reisner had published an article.

'To Anna Akhmatova' (1929). Stanza 7 refers to Akhmatova's poem 'Lotova zhena' (1922-24), which ends: 'But my heart will never forget the woman / Who gave her life for a single glance.' Stanza 8: in a review of Akhmatova's poems Pasternak had written that there was in them 'an original dramatism and the narrative freshness of prose'; in 1929 he sent her the poem here translated and told her he sensed an electric force always issuing from her.

'To Marina Tsvetaeva'(1929). Pasternak, living in Moscow, was in correspondence with Tsvetaeva, who was living in France. Her poem 'Toska po rodine' (1934) was written in response to his poem, echoing the refrain 'I don't care' ('Mne vse ravno') it attributes to her.

'To the Meyerholds' (1929). Addressed to the theatre director Vsevevolod Emilyevich Meyerhold (1874-1940) and his wife, the actress Zinaida Nikolaevna Reikh (1894-1939), the poem is Pasternak's response to their production of (and performance in) *Gore umu* [sic] at which he was present on 25 March 1928. On 26 March he wrote a long, thoughtful and admiring letter to Meyerhold saying, *inter alia*: 'I know the theatre very little and am not drawn to it ... This is the first and only time I have found myself in the *theatre*, understood what it means and believed in the conceivability of this art ... When I feel the breath of a genuine talent, it turns me into an inexperienced child, I become utterly attached to the work, feel shy of its author and make excessive use of my handkerchief.'

'(Chopin)'. Untitled, but with a note, 'Kiev VII, 1931'.

'(February)' (1913). Untitled; dedicated to his university friend Konstantin Loks.

'Dream' (1913, revised 1928).

'Snowstorm' (1915). This is the first of a pair of poems under this title.

'Winter Morning' (1922). This is the first in a group of five poems under this title.

Cesare Pavese
Italy

Translated by Martin Bennett

Tolerance

Noiselessly it rains upon the meadow of the sea.
Not a soul passes along the unswept streets.
And down from the train steps a solitary female:
from beneath her coat flashes a stretch of silk
and legs disappearing inside a dingy doorway.

The whole town seems submerged. Dusk drips cold
across every threshold, and here and there a chimney
tinges shadow with bluish smoke. Chequered gold
by chequered gold, lights are switched on, including hers
behind the half-open shutters of the blackened house.

Come morning, a sunstruck sea as the cold continues.
A woman, half-dressed, is washing off her lipstick
at the fountain, streaking its water pink. Her hair
is a garish ginger, not unlike the orange skin
that scatters the ground. Stretched there with her wet look,
she plays the matinée idol for a wide-eyed urchin.
Around the square bleary women fling the shutters open –
their husbands still dozing somewhere within . . .

When evening comes back, the rain accompanies it,
hissing over newly-lit braziers. Fanning the coals,
the wives glance across at the blackened house,
the deserted fountain. But that set of shutters is battened
tight; only inside there stands a bed, and on it
a red-head is busy, striving to make ends meet.
Night brings rest to the town and all its citizens
except the red-head whom dawn'll find at the fountain,
washing off her lipstick, soaping her arms and legs.

What's going through Deola's mind

Deola whiles away the morning by sitting in a café
and nobody even sees her. At this hour throughout the city
everyone's scuttling under still cool sunlight. She, however,
luxuriates in a lack of business, smokes, breathes air
mostly her own. Back at the pensione she'd be asleep by order,
if only to regather her powers for another stint
upon the duvet filthied by the boots of customers,
those pains in the spine. Things on your own are different.
Work's less like slavery, something you can take
or leave. The gentleman yesterday, waking her early,
kissed her, then insisted she accompany him to the station
and see him off (*'Darling, I'd stay with you here in Turin
if I could'*).
    She's a bit dazed, but otherwise feels fine,
in freedom a newfound pleasure, time to drink her milk
and nibble brioches. This morning she's half-way to being 'Signora'
and, if she spies passers-by, it's merely to stave off boredom.
At the pensione she'd be catching some duty sleep, such a fug
in there, it's small wonder the Madame goes out walking.
To work the local dives and nightspots requires assets
that, at the age of thirty, are in increasingly short supply.

Deola sits readjusting her profile in the mirror,
scrutinising herself in the cool clear glass. A bit off-colour,
but it has nothing to do with the hang of smoke. She furrows her brow.
You need a steel will like Mari's if you're to survive
back there (*'because, dear girl, men visit the pensione
to satisfy the very yearnings which girlfriends and wives
don't want to know about'*) and yet Mari would work
tirelessly, with brio even, and somehow kept her health.
Deola doesn't pay the passers going by the café
another thought now she works evenings only, contenting herself
with leisurely pick-ups at a local dance-place. Glancing
at a customer, playing footsie, she lets the orchestra
orchestrate her new career as an actress in a love scene
with some rich young lead. A single pick-up per night
and she can make do. (*'Maybe yesterday's gentleman
will take me with him after all.'*) To stay alone from choice,
and sit inside the café. To be one's own woman.

Donne Appassionate

At twilight the girls come down into the water
as the sea, outstretched, withdraws. Within the wood
each leaf twitches, and cautiously they tread back
across the sand onto the bank beyond. Only the surf
continues, away into the distance, its restless games.

The girls are afraid of the seaweed that lurks
beneath the waves, how it clutches both legs and shoulders:
so naked, after all, is the human form. Hastening upward,
they call to each other by name, keep their eyes peeled.
Even the shadows, in the dark depths of the seabed,
are enormous: they seem to flit this way and that,
as if magnetised by each passing body. The wood, then,
is something of a refuge in the setting sunlight
except the girls prefer to remain out in the open,
seated on a sheet laid cosily across the shingle.

So there they are all huddled, clasping that sheet
about their legs and contemplating the sea outspread
like a meadow in the waning light. Yet in a meadow
which of them would now dare to lie down naked?
From the sea weeds would leap, licking their feet
as an aperitif before swallowing the body whole.
Down in the sea sometimes there are eyes which flicker.

Out skinny-dipping on her own in the pitch darkness
which exists only between moons, some unnamed stranger
disappeared one night and she has never been seen since.
Big girl, they say; she must've also been dazzlingly white
or those eyes at the sea floor could not have reached her.

Cesare Pavese
Italy

Translated by Marco Sonzogni and David Wheatley

Cesare Pavese, *born in 1908, is most famous today as a novelist, and as one of Italy's leading translators of American literature. After his suicide in 1950, the manuscript of* Death Will Come and Will Wear Your Eyes *was found in his desk. It was published in 1951 (Einaudi, Turin). Geoffrey Brock's translation of the sequence appeared in MPT 11.*

Marco Sonzogni *is the Editor of* Translation Ireland *and of* College Green, *and edited* Or volge l'anno – At the Year's Turning. An Anthology of Irish Poets Responding to Leopardi *(1998). He teaches Italian at University College Dublin.*

David Wheatley *is a lecturer in English at the University of Hull, a critic and a poet. Two collections of his poetry,* Thirst *and* Misery Hill, *were published by Gallery Press.*

from **Death Will Come and Will Wear Your Eyes**

11

The gleam of dawn
breathes with your voice
at the end of empty streets.
Grey light your eyes,
sweet drops of dawn
on the dark hills.
Like dawn wind
your step and your breath
flood the houses.
The town shudders,
the stones reek –
you are life, the awakening.

   [20 March 1950]

13

Death will come and will wear your eyes –
the death that is with us

from morning to evening, sleepless,
deaf, like an old regret
or an absurd vice. Your eyes
will be a futile word,
a cry kept silent, a silence.
Thus you see them every morning
when alone you stoop over yourself
in the mirror. O dear hope,
that day we too will know
that you are life and nothingness.

Death keeps an eye on each of us.
Death will come and will have your eyes.
It will be like giving up a vice,
like watching a dead face
re-emerge in the mirror,
like listening to closed lips.
We will go down into the vortex mute.

[22 March 1950]

15

I will pass by Piazza di Spagna

It will be a clear sky.
Streets will open
on the hills with pines and stones.
The turmoil of the streets
won't change that stillness in the air.
The flowers sprayed
with colour will make eyes
at the fountains like amused
women. The stairs
the balconies the swallows
will sing of the sun.
That street will open,
the stones will sing,
the heart will beat shaking
like fountain water –
this will be the voice
that will climb your stairs.
The windows will know

the smell of the stone and of
morning air. A door will open.
The turmoil of the streets
will be the turmoil of your heart
in the lost light.

It will be you – still and clear.

   [28 March 1950]

Halina Poświatowska
Poland

Translated by Anna Gąsienica-Byrcyn

Halina Poświatowska *(1935-1967) published three collections of poems between 1956 and 1963, and two more collections were published posthumously. She studied at Smith College and Jagiellonian University in Cracow where she graduated with an MA in History of Philosophy. Her health was delicate and she was operated on twice for a serious heart disease; she died in 1967 at the age of 32. For her literary work, Poświatowska posthumously received the Pierścień award at the Gdańsk Autumn Literary Festival in 1967. She is well known and widely read in Poland. In 1997 four volumes of her collected work appeared in Cracow.*

Anna Gąsienica-Byrcyn *is a graduate student at the University of Illinois and was awarded a PhD in 2000 for her thesis on 'Aspects of Myth in the Poetry of Halina Poświtowska'.*

from **Dzień dzisiejszy**

inside me
a tree grows
the branches cling
to my veins tightly
the roots
drink my blood
dry my lips
turn brown
inside me
hunger

from **Oda do rąk**

Greetings to you my palms, my grasping fingers, and my finger smashed by the car door. My palm X-rayed looks like a sprained wing, like a tiny piece of bone drawn by its own contour. My left hand's annular finger once decorated by a ring is widowed now, deprived of its adornment. The one who gave me the ring long since has no fingers. His arms are woven with the tree's roots into one.

My hands have so often touched the frozen palms of the dead, and the warm, strong palms of the living. They know how to caress unusually by touch losing the space that separates existence from existence, and heaven from earth. My hands knowing the pain of helplessness cling to each other like two frightened birds, homeless, blindly seeking everywhere the trace of your hands.

*

the river flows inside me

with infinite patience
I caress the rock
I run my fingers
along its sharp edge
so the rock would soften
humbly
and cling to my lips

the river flows inside me

I wash leaves for the trees
and deceitfully
from under their feet
I eat up the golden sand
so they would move inside me
with their swaying twigs
so they would touch my lips

the river flows inside me

I stretch my hand
over the cat's back
fur sings
panic grows in the boughs
trees
flutter

*

they said about my eyes: they stare
but my restless eyes
danced on the tips of my fingers
to the sound of a furious unwritten melody

the melody chimed in my ears
which they said simply existed
but they were kneeling and were immersed in listening
with closed eyes

my lips – they said
are not lips
but a hot glowing flame
dashing out sparks of words
the words they were unable to understand

my legs they said – but this is a lie
I am dressed in the gold of the earth
in a shining
silver skirt
made of angel feathers

from **Wiersze wybrane**

madonnas with infants in their arms
soothe the sadness of the universe
peaceful in their tenderness
eternal in their half-smile

the walls whitened with worry
congeal in perfection
the corners cling to each other
the proper dimensions blossom

and there is a garden
water lilies bathe in the pools
a woman with slender fingers
holds a boy on her knees

*

I broke off the branch of love
I buried it in the earth
and look
my garden has blossomed

one cannot kill love
if you bury it in the earth
it grows back
if you toss it into the air
it grows leaflike wings
dropped into the water

it flashes with gills
immersed in the night
it shines

so I wanted to bury it in my heart
but my heart was home to my love
my heart opened its heart's door
and it rang out with song from wall to wall
my heart danced on my fingertips

so I buried my love in my head
and people asked
why my head has blossomed
why my eyes shine star-like
and why my lips are brighter than the dawn

I wanted to tear this love to pieces
but it was supple it entangled my hands
and my hands are bound with love
people ask whose prisoner I am

Aleksandr Pushkin
Russia

Translated by Stanley Mitchell

Stanley Mitchell, *Emeritus Professor of Aesthetics (University of Derby), is an Honorary Senior Research Fellow in the Department of the History of Art at University College London. He has published translations of Lukács and Benjamin. Readers will remember that his translation of the first chapter of* Eugene Onegin *appeared in MPT 11, to be followed in MPT 15 by the first two stanzas of Chapter Two, presented as work in progress. We reprint those two stanzas in their revised form, together with the remainder of Chapter Two, again as work in progress. Stanley Mitchell's translation of the entire poem is to be published by Penguin Classics.*

from **Eugene Onegin, Chapter Two**

> O rus! (Horace)
> O Rus'![1]

One
The country place where Eugene suffered
Was a delightful little spot;
The innocent might there have offered
Blessings to heaven for their lot.
The manor house stood in seclusion,
Screened by a hill from wind's intrusion,
Above a stream. Afar there stretched
Meadows and golden cornfields, patched
With dazzling, multi-coloured flowers;
Villages twinkled, herds would pass,
Roam here and there through meadowgrass,
And, in its thick, entangled bowers
A vast, neglected garden nursed
Dryads, in pensive mood immersed.

Two
The noble castle was constructed
As castles should be, solid-based,
Designed for comfort, unaffected,
In sensible and ancient taste,
With lofty rooms throughout the dwelling
And damask from the floor to ceiling,
Portraits of Tsars upon the walls

And stoves with patchwork coloured tiles.
Today all this is antiquated,
I really cannot fathom why;
Of course, Onegin passed it by,
Unable to appreciate it,
Since he would yawn, indifferent to
An old interior or a new.

Three
Into the very room he settled,
Where some forty years till his demise
Uncle with stewardess had battled,
Looked through the window, swatted flies.
All was quite plain; the oaken floorboards,
A table, down divan, two cupboards,
And not an inkspot anywhere.
Onegin opened up the cupboards; there,
In one lay an expenses manual,
The other stocked liqueurs of fruit
And jugs of *eau-de-pomme* to boot
Next to an eighteen-o-eight annual.
The old man, by much work perplexed,
Consulted not another text.

Four
Alone among his acquisitions,
Merely to while away the time,
He undertook to make revisions
And introduced a new regime.
A lonely sage in deepest Russia,
He eased the ancient *corvée*'s pressure,
Replacing it with light quit-rent;[2]
The serf blessed destiny's intent.
But Eugene's thrifty neighbour, flurried,
Fell sulking; in his corner he
Envisaged a catastrophe;
Another slyly smiled, unworried.
Yet all were absolutely frank:
Here was a highly dangerous crank.

Five
At first they all rode up to greet him;
But at the back porch every day
A stallion from the Don would meet him

As soon as on the carriage way
Their home-made carts could be detected,
When off he gallopped unaffected.
Outraged by this behaviour, they
Withdrew their friendship straightaway.
"Our neighbour is a boor, as mad as
A freemason, a crack-brained ass;
Drinks only red wine by the glass;
Won't stoop to kiss the hands of ladies;
It's 'yes' and 'no', not 'yes, Sir', 'no,
Sir'. All agreed this was *de trop*.

Six
Just at this time a new landowner
Had driven down to *his* estate
And was received with equal honour
As cause for neighbourhood debate.
By name Vladímir Lensky, wholly
Endowed with Göttingenian soul, he
Was handsome, in his youthful prime,
A devotee of Kant and rhyme.
He brought from Germany's misty milieu
The fruits of learning: dreams inspired
By liberty; a spirit, fired
By lofty thoughts and quite peculiar;
A speech with ever-rapturous air;
And curling, shoulder-length black hair.

Seven
Corruptions's chill had not yet harmed him,
He had not fallen yet from grace,
An amicable greeting warmed him
As did a maidenly embrace.
Of heart's affairs he had no notions,
Hope nursed his juvenile emotions,
And worldly noise and glitter still
Lent his young mind a novel thrill.
With sweetest fancy he would cradle
His doubting heart's uncertainty.
He looked upon life's destiny
As some enticing kind of riddle
To solve which he would rack his mind,
Expecting marvels of mankind.

Eight

He held that he should be united
To a kindred soul, who pines away,
Fearing her love is unrequited
While waiting for him every day;
He held that friends would raise a banner,
Wear fetters to defend his honour,
And would not cease to fight before
They smashed the arms his slanderer bore;
That there were some whom fate had chosen,
Blest comrades of humanity;
That their immortal family
Would in a future time emblazon
Our world with overwhelming rays,
Endowing us with blissful days.

Nine

Compassion, virtuous indignation,
A pure love for the common good
And glory's torment and elation
Had stirred from early days his blood.
He with his lyre roved ever further;
Beneath the sky of Schiller, Goethe
His soul burst into sudden flame,
Kindled by their poetic fame;
The Muses of sublime creation
He, happy one, did not disgrace,
But proudly in his songs made place
For sentiments of exaltation,
For yearnings of chaste reverie
And charms of grave simplicity.

Ten

Of love he sang, to love obedient,
His song possessed the clarity
Of simple maidens' thoughts, of infant
Slumber and of the moon, when she
Shines in the sky's untroubled spaces,
Goddess of sighs and secret places;
He sang of parting, and despond,
Vague somethings and the *dim beyond*,
And also of romantic roses;
He sang about those distant spheres
In which he'd long shed living tears

Where silently the world reposes;
He sang about life's fading scene
While he was not yet quite eighteen.

Eleven
Where only Eugene in their desert
Could judge his worth and quality,
He did not care at all to hazard
His neighbours' hospitality;
He fled their noisy conversations;
Their sensible deliberations
On haymaking, on liquor, wine,
On kennels, on their kith and kind
Did not excel in sensitivity,
Nor in poetic fire or wit,
Nor in intelligence, nor fit
With any art of sociability;
But the comments of their spouses dear
Were far less sensible, I fear.

Twelve
Lensky, a wealthy youth and handsome
Was seized upon as marriageable;
Such in the country was the custom;
All daughters were eligible
To court their *semi-Russian neighbour;*
When he arrived, the guests would labour
To drop a hint and to deplore
The dull life of a bachelor;
To the samovar they beckon Lensky,
Where Dunya's stationed, pouring tea,
They whisper to her: "Wait and see!"
They bring in a guitar; and then she
Begins to shrill (good God!) and call:
Oh come into my golden hall . . .

Thirteen
But Lensky, not, of course, intending
To bear the bonds of marriage yet,
Looked forward warmly to befriending
Onegin whom he'd newly met.
Not ice and flame, nor stone and water,
Nor verse and prose are from each other
So different as the two men were.

At first, since so dissimilar,
They found their meeting dull, ill-fated;
Then got to like each other; then
Rode everyday together, when
They soon could not be separated.
So (I'm the first one to confess)
People are friends from idleness.

Fourteen
But still, this idle friendship's better
Than our assault on prejudice:
We call, as if it doesn't matter,
All men, save us, nonentities.
We all aspire to be Napoleons;
Two-legged creatures in their millions
Are but a useful tool for us,
Feeling we find ridiculous.
Onegin showed much more perception
Than many; while he knew his mind
And on the whole despised mankind,
There is no rule without exception:
True worth in some he did detect
And treated feeling with respect.

Fifteen
He heard out Lensky with indulgence.
The poet's fervent talk, his mind,
Still hesitant in forming judgments,
His gaze with inspiration blind –
All this was novel to Onegin;
He tried to stop himself from making
Remarks, that were unkind or cool
And thought: I'd really be a fool
To spoil his rapture with rejection;
His day, without me, will arrive;
So, in the meantime, let him thrive,
Believing in the world's perfection;
Forgive the fever of the young,
Their ardour and delirious tongue.

Sixteen
Engaged in constant disputations,
They speculated on the source
Of pacts drawn up by vanished nations,

On good and evil and the course
Of science, on old prejudices,
And secrets in the grave's abysses,
On destiny and life in turn –
All qualified for their concern.
The poet, in argument refulgent,
Recited self-obliviously
Fragments of Northern balladry,
And Eugene, who remained indulgent,
While little grasping what he heard,
Listened to Lensky's every word.

Seventeen
More often, though, it was the passions
Which occupied my anchorites.
Free from their stormy depredations,
Onegin spoke of their delights
And sighed, regretting their enticement.
Happy who tasted this excitement
And in the end could loose its knot,
Still happier who knew it not,
Who cooled the heat of love by parting,
Changed enmity to obloquy;
Yawned with his wife in company,
Remained immune to jealous smarting,
And was not predisposed to lose
An heirloom to a crafty deuce.[3]

Eighteen
When to the banner we have gathered
Of sensible tranquillity,
When passion's flame at last is smothered
And we as an absurdity
Consider its caprices, surges,
Belated signs of former urges –
Resigned, but not without a tear,
We sometimes like to lend an ear
To tales of other people's passions,
And these stir up the heart again.
Exactly thus, a veteran
Will gladly eavesdrop on confessions
Of young, mustachioed blades who strut,
Oblivious of him in his hut.

Nineteen

For flaming youth is quite unable
To keep its thoughts and feelings close,
But always is prepared to babble
Out loves and hatreds, joys and woes.
Of love a self-declared survivor,
Grave Eugene heard his friend deliver
His heart's confession lovingly
And tell his whole biography;
A simple soul, not seeking glory,
He laid his trustful conscience bare.
Eugene with ease discovered there
The poet's young, romantic story,
A tale of copious feelings – or
A chronicle we've heard before.

Twenty

Ah, how he loved, we cannot know it,
Today such love's anomalous;
Only the mad soul of a poet
Is still condemned to loving thus.
Always and everywhere one vision,
One single, customary mission,
One single, customary grief;
Not distance with its cool relief,
Nor lengthy years of separation,
Nor hours devoted to the Muse,
Nor foreign beauties he might choose,
Nor merriment, nor meditation
Had changed in him a soul whose fire
Was lit by innocent desire.

Twenty-One

Scarcely a youth, not yet essaying
The torments of the heart, he fell
In love with Olga, watched her playing
The games of a young demoiselle;
By overshadowing oaks protected,
He shared the games that she selected;
Their fathers – friends and neighbours, they –
Foresaw their children's wedding day.
Under a humble porch the maiden,
Endowed with innocence and grace,
Blossomed beneath her parents' gaze,

Like lily of the valley hidden
In densest grass, unbeknown by
The passing bee or butterfly.

Twenty-Two
By her the poet had been given
His early dreams of ecstasy,
And thinking of her would enliven
His pipe's first moans of melody.
Farewell to golden games now over!
Instead he looked for woodland cover,
Seclusion, stillness, and the night,
The stars and heaven's brightest light,
The moon amid her constellation
The moon to whom, when evening nears,
We dedicated walks and tears,
Our secret sorrow's consolation . . .
But now we only see in her
A substitute for lamplight's blur.

Twenty-Three
All modesty and all docility,
Always as merry as the morn,
As simple as a life of poetry,
As charming as love's kiss newborn,
Her eyes as azure as the heaven,
Her flaxen curls, her smile so even,
Her movements, voice, her slender stance,
These made up Olga . . . but just chance
On any novel at your leisure,
Her portrait's there – it's very sweet,
And even I found it a treat,
But now it bores me beyond measure.
Reader, I shall, if you'll allow,
Turn to the elder sister now.

Twenty-Four
Her elder sister was Tatiana . . .
This is the first time that we grace
Our novel in this wilful manner
With such a name, so out of place.[4]
What of it? It is pleasant, sonorous;
But well I know that it is onerous
With memories of olden days

Or housemaid domiciles! A craze
We must admit to is the gaudy
And graceless names we're apt to choose
(Our verse deserves still more abuse);
Enlightenment is not our *forte*,
It's simply opened wide a door
To affectation – nothing more.

Twenty-Five

So she was called Tatiana. Lacking
The beauty of her sister and
Her rosy freshness, not attracting
The eye in that secluded land,
A wayward, silent, sad young maiden,
Shy as the doe in forest hidden,
She seemed inside her family
A stranger, an anomaly.
She could not snuggle up to father
Or mother; and, herself a child,
By children's games was not beguiled
And would not skip or play but rather
Would quietly through a window stare
And all day long not move from there.

Twenty-Six

A pensive mind was her attendant
Already from her infancy
And filled with reverie resplendent
The flow of rural liberty.
Her delicate fingers knew not needles;
Embroidery seemed made of riddles;
To animate a linen cloth
With silken patterns she was loath.
Desiring to assert her power,
The child diverts her pliant doll,
Encouraging with pastimes droll
The world of etiquette to flower,
And to her doll with gravity
Imparts mammá's morality.

Twenty-Seven

But even in these years Tatiana
Never picked up a doll or chose
To tell it in a grown-up manner

Of town events and fashion shows.
Averse to childish pranks and banter,
She liked instead, when it was winter,
To read a fearful tale at night,
Which gave her heart much more delight.
Whenever nurse would fetch for Olga
A company of little friends
To play upon the manor lands,
She found their games of catch too vulgar.
Their ringing laughs and jollity
Wearied Tatiana equally.

Twenty-Eight
She liked instead to fix her eyes on
The moment of the dawn's advance
When, fading on the pale horizon,
The stars complete their choral dance,
And at its edge the earth is glowing
And the wind that heralds morn is blowing,
And by degrees the day ascends.
In winter when the night extends
To half the world for so much longer,
And longer too the lazy East,
When moonlight is bedimmed by mist,
Continues to repose in languor,
Awakened at her usual time,
By candlelight from bed she'd climb.

Twenty-Nine
Fond early on of reading novels,
For only they would make her glow,
She fell for the deceiving marvels
Of Richardson and of Rousseau.
Her father was a decent fellow
Of eighteenth century mould, but mellow
Who found no harm in books, which he,
Not having read at all, would see
As empty playthings, unengrossing.
He cared not that a secret tome
Would lie till morning, quite at home,
Beneath his daughter's pillow dozing.
And yet his wife enthused upon
The narratives of Richardson.

Thirty

Her love for them was not connected
With her perusing Richardson,
Nor with the fact that she rejected
Lovelace for virtuous Grandison.
But in the past Princess Alína,
Her Moscow cousin, when she'd seen her,
Had talked about these gentlemen.
Her husband was her fiancé then,
A bond to which she'd not consented;
She sighed after another one
Whose heart and mind had far outdone
The simple love of her intended;
This Grandison was smart at cards,
A fop and Ensign in the Guards.

Thirty-One

Like him, according to the fashion,
She always dressed to look well-bred;
But soon, without the least discussion
The girl was to the altar led.
And, to dispel her dreadful grieving,
Her husband soon was wisely leaving
To take her to his country seat
Where God knows whom she was to meet;
At first she raved and sobbed and ranted,
All but divorced her husband, then
Took part in household matters, when
She grew accustomed and contented.
God gave us habit to redress
Our yearnings after happiness.

Thirty-Two

With habit's help she soon recovered,
Although her grieving heart still bled;
Something momentous she discovered
That made her feel quite comforted:
Between her household work and leisure
She ascertained the perfect measure
For governing her husband's life,
And then became a proper wife.
She drove out to inspect the farming,
She pickled mushrooms, spent and saved,
Foreheads of new recruits she shaved,[5]

Enjoyed a weekly bathhouse warming,
Beat maidservants who made her cross –
She, not her husband, was the boss.

Thirty-Three
Once she'd have written verses in a
Young maiden's album with her blood,
Have called Praskóviya – Polína
And made a song of every word.
She wore tight stays to suit convention,
A Russian N just like a French one
She learned to utter through her nose;
But all of this soon met its close:
Stays, album and Princess Alina,
Her sentimental verselets, all
She now forgot, began to call
Akul'ka previous Selina,[6]
And finally appeared, becapped,
Inside a quilted housecoat wrapped.

Thirty-Four
But still her husband dearly loved her,
Upon her schemes he did not frown,
In all he cheerfully believed her,
And ate and drank in dressing-gown;
His life with undemanding labours
Rolled gently on; sometimes his neighbours,
A kindly group and casual,
Met of an evening in the hall,
Complained, engaged in tittle-tattle
And chuckled over this or that
Till it was time for tea, whereat
Olga was told to fetch the kettle;
Then supper came, and close of day,
When all the guests would drive away.

Thirty-Five
They kept, while tranquilly existing,
The customs of antiquity,
Indulged themselves at Shrovetide, feasting
On Russian pancakes (or *binȳ*);
They fasted twice a year for sinning,
They loved round swings, which sent you spinning,
And choral dances, guessing songs.

On Trinity, among the throngs
Of yawning peasants at thanksgiving,
They touchingly shed tears, three drops
Upon a bunch of buttercups;[7]
They needed *kvas* like air for living;[8]
And at their table guests were served
In order, as their rank deserved.

Thirty-Six

And thus the two of them grew older
Until the grave invited down
The husband and the erstwhile soldier,
And he received a second crown.[9]
He died approaching midday dinner,
Mourned by a neighbour at the manor,
By children and a faithful wife
More truly than occurs in life.
He was a simple, kindly *barin*,[10]
And there, above his last remains,
A solemn monument proclaims:
"The humble sinner, Dmitrii Larin,
Slave of the Lord and Brigadier
Beneath this stone reposeth here."

Thirty-Seven

His own penates reinstating,
Vladímir Lensky soon stood by
His neighbour's grave where, contemplating,
He blessed the ashes with a sigh;
And sorrow long his heart affected,
"Poor Yorick," he exclaimed, dejected,
"He used to carry me aloft,
And in my childhood days how oft
I'd play with his Ochákov medal!"[11]
He destined Olga as my bride,
Would say: Perhaps I shall have died . . ."
True sadness pricked Vladímir's mettle,
He there and then inscribed for him
A gravestone madrigal or hymn.

Thirty-Eight

Still there, in tears, he wrote another
To mark the patriarchal dust
Of both his father and his mother . . .

Alas, each generation must
By Providence's dispensation
Rise, ripen, fall in quick succession
Upon life's furrows; in its wake
Others the selfsame journey take . . .
So, too, the heedless tribe now living
Grows up, gets animated, seethes,
Sees off its forefathers with wreaths.
But its time, too is soon arriving,
And one fine day our grandsons will
Hurry us out with equal zeal!

Thirty-Nine
Meanwhile, dear friends, enjoy the pleasure
And lightness of this life which I
Find meaningless in such a measure,
I almost wish to say goodbye;
'Gainst ghosts I keep my eyelids lowered,
Yet distant hopes have sometimes flowered,
Arousing once again my heart.
I'd find it grievous to depart
Without the tiniest recognition.
Not courting praise, I live and write,
But still, it seems, I'd take delight
In winning fame for my sad mission
So that the merest line I've penned
Will hail me like a faithful friend.

Forty
And someone's heart it will awaken;
And this new strophe that I nurse
Will not in Lethe drown, forsaken,
If destiny preserves my verse.
Perhaps a future ignoramus
Will comment when my portrait's famous
(A flattering hope!): "Now who is he?
He's someone who wrote poetry!"
I offer *you*, then, my oblations,
Admirer of Aónia's maids,
O you, whose memory never fades,
And saves my volatile creations,
Whose hand, ensuring my renown,
Will pat the old man's laurel crown![12]

Notes

1   The old form for *Rossiya* (Russia)
2   A *corvée* was the unpaid labour due from a serf to his owner; the form of quit-rent described here was paid by the serf in commutation of his *corvée* or in consideration of being allowed to ply a trade elsewhere.
3   The 'crafty deuce' refers to the hazardous role of the card in banking games such as faro or stuss.
4   Tatiana was a peasant name. In a note Pushkin writes: "The sweetest-sounding Greek names such as, for example, Agafon, Filat, Fedora, Fekla etc. are used by us only among the common people". Pushkin's names are Russified.
5   This was a way of distinguishing often undisciplined serfs, who were to join the army.
6   In the two cases mentioned, the future Mrs. Larin restores a fashionable and gallicized pseudonym (e.g. Polina/Pauline) to its peasant and Russian original.
7   A way of atoning for sins: the number of teardrops represents the number of sins.
8   Russian national soft drink (sometimes mildly fermented), usually made of leavened rye dough or rye bread with malt. There are other varieties in which honey or fruit is used.
9   The first crown is the wedding crown.
10 The term *barin*, which is used in some English-language history texts, means 'squire' or 'landowner'.
11 Ochakov was a fortified Moldavian town and port on the Black Sea, some forty miles West of Odessa. It was seized from the Turks by Suvorov in 1788 and became Russian by the treaty of 1792. The commemorative medal was given to all officers who took part in the campaign and therefore does not distinguish Larin who, as a brigadier (a general's rank), might have expected the more illustrious 'order'. The commentator Lotman suggests that Pushkin's award keeps Larin ordinary.
12 Alongside the future ignoramus, Pushkin addresses his future devotee. The 'old man' refers to Pushkin, should he live that long. A Latin teacher at Pushkin's lycée would, before embarking on a classical text, declare: "Let's pat the old man on the head".

I am indebted, in compiling these notes, to the commentaries of Nabokov, Brodskii and Lotman.

Alexander Pushkin
Russia

Translated by Timothy Ades

Timothy Ades' 33 Sonnets of Jean Cassou *won a BCLA/BCLT award in 1996. His* Homer in Cuernavaca *by Alfonso Reyes is now in print.*
   Timothy Ades writes: *Thirty versions of this poem appeared in MPT 15: a transliteration and a literal version had been sent to thirty paladins. I was set the same exercise at a recent summer school.*

Worldly Power

When the grand, when the solemn celebration was in train
And the Lord on the cross was expiring in His pain,
At the side of the life-giving Rood
Sinful Mary, and the Virgin most holy and good,
A pair of women, stood;
Who could reckon up their anguish? No-one could.
But to-day at the foot of the hallowed Rood,
As it might be the city governor's entry,
We see not women but men, not saints,
But with rifles and shakos, two fearsome sentries.
Say, why the custodial vigilance?
Is the crucifixion a treasury fief?
Were you nervous of mice, or perhaps of a thief?
Would you add to the glory of the Tsar of Tsars?
Or are you the master's rescuers,
A security force for the thorn-crowned Christ
Who subjects his flesh to the nails and spears
And the flails of his executioners?
Is the common herd not sufficiently nice
For the one who saved mankind by His sacrifice,
And the sauntering scions of the civilised class?
Will you suffer not the people in freedom to pass?

Salvatore Quasimodo
Italy

Translated by Marco Sonzogni and Gerald Dawe

Salvatore Quasimodo *was awarded the Nobel Prize for Literature in 1959. This year is the centenary of his birth in Sicily in 1901, and the translations here are dedicated 'in memory of Salvatore and for Alessandro' (his son).*

Gerald Dawe *is the author of five collections of poetry, most recently* The Morning Train *(1999). He has also published* Stray Dogs and Dark Horses: Selected Essays *(2000). He teaches at Trinity College Dublin.*

The poems here are selected from the section Poesie disperse *in* Poesie e discorsi sulla poesia di Salvatore Quasimodo, *edited and introduced by Gilberto Finzi, with a preface by Carlo Bo (Mondadori; Milan, 1973).*

from **The Night Fountain (Selected uncollected poems)**

Primroses

Blood clots hanging over torn green velvet.
Ah, the wounds of the fields!
Spring has broken the veins of swollen breasts
breathing in deep the sweet air.
Wind gusts with eager lips. A kiss!
And the blood-red primroses float
on the waves without stirring.

Birthday

Shipwreck of crimson trees:
the light moves,
sweet start of the day,
for the grass, for the water,
a gift of joy.

The sky swells with clouds and leaves,
dark cars full
of fog make noise.
My heart couldn't bear
a heavier pain.

A light ferment, I listen to myself:
mirroring the green
a net of veins and flowers
spreads;

it breathes loving:
the voice
is the first shiver in the air.

The Flower of Silence

A little cypress, the capital of a Doric column,
and the fresh sky of the mild
majolica-coloured morning.

Sorrow, an eternal spring of good things,
here is your temple, your sacred stone
for the sleep that knows no torment.

Not the scented feathers of alcoves
but the red caresses of a lit hand
will give you, intact, the flower of silence.

Serenity

Don't throw away leftovers of bread;
there's someone behind your door,
there's someone whose hope is never dead

until they see your twisted face.
Serene, the light of morning
silently covers the dead dawn

and sleeps in its childlike eyes.

The Burning Myrrh

So will we sing, will we sing in vain
all the roses in our greenhouses,
the bitter perfume of rich lands,
lakes of *ciano*-painted dreams;

dawn owls risen from a wash-basin
of blue cornflowers and violets
withered at once before the sun,
big and serene like a sacred fire?

Stars fly over our heads
like butterflies that with the slow whirr
of white wings over deserted fields
go into the dark looking for flames.

Ciano: a literary term meaning 'blue'.

The Night Fountain

The scent of an orange blossom, an enchanted night fountain,
when sleep escapes me
I call you with the names of most delicate flowers
– my bread with the white cross
all stars and snow – .

When the violet jumps
on the walls of greenhouses
I look in the crimson
for your eyes so calm
like the eyes of a lamb,

and yet they hurt me so much
like words of farewell,
like words that remain
unspoken in the heart
for fear of finding them no good.

I left two kisses on your orchid body,
they looked like two little flowers
like those which grow at the roadside,
so small, suffering the cold,
and outside the dappled sky bore my fever

and I thought I was happy.

The Swallow of Light

Love is a swallow of light
that flies from my garden to yours
and embroiders crystal words
in the night that unfolds like a cloud of myrrh.

Are you harmony, perhaps, closed
in my heart like a violet
that, disillusioned, looks in the sky
for the first ray, the first sparkle?

In the morning the swallow drinks at a well
where water is a bunch of butterflies
that talk about flowers
near three little cypresses,
three small sleeping dreams.

Pray that the well will never dry;
with joined hands I will listen
to gold music rustle on the sunset's harp
or the half-closed wisteria, like eyelids
in the melancholy of one who said

"Goodbye"!

Jacques Réda
France

Translated by Jennie Feldman

Jacques Réda, *born in Lunéville in 1929, is one of France's leading poets. A former editor of* La Nouvelle revue française, *he has published several volumes of poetry including* Amen, Récitatif, La tourne *and* Retour au calme *(Gallimard 1968, 1970, 1975, 1989) and the prose poems,* Les ruines de Paris *(Gallimard, 1977, 1993). His most recent collection is* La course *(Gallimard, 1999). He has also written books on poetry and jazz. In 1997 he was awarded Le Grand Prix de la Poésie by the Académie Française, and in 1999 the Prix Goncourt for poetry.*

Jennie Feldman *was born in South Africa, graduated from Oxford University, and now lives in Haifa, Israel. A former producer and presenter of radio documentaries, which won three international awards, she is now completing her first full collection of poems, and preparing a volume of translations of poems by Jacques Réda.*

from **Récitatif**

Hotel Continental

Solitude is chill and soft on the tongue that names it
And lifts the soul a little in broken light;
That's when – out of the desertion, the severing – a figure
Rises and beckons in its turn under wallpaper leaves,
In the wardrobe's creak and the margins of a book
That can't be read by the distant gaze turned on us.
But there's no pronounceable name for this pit that divides
The self in two, and makes of every heartbeat
A marked door slamming when eviction's done.
Here I am with one more stair to go,
Where a chair's consoling presence waits
And reassurance murmurs from the basin;
Where even solitude withdraws its hand from mine
And leaves me, like that day after you'd gone,
When standing in the rain I saw a circle of time
Impossible to reckon, and inside it
The little park gate clashing iron on iron.

from **Amen**

Autumn

Ah, a sound I recognize – autumn's rambling gust
Here already; deep inside the forests it breeds thunder
Silently, and cripples overloaded orchards.
A solemn wind that's like us, speaking our language
Where disaster sings an undertone.
                                    Let us offer him
The roses' waning, smells by the cartload slowly pouring
Into the valley, and stanzas of birdsong he unravels
In the warmth that cupped our sleep.
                                    This evening's
Sky long shut within its brightness, expands and breaks away
Dragging the horizon of its slant sail; and the blue
Once our habitual threshold, moves off in long strides
Through the creased vale lying open for the rain to read.

Umberto Saba
Italy

Translated by Simon Carnell and by Robert Chandler

Umberto Saba *(1883-1957) was born to a Jewish mother in Trieste, where he lived for much of his life working as an antiquarian bookseller. During the German occupation in the Second World War he was in hiding in Florence. His poetry is autobiographical and shows an early interest in psychoanalysis. His collected poems wre published in 1988* (Tutte le poesie, Meridiani).

Simon Carnell *is a freelance writer and lecturer, and has published poems in many journals, including* London Review of Books, London Magazine, Times Literary Supplement, Harvard Review. *He is currently compiling his first poetry collection. His interest in Saba began as an interest in Trieste, and he notes in Saba's work a 'quite subtle political resonance – combined with an engaging directness and deceptive simplicity'. An earlier version of 'The Pig' was first published in* Thumbscrew.

Robert Chandler *is a prolific translator of prose and poetry, especially from Russian. His co-translations with Elizabeth Chandler and Angela Livingstone of Andrei Platonov's fiction have been published by Harvill Press.*

The Goat

You spoke with a goat.
It was alone in a field, it was tethered.
Stuffed with grass, soaked with rain,
it was bleating on.

That monotonous bleat –
it answered to your condition.
You responded at first
as a joke; then because sorrow's eternal,
and speaks with one unchanging voice.
That's the voice you heard,
crying in a solitary goat.

In a goat with a Semitic face
every other hurt complained,
that of all creaturely existence.

[SC]

The Pig

The swill, the flower of filth, is purified
by his instinctive hunger for it.
Take it away and he shrieks like a spanked child.

But what for him is a great treat
is, to my way of thinking, a torment.
He's no inkling as to why the farmer's wife,
chasing the poor thing around the yard,
wants him porky and well stuffed:
clueless, like the rest of the living,
as to what he's destined for
when he's reached perfection.
If I look out of his eyes, switch skins,
I can feel the knife, the cut throat scream
as the dog barks amongst the onlookers,
and the farmer's wife laughs in the open door.

I'm the one fighting back the tears,
looking into the porker's beatific face.

   [SC]

Thirteenth Match

On the terrace a sparse crowd
tried to keep warm. And when the sun
ducked behind a house, the action
on the field clarified:
red shirts chasing white shirts,
back and forth,
in a peculiar iridescent light
which kept the night at bay.
The wind diverts the ball from its path;
Dame Fortune slips
the blindfold back over her eyes . . .

And it's good
to be gathered in a small crowd –
frozen like the last men
on a hill –
watching the very last game.

   [SC]

Ulysses

In my youth I would sail along
The Dalmatian coast. Islands appeared
On the glassy sea, white gulls sometimes
Pausing above them, intent on prey, –
Slippery, draped in weed, emeralds
Glittering in the gold sun. When high
Tide and night extinguished them, sails
Slipped off into the deep, to leeward,
Fleeing their threat, to the no-man's land
That has become my kingdom. Harbour
Lights are for others. I am called
Oceanwards by my untamed spirit,
By this painful, unquenched, love of life.

[RC]

Egon Schiele

Translated by Will Stone and Anthony Vivis

Egon Schiele *(1890-1918) is best known as a painter of tortured portraits and lyrical landscapes. He was the youngest of the Viennese Expressionists who in 1909 rebelled against the Academy and formed the* Neukunstgruppe *('New Art Group') – his fellow rebels were Gerstl and Kokoschka. Schiele died in the influenza epidemic at the end of the Great War, some six months after finally achieving acceptance and success with his one-man show at the Vienna Secession in March 1918.*

1910

I was first to see the eternal avenues of spring, the raging storm
and had to take my leave, – endlessly of all the locations of life.
in those early days the level lands were around me, at that time
I had already heard and smelled the miracle flowers, the speechless
gardens, the birds. The birds? – in whose eyes I saw myself pink
with shining eyes? – The birds are no more. – Often come autumn
I would weep with half my eyes. Then I delighted in the glorious
summer and laughed, as in summer I painted for myself the white
winter. In spring I dreamt of the universal music of all living things.
Until that time there was joy, then began times of idle leisure and the
lifeless schools. I encountered endless dead cities and mourned myself.
At that time I experienced my dying father. My brutal teachers were
always my greatest foes.
Now I must rekindle my life!
At last I can see the generous sun once more and be free.

Visions

Everything was dear to me –
I wanted to look at the angry lovingly,
so that their eyes must reciprocate;
and I wanted to offer gifts to the envious and tell them
I am worthless.

... I heard tender swelling winds sweep through
lines of air.
And the girl

who read aloud in a lamenting voice
and the infants,
who gazed at me with huge eyes and on my return look
snuggled up,
and the far off clouds,
which gazed upon me with virtuous folded eyes.

The white pallid girls showed me their black
legs and red garters
and spoke with black fingers.
I, however pondered the far worlds
of finger flowers –
and whether I myself am there
I was hardly aware.

I saw the park: yellow-green, blue-green, red-green, violet-green,
sunny-green and shudder-green –
and listened to the blossoming orange flowers,
then I bound myself to the oval park wall and listened
to the gaunt-footed children,
who were touched with blue and streaked with grey
by the pink bows.
The tree column led lines exactly where they sat down
long around.
I pondered my coloured portrait visions,
and it struck me
that only once had I spoken
to all of them.

Music While Drowning

In no time the black river yoked all my strength
I saw the lesser waters great and the soft banks steep and high.

Twisting I fought
and heard the waters within me,
the fine, beautiful black waters –
then I breathed golden strength once more.
The river ran rigid and more strongly.

Antun Branko Simic
Croatia

Translated by Courtney Angela Brkic

Antun Branko Simic *(1898-1925) was born in Herzogovina and led a difficult life, dying of tuberculosis at the age of twenty-seven in Zagreb. Only one collection of his work was published in his lifetime, but it paved the way for much of contemporary Croatian poetry. Initially influenced by German expressionism, he quickly found his own voice. Though apparently cold and rational, his poetry is deeply passionate, and much concerned with physicality, God and death. He wrote numerous articles, polemical works and essays, and helped to found several literary magazines.* Sabrana Djela *(Selected Works) was published posthumously in 1960.*

Courtney Angela Brkic *graduated from the College of William and Mary in 1994. She studied in Zagreb, Croatia, with a Fulbright Scholarship (1995-1996) and remained in the region until 1999. She has worked as an independent translator, and is currently studying for the MFA in writing at New York University with a New York Times Fellowship.*

The Return

You do not even sense
that I have returned and am near at hand

At night when the silent moon murmurs in your ear
know:
it is not the moon circling your house
I am wandering on the blue paths of your garden.

When walking on the road in the dead noon light
you stop,
frightened by the cry of a strange bird
know:
that was my heart's call from the near banks

And when you see some shadow move in the twilight
from the far side of the dark, silent water
know:
I am walking, proud and exultant
as if beside you.

My love, my friend and I

On my love's body
your gaze
rests
caresses
slips and falls
like a dead black bird

Your lust howls and howls
around the body of my sweetheart

Your gaze and mine
a collision of hatred
scrapes
bursts
hurts and hurts

Through space
the red stream
of my blood
sprays

Famished death eats the heart

Paul Snoek
Belgium (Flemish language)

Translated by Kendall Dunkelberg

Paul Snoek *was the pseudonym of Edmund Schietekat, born in 1933 near Antwerp. One of Belgium's best-known postwar poets and a member of the second generation of experimental writers in Flanders, he published twenty volumes of poetry between 1954 and 1982. He received many prizes, including the Belgian Triennial State Prize in 1968 for* De zwarte muze *(The Black Muse), from which the poems here are taken. He was a director of the Flemish PEN Centre, and was also well known as a painter, motocross racer and television talk show panellist, whilst leading a busy private life in business, arts administration and antique dealing. He was killed in October 1981 when the car he was driving struck a crane on a country road in West Flanders. Translations of poems by Snoek appeared in the First Series of* MPT *(27-28, 1976).*

Kendall Dunkelberg *is a poet who has published translations in many American magazines. In 1997 he was guest editor and translator for a special Dutch and Flemish issue of* The Literary Review. *His translation of Snoek's trilogy,* Hercules, Richelieu and Nostradamus, *appeared in 2000 (Los Angeles: Green Integer).*

Memoirs

How can it be?
Originally I had hoped
to go through the house unnoticed
disguised and superfluous as a human
between the houses and their people.

And to bear my grief daily
until it turned translucent
and bearable as daylight.

I thought it was sufficient
to sob for a night in a long, thick bed,
and to cry once down to the heartbone.
But no.

I am used to crying in the first person
and alone.
I make like I smile
and with all my body parts inhabit my body.

How can it be,
that I didn't know that grief
evens the fierce relief off of love
and that life is no zenith
but a standstill?

And yet it is sad
that no smuggler's slang exists,
no convenient code
in which I secretly could write
about the phenomenon homesick
and make like I'm writing about the moon,
yes, writing thick books
about the so-called moonlight.

But in reality
about the house I lived in
and still have abandoned
with in my marrow the warmth
of yet so much future regret.

My skin turns white from it
and still whiter my shiver.
When I read in bright mirrors
the old texts about the eye.

The turned-to-porcelain eye.

When I see how clear the tracks are
that my shadow left behind in my past.
My shadow, people,
who out of loneliness
the body of his bearer
no longer preserves, no longer recognizes.

A slang, like I said
with which I could write
about the heart and its thermal slowness.

About love
in the abandoned house of my memory.

About my life
of which I vaguely remember the future.

Datemark

Hello man, hello unknown, my it's nice
that we don't need to recognize one another
but calmly and each to his own
abide in the good cell of silence.

We are not bound by fear or fondness.
A strange peace innerly separates us.
And they who are friend or foe, envy us,
for we are centuries-old strangers.

Nice, that we simply pass each other
like shoulders, shadows, or backs in the rain.
We can't be found. We form the void.
The future is our only memory.

We are simultaneously the resting equilibrium
in a complete and anonymous movement
of strange and totally unknown
twins of loneliness.

Message

No one believes me. It is too simple.
Each day I awake from my sleep, numbed
like after an explosion, with lead in my lips
with dust and print in my hair.

And it continues and remains dangerous.
I never clamber out of my pit, yet I admire
heavenward the everyday landscape:
the blue sky is blue, so blue.

I make myself comfortable. I toil
and throw a little earth on high, like so.
And I sing whole days long for peace,
in this manner I dig myself deeper to protection.

I sing and dig until I'm tired and hoarse from it,
for what you want to forget, you must repeat often.
As long as no one hears me I am safe.
(*Bombs always fall on the same place.*)

Honest to god

It has actually happened that at night in bed
I have shone a little light so I could see myself.
(*I even dare to mail just received letters
unopened, so I can again be the recipient.*)

I think that I have lost myself from sight
and have halfway gotten lost in the somewhere.
Since every day I find it more and more strange
to catch myself being present.

Honest, sometimes it happens in the morning
I stare at myself in the mirror like at a stranger
who I can no longer remember
where I met before.

Until it comes to me that I saw him days
before in that other mirror.
(*If this now has something to do with dying,
I dare not say. If I see myself, I'll ask him.*)

Luís Amorim de Sousa

Translated by the poet, and by Marc Widershien and Alberto de Lacerda

Luís Amorim de Sousa *was born in Angola in 1937. He grew up in Lisbon and Lourenço Marques, now Maputo, the capital of Mozambique, and left for London in 1959. He has lived his entire adult life abroad, mainly in London and Washington DC. Luís Amorim de Sousa has published four collections of verse and two autobiographical narratives. Another book of verse is due out this year. He is married and lives in Hampstead.*

Except for 'Private Scene', the poems here are unpublished.

Private Scene

obsessed with books
I'll undoubtedly never read
I perceived that you've undressed
near the radiator

the line which the eye pursues
if not with care then with metrical rigour
finds another cadence in your flesh
already flushed by the warmth

another thought presents itself
explicit innuendo seized upon
contrary to my body's gravity
the book stays open on the carpet

> [MW and AdL in *Modern Portuguese Poetry*, Selection and Introduction by Alberto de Lacerda, *The Journal of the American Portuguese Society*, New York, 1978]

from **The Insect on the Leaf**

Four with the letter S

I
I always think of you
on rainy days

too much sun
beach weather
troubled you

       – climate for infidels
                        you'd say
when the cold came
it was worse

you hardly moved
you grew
    a little smaller

and then it rained

the trees swelled up
the hills
seen from the window
resembled camels asleep

all that you had to see

holding your gaze beyond
the window sill
you looked and looked
until your breath fogged you out

and thus you stayed
and I've kept you

a fading mezzotint against the glass
a flood of things
               come to mind

   IV
the fortune teller
turned up the jack of spades
and said
    a prince for you

you gave her in return
guava preserve

the sunset
went indigo

later there was
a story to do with ships
a tango
on the verandah
of the colonial house

an intense glow
grew pale in the palm grove

now you watch the tv soaps
your prince
    fears the damp
no longer rides out to hunt

during the ads
you mollify your sauces in the kitchen

behind the spice-rack
                you keep
    a playing card

from **O Verbo Trafalgar**

II
every man to his junk shop
        says EP
my own was in Cecil Court
the antique shop
on the right
coming down Charing Cross
                Road

a deep recess   a window
always very
poorly lit
babylonic dust accumulating
over sarcophagi
daggers   Roman vases
helmets   fragments of papyrus
and suspended from a hook

gilt frames longing to hug
ancestors and still lives

St Martin´s Lane
runs over the other side

on and further down a bit
and there it is
      the river

          Hungerford Bridge
          Waterloo Bridge

   and the Thames curling a bend
towards and beyond St Paul´s

      from there
      I made my way back

the Embankment
with its military concerts in the rain
gathered old ladies
holding their crooked umbrellas
startled
when the cannons boomed

   and the river
   moving on

I walked all over London

every time I had the chance
I returned to Cecil Court

   [LdS]

Alain Suied
France

Translated by Steve Light

Alain Suied, *poet, essayist and translator, was born in Tunis. When he was eight years old, his family moved to Paris. He published his first collection of poems,* Le Silence, *at the age of nineteen, and some fourteen volumes since then, including* La lumière de l'origine *(Granit, 1987), which was awarded the Verlaine Prize of the Académie Française. He is well known in France as a translator of American and English poetry, including the work of Dylan Thomas, Keats, Blake and Pound, and for his critical essays on poets ranging from Heine to Celan.*

Steve Light *has published works on philosophy, two volumes of poems, and* Somewhere between Philosophy and Music: Lyrico-critical essays on Poetic Modernity. *He translates from French and Italian; excerpts from his version of Sergio Solmi's* Meditazioni sullo Scorpione *appeared in MPT 9.*

Generations

From what you do not say
to my appeal – towards
the lost word

there is a shadow

visible and invisible
precise and impossible
missing and present.

From your memory
to my forgetfulness – towards
the lost country

there is a shadow

which measures the extent
and the limit
of our light.

Realm

You are the child of history
you are also the child's forgotten history:
it is written in invisible ink.
Everything speaks of the realm you have deserted.
The message, effaced, returns:
you are the child of memory
you are also the child's forgotten memory.
Everything speaks of the unknown realm
which you find once more with each and every step.

Lack

Pain knows
the precise weight
of the world.

Pain remembers
the precise cry
of separation.

Pain carves out
the precise space

which our
words lack.

But no-one knows
the precise tenor
of the world.
No-one remembers
the precise meaning
of separation.

Pain carves out
the precise illusion

which our
certitudes lack.

What is

What holds
us to
the earth?

A familiar
shadow?
A lost élan?
An absence
of knowledge?

Lack alone
makes us be

at the heart
of the question
a cry tears
the night of
our forgetfulness

What holds
us to
the world?

A lack
in which
an impossible
presence reigns

Jesper Svenbro
Sweden

Translated by John Matthias, Lars-Håkan Svensson and Göran Printz-Påhlson

Jesper Svenbro *is one of the leading Swedish poets of his generation. He was born in 1944 in the small town of Landskrona in southern Sweden, a region which has remained important to him despite a long residence abroad. An internationally renowned classical scholar, Svenbro has had his most important works (chiefly written in French) translated into English.* Phrasikleia, An Anthropology of Reading in Ancient Greece *was published by Cornell University Press and* The Craft of Zeus, *in collaboration with John Scheid, by Harvard. He has published nine volumes of poetry in Sweden. The poems here are part of a selection of poems to appear in English translation from Northwestern University Press. Svenbro lives in Paris where he holds a post at the Centre National de Recherche Scientifique.*

John Matthias *is an American poet, critic and translator. He has published nine volumes of poetry in the US including* Swimming at Midnight: Selected Shorter Poems, Beltane at Aphelion: Collected Longer Poems *and, most recently,* Pages: New Poems and Cuttings. *He co-edited and co-translated with Göran Printz-Påhlson the Anvil Press anthology* Contemporary Swedish Poetry. *Matthias teaches at the University of Notre Dame and is poetry editor of* Notre Dame Review.

Lars-Håkan Svensson *has translated poetry and prose from Greek, Latin, French, Italian, Danish and English. His translations from English include books by John Matthias, Paul Muldoon and Les Murray. He has recently published a selection of the correspondence between Tomas Tranströmer and Robert Bly, translating Bly's letters into Swedish as well as those written in English by Tranströmer. Svensson teaches at the University of Lund.*

Göran Printz-Påhlson *is a well-known poet, critic and translator. He collaborated with John Matthias on the Anvil Press anthology* Contemporary Swedish Poetry. *Bonniers has published his* Collected Poems *and a recent volume of essays. Having taught at Cambridge for many years, he now lives in Malmo. Svenbro's 1979 volume,* Sarimner, *was dedicated to Printz-Påhlson.*

Three-toed Gull, Sighted Near the Lighthouse of Kullen

I was familiar with the sense of soaring from the music
of Lars-Erik Larsson: he must have seen
the same water surfaces as I, been filled by the same light
along the same curving coastline,

and felt the slowly rising movement of the summer
in an outer world which already was an inner one:
it was as if one stood and looked northwest
where the northern Sound has imperceptibly become the Kattegat
on a day when all the sea is placid and the sky light-blue
and a hazy fog seals the horizon –
the blank shining ground-swell
with a single floating tuft of seaweed
or a bit of plank which heaves, heaves
slowly mirroring itself, while the sea's
cool and intensely shining mist
rises up in microscopic crystals of salt –
soaring in the air where the Sound opens out
on an unfathomable beyond and a single three-toed gull
which, battered from some afterworld of flight,
comes in view as flying's sole survivor
gliding inland towards the lighthouse at Kullaberg –
Winddriventhing at rest in the bluest of hazes
or perhaps an optical illusion in the prisms of the lighthouse
open toward monotony of air –
all alone on a summer's day,
which sees the loss of the horizon,
takes a giddy gyroscopic turn and topples over in memory
without a sense of anything but height and depth
as if shutting its eyes to the infinite
with wings spread wide, rising and sinking and soaring
seems to free itself at last
from the immense and sparkling blue.

[JM/L-HS]

Sunlight on The Sound

Because my father had grown up in Helsingborg,
I had the strongest feeling every time we visited
of his belonging there:
his kinship with the city so impressed me
that I made it mine.
From my grandmother's apartment
we had an excellent view of the Sound:
Kronborg Castle was straight across
in the sun, its roofs green with verdigris.
Ships of different kinds steered to the south or north.

Ferries and sailing boats shone white . . .
This is what I am thinking of this morning
having woken from a dream
that seemed to take place on the beach
just north of Helsingborg.
My dream is like a poem of light.
And every time I go over it in memory
it remains unchanged:
not a boat can be seen at sea,
not a single person on the land.
The sea and sky are blue. A southwesterly breeze.
I am standing on the sandy beach in the sun
and seeing the horizon open in the northwest on immensity beyond.
I turn my gaze to the west
and I am saying aloud in my dream
where for an instant words and visual impressions
correspond in every way: *The sunlight on the Sound.*
In my dream it is as though these words
composed a truthful
and exhaustive statement about the world –
as if I wouldn't be able to add the smallest adjective
without obscuring the sun.
I couldn't add a single word.
Nor could I subtract one.

[JM/L-HS]

The Idea of the Sound

When, sometime in the early sixties,
we tried to reformulate the idea of the Sound,
Paul Eluard's poem 'Bathing woman
from light to darkness' was our only axiom:
with just this poem for our intellectual baggage
we took the boat to Hven
one May morning in a western wind
with "Eluard clouds" sweeping across the entire sky –
in joint formation as far as you could see!
When we started it was early.
The day was a circle drawn with a pair of compasses.
We walked along the long beach of the island widdershins:
saw how the maritime light would change
for every hour in the periphery:

this was "the order of splendour, the order of stones",
mentioned in our poem.
And we could hear a drawing-pencil being used –
or was it the sea that made this whispering sound?
Imperceptibly we went to meet the sun.
In our thoughts the idea of the Sound
– two beaches, streaming salt water –
appeared as a dazzling abstraction
of lines, angles, infinity.
We felt the salt on our skin, the sand in our eyes . . .
For a long time the sunlight cut its prisms.
But when, late in the afternoon,
we finally reached the point in the poem
which lies about a kilometre south of Bäckviken
the sun was sinking, the sandy cliffs
already casting long shadows towards the east
across the green depths where we had arrived in the morning.
The stone blocks which we were sitting on
were still warm from the sun,
all we heard was the roar of the sea,
the corrosive wind had exhausted all our senses . . .
Here the island was suddenly left to the waves:
no houses could be seen,
the bay before us seemed to have gone out –
and as in ancient times it would once more have been possible
to go to sleep in the sea.

[JM/L-HS]

Sound-image

The irregularity of my piano-playing sometimes means
that when I sit down in front of the keyboard
and begin to play a few bars of some piece
I may have played for years – a prelude, a minuet –
I suddenly lose my memory of it:
a great chasm of forgetfulness then opens up
and the music is silent. How is memory
to be made whole again? The sound-image seems to have disappeared.
One way of making the music return
has been to think of the room where I once learned
to play in my childhood: to concentrate –
not on the music but on the room

with its cool freshness on a summer's day
when the sounds of the neighbourhood turn silent and the sunlight
from the room opening onto the garden is reflected, vibrates
there in the dimness of a deep green velvet,
is refracted in the chandelier's iridescent prisms, reflected
without tinkling on the ceiling or the walls.
Behind me are the pastel painting of sailing-boats on the Sound,
the sofa purchased at the turn of the century in Helsinborg,
mirrors and silver, and I feel as well my grandmother's presence
beside me on a chair near the keyboard
where my fingers now are running easily and without trembling
across the white keys and the black
as if I were walking on a well-known path,
a passage, corridor or staircase just now rediscovered
in my memory's furthest recess, in its sounding labyrinth,
and she is seventeen as in that photograph,
her curly hair pinned up, the suggestion of a smile –
the year must be 1900, her lace collar is white
and she is looking at me with her large grey-blue eyes,
looking at me with love.

[JM/L-HS]

Stalin as Wolf

The position of the wolf was once secure in political theory
before it was driven by urbanization back to that final wilderness,
e.g. Siberia, where it lingers still without, to anyone's notice,
affecting contemporary politics. The plains sparkle in sunlight
as a helicopter rushes over the landscape: stunted birches
appear and disappear out on the snow-covered tundra
where all at once a wolf can be seen: it runs, it trips,
looks backward: someone has edited-in the hot gasps
of a dog to make us hear its fear: it is filmed close-up
and the camera is slightly jarred when the helicopter gunner
fires. The wolf is hit, rolls over in a swirl of snow,
then everything is still. Every year in the Soviet Union
more than 22,000 wolves were killed according to recent
statistics, and perhaps it is even yet a silent requirement
of Russian polity – menacing, inaccessible – which would explain
the cynical, obsessive precision of the hunting methods
both in the filmed sequence noted above, which,
with no comment, introduced a documentary on modern Siberia,

and also on the inner tundra where the wolf howls with hunger
in a nightmare only partially reclaimable. The facts about wolves
in Sweden at my disposal allow no conclusions, and yet,
within its territory, the wolf has developed local, independent
clans which have been identified as distinctive species. About
the role of the wolf in Russian politics 1875-1953, however,
we know more than we suppose: Stalin's most wolf-like characteristic
was distrust, which grew in proportions never foreseen by classical
lupine theory. As early as in Aesop we can find sufficient examples
to maintain that Stalin's role in political theory is basic:
the Wolf as Butcher masters to perfection the partition technique
which is the base of political equality. The jaws of the wolf
equal the Knife, and classical myth provides again the scenario
which ought to have haunted us earlier: hunting the Wolf became
in the Thirties a dominant trait in Soviet politics; he who wrote
"All power to the Soviets" three years before Kronstadt was now
the uncontested Butcher, the principle of absolute mistrust
had triumphed over Equality and the pack closed ranks around Stalin
in the whirling snowstorm. The Bolsheviks had certainly planned
an equitous banquet of wolves, but forgotten the moment when Knife
turns into Weapon and the feast into its opposite. The gasps
haunt me, the plains sparkle, the film invades the memory:
am I willing to test that project now when Stalin's crimes
are rostered and surveyed, now when his blood-thirst, along with
the prospects which made it possible, have all been analysed?
Zoologists can emend, on essential points, classical mythology,
refract the Stalinoid language: lacking both project and theory
the pack makes real the apophthegm: "To each according to his need,
from each according to his ability." It refutes the picture
that pursues me and, in the end, obliges me to abandon
my language: gazing at Stalin, letting the wolf run off.

[JM/GP-P]

Lőrinc Szabó
Hungary

Translated by George Held and Katherine Mayer

Lőrinc Szabó *(1900-1957) was a notable lyric poet and a translator of English-language poets, including Shakespeare and Emily Dickinson. The poems here are from his sonnet sequence,* The Twenty-sixth Year, *written between 1950 and 1956 to commemorate the suicide in 1950 of the woman who had been his lover for twenty-five years.*

George Held, *born in 1935, teaches English at Queens College, City University of New York. He co-edits* The Ledge, *and has published two chapbooks,* Winged *(1995) and* Salamander Love and Others *(1998). A collection of his poems,* Beyond Renewal, *is due to appear, and he is completing a collection of sonnets,* After Shakespeare .

Katherine Mayer *is a member of the Hungarian minority in Komárno, Slovakia, where she teaches high-school English. She has published a children's book in English,* Dusty *(London, 1996).*

Even if . . . ?

I am joyful that I love you this way,
in this hot and painful way: I exist
to watch over you: I don't even call you,
yet you are here: your troublingly lovely
dream eyes watch over my destiny,
and as old landscapes or years light up,
you light up, and I feel: you feel in your heart
the penitent tenderness of my heart.
This very joyfulness now, this very pain,
this unites us; and most (oh, immensely,
totally!) when across your lovely face
runs a smile, slightly mocking, but fully
knowing, trusting, and starts its provocation:
"This way, even if I were still alive?"

From a Crumbling Rock

But what you were or what you were like,
now that you are not, and since I can't think
that in the star-stirring universe
you should meet me on another sandbar

and give me everything again, my dear,
that during twenty-five years in your heart
and in your young soul I loved so dearly,
and since my life also proceeds to sink:
from my rock (crumbling rock! the year you died!),
since our feelings and beings stopped blending,
I've done nothing but stare at eternal time
and I'm struck dumb to see that in the ceaseless
turbulence everything that ever was
has such exquisite insignificance.

Jan Twardowski
Poland

Translated by Sarah Lawson and Małgorzata Koraszewska and by Ryszard J Reisner

Jan Twardowski *is a priest who lives in Warsaw. Though hardly known abroad, his work is very popular in Poland, where he is probably the best known of Polish poets.*

Sarah Lawson *is a writer and translator (from French, Spanish and Dutch) who was born in Indianapolis and educated at Indiana University and at Glasgow University, where she took a PhD in English in 1971. She now lives in London.*

Małgorzata Koraszewska *holds a degree in sociology from the University of Warsaw and a diploma from the University of Lund. She lived for many years in Sweden and England, but has now returned to Poland. She translates, chiefly non-fictional works, from English into Polish.*

These two translators have collaborated on the translation of many of Twardowski's poems; some of their versions appeared in MPT 11 and MPT 13.

*

Dogmatists are making noises in Latin
moralists are droning over the little trough of human conscience
apologists are creaking – crucified on the cross of faith
preachers are repairing a loudspeaker so as to be heard better

philosophers are grumbling about St Thomas, already filed
with the old yearbooks of saints in the archive of Paradise
martyrs are counting up blows to their faces
the pumpkin of sin has at last fallen on the heads of sticklers
organists are licking sounds –
believers have split into warring camps

And only in the plain open land
in the breath of a herb –
on your knees admiring the sky-drifts
can you still find Silence

The Quail

Quail, you who always sound loudest
at sunrise and sundown
isn't it so that there are only two pure moments
the early one light and the other at twilight
when God gives a day and when He takes it away
when somebody sought me and when I'm superfluous
when somebody loved me and when I'm left alone
when I am born and when I die
those two seconds which will always come
the one white the other dark
so very genuine that both are naked
so far beyond us that we are no longer there

[SL/MK]

In March

In March appears
the rook
magpie
lapwing
tawny owl
heron
post-communist comrade crow
only God is not seen
doesn't wish to upset the non-believers

All is important

The universe can't embrace Him
but a crèche proved ample
Almighty but cannot do all
for He himself patiently asks for love
close but as if He wasn't present
weighty for so wise, that He knows how to be happy.

Sometimes during procession bad weather strikes
the bishop drenched like a duck
maybe by chance someone will think
that he wanted to go for a dip

don't be shocked
all is important among things eternal
God's smile that's a grace that grasps the ridiculous
in a world where world fears world
shelter me in the calm of Your paradoxes.

Not so not so

My soul does not believe me
my heart has some personal doubts
my mind doesn't listen
my health is slipping
my youth has passed away
my family snapshots do not live
my country is now different
even hell has misled for it's cold

i covered myself completely so i couldn't be seen
but a tear ran out
and undressed stark naked

Painter after death

I was painting the sky gold
ecological green
like a hazel that has many fruit – in red
variegated like village roosters
but here sky is like the skyblue sky

overheard written down

The door shuudered – *who is it?*
– *death*
entered slight teeny-weeny with a scythe like a matchstick
Surprise. Eyes agog
and it
– *I came for the canary*

[RJR]

Giuseppe Ungaretti
Italy

Translated by Andrew Fitzsimons, by Stuart Flynn and by Andrew Frisardi

Giuseppe Ungaretti *(1888-1970) was born in Egypt where his father was a labourer on the Suez Canal. He left Egypt in 1912 and lived for three years in Paris, where he met Apollinaire, Picasso, Braque, Modigliani and Cendrars, and published his first poems. He returned to Italy in 1915 and saw active service in the First World War, an experience that strongly informed much of his early poetry, including some of that represented here. He was a member of the 'Hermetic' school of poets in the Thirties, and is generally thought impossible to translate.*

Stuart Flynn's *original poetry and translations from Ancient Greek, Latin, Italian and German have appeared in various magazines. A pamphlet of his poems appeared in February 2000 (Acumen Publications). He has published translations of many Italian poets, including Petrarch, Cavalcanti, Gabriele Rossetti, Leopardi, Carducci, Quasimodo and Pasolini. His translations from Novalis'* Hymns to the Night *appeared in MPT 16. He lives in London.*

Stuart Flynn writes: Ungaretti's style is one of extreme compression, which presents significant difficulties to the translator. He seeks to strip his verse down to the point of maximum minimalism, where a single word is often loaded with connotations that are almost impossible to render in another language. His poetry, even the earliest, is also very modern, particularly when compared to the writing of many of his contemporaries in this country, and retains its freshness and relevance today.

Eternity

Between the tended flower and one given
the unsayable divide

Boredom

This night too will pass

This loneliness doing the rounds
on the wavering shadows of tramlines
over the glistening asphalt

I see the heads of the cabmen
half-asleep
nodding

Memory of Africa

The sun razes the city

Vision fades

Even tombs give up the ghost

Casa Mia

Surprised
after so long
by a love

I thought I'd scattered
to the world

[A Fitzsimons]

Another Night
                    (Vallone, April 20, 1917)

In this darkness
with frozen hands
I can make out
my face

I see myself
abandoned in the infinity

The Unchanging

The ship moves, alone
In the quiet of evening.

Light glows from the houses
In the distance.

In darkest night
The sea disappears.

It remains alone, unchanging,
A rumble that fades away . . .

It renews itself . . .

Soldiers
(Bosco di Courton, July 1918)

They stand
like leaves
on the trees
in autumn

Wanderer

In no part
of the world
can I
settle down

In every
new place
I meet
I find myself
dissatisfied
so that
I am
immediately
tired of it

And it always feels
alien to me

Being born
to return to eras
already too familiar

I crave
a single minute
of fresh life

I seek
an innocent land

> [S Flynn]

Statue
>   (1927)

Petrified youth,
O statue, o statue of human depths . . .

After much journeying the mighty tumult
wears down a rock
to flowering lips.

Pilgrimage
> (Gully of the Isolated Tree, August 15, 1916)

Trapped
inside these bowels
of rubble
hours and hours
I dragged along
my carcass
worn down by mud
like a shoe sole
or like a seed
of white thorn

Ungaretti
man of sorrow
all you need is an illusion
to feel courageous

A searchlight
over there
creates an ocean
in fog

> [A Frisardi]

Mihai Ursachi
Romania

Translated by Adam J Sorkin with Ileana Orlich, Georgiana Farnoaga and Doru Motz

Mihai Ursachi *(born in 1941) is one of Romania's most honoured writers. He defected from Romania in 1981 after a term of imprisonment in solitary confinement, imposed because of an earlier attempt to escape by swimming the Danube. He went to America, taught swimming in California, and learned English whilst working as a garage mechanic in Austin and as German instructor at the University of Texas. He returned to Romania after the 1989 revolution, became Director of the National Theatre in Iași, but lost his post in 1992 because of his opposition to the government. In the same year he was awarded the Mihai Eminescu poetry prize, the first such award since the War.*

Adam Sorkin *is Professor of English at Penn State Delaware County. He has published thirteen books of literary translations, including Liliana Ursu's* The Sky Behind the Forest *(with the poet and Tess Gallagher, 1997), which was shortlisted for the Weidenfeld Prize. His collaborative translations have appeared in nearly 200 literary magazines.*

Ileana Orlich *is Director of the Romania Program at Arizona State University at Tempe. She has published many essays on Romanian poets and prose writers.*

Georgiana Farnoaga *teaches Romanian at UCLA and has co-translated books of Romanian poetry and stories.*

Doru Motz *is a broadcaster, producer and simultaneous translator for the Voice of America in Washington, DC. He has published over forty books, and is also a typographer and designer of fonts.*

The Parable of the Instant and the Listener Inside the Clock

... It seemed I existed inside a colossal grandfather clock: the small
    toothed wheels
(they were myriad) rustled like leaves; the great toothed wheels snarled
and thundered, so loud they almost could not be heard.
Multiple systems of pulleys screeched and groaned periodically,
like victims of torture; at equal intervals,
hammer blows pounded with mighty power,
like the vowels in the word "dead." And there were
other sounds, muffled, like prolonged insinuations,
late, self-consuming echoes and decisive syncopes. For an endless time,
or perhaps in that second alone, it seemed

I became concentrated into *hearing;* although I was
only the tympanum meant to go on listening for all of eternity
and for each distinct instant.
In that very instant,
I heard, of a sudden: "This is the moment."
"This is the moment, this is the moment, this is the moment."
I consulted my little silver watch. It was that moment.

   [AJS/IO]

The History of the Great Clock and the Blind Man

A huge clockwork, in the wilderness of stones,
like an immense basilica-mosque. None
among you, travellers, has traversed that realm
known as "The Great Stone Clock." Some say its melancholy sound
can be heard absolutely everywhere on earth,
but it's much likelier for it never to be heard anywhere
(or, since we hear it continuously, habit makes us hear it not at all).
What seems strange to me is that the watchman, blind and poor,
always is counting something, using for this purpose
the small mummy bones of his hands. He counts in haste,
and sometimes his blind face, as parched as an old palimpsest,
appears to glow with hope and joy. Then he stares with his
empty eye sockets at the Great Clock.
Soon he is absorbed again in his wretched calculus,
and no one disturbs the great silence all around.

This, worthy travellers, is the history
of the Great Clock and the Blind Man,
Now I've told you, so I'll keep still.

   [AJS/IO]

Rebuke

When you rebuke me as the maddest of men,
I gnaw on my moustache silent and forlorn;
you won't understand
that I'm the ever-suffering badger,
blood-brother to the cuckoo;
that I'm the ursine winemaster of secret vineyards,

ursus horribilis close upon the seed of silence;
ravenous and dumb,
with voice only for celestial weddings.

   [AJS]

The Crown of Straw

A ball of clay launched in violence from a blind slingshot,
this globe of pain hurtles far into chaos,
bearing my love: What good,
elaborate lute songs? What good,
magniloquent twilight of violet hues?
The voice on the face of the waters
you don't hear, don't believe, don't speak about.

Behold my ancestors' patch of earth; here they ploughed
ten thousand years; here their gentle oxen drowned in clay
at the foot of the skies. May they rest in peace,
the gentle ones, may the eternally restless find their rest.
Their field is the azure, stars their grain:
but a crown of straw, a wreath of nonredemption, adorns my brow.

A restless plummeting into the unplumbed precipice
of the sky . . . What good,
the dizzy drunkenness of the forest in bloom? What good,
the fiery madness of an impossible thought?
Oh, won't these eyes ever open upon
their salvation? Never
will I cease to love the impossible.
A crown of straw adorns my head.

With boundless love, the abyss
swallows me, the abyss embraces
this sphere, which is
His tear.

The weeping on the face of the waters
you don't hear, don't believe, don't speak about.

   [AJS/GF]

The Aviary

Celestial algebra! The melodious crystal of the raven's skeleton (when ravens fly, they strum austere vibrations in the ether, syntagmas of ice). "This explains a multitude of things."

*

And similarly: there exists a bird which, on summer mornings (the sky – the cruelty of Prussic acid), cracks the whip far too harshly. Oh, flagellated bucolic odours – the masochistic silence of nostalgia: *Pit-palac! Pit-palac!*

*

As for the fatuous cuckoos, who I hear have nested in many a grove and coppice, yes, even in urbanized areas, what can I say? Their solitude, proverbial, it turns out is simply a tall tale. (Their voices hoarse with lust – obese chanteuses!)

*

Solemn bird,
who are you
covetous
of my solitude?

Why keep being born,
to fatten yourself
on solitude?

"My blood –
the purple of solitude.
Out of the flames,
eternally for the flames,
into the flames . . . "

*

Black seeds of nonsalvation . . .

"When she sees water of good omen
she runs off like a madwoman;
when she sees bad water with a stink
she muddies it and bends to drink."

Never will you find your twin, oh solitary wing beating in the unfathomed abyss of the sky! White wing . . .

*

And should you come, beating your immense wings (capacious white heart, *anima mundi*), when the great blizzard pronounces its cyanotic verb, you will keep me from following. By the gate stands a willow tree, its leaves always stirred in soft motion. Maybe you will recognize that place. If you come, you will halt there. The sky is a deep blue-violet. No, it's not out of mercy that you'll come, but mere chance.

*

You will find a sick eagle, a poor dying bird.

[AJS/DM]

Liliana Ursu
Romania

Translated by Michael M Naydan, Tess Gallagher and the poet

Liliana Ursu *has published seven collections of poems in Romania and works in Bucharest as an interviewer on literary topics for a national radio programme. Translations of her poems have appeared in about forty American and British literary journals, and two collections of her poems have been published in English translation:* The Sky behind the Forest *(Bloodaxe, 1996) and* Angel Riding a Beast *(Northwestern University Press, 1998). Since January 2000 she has been a writer-in-residence at the University of Louisville.*

Michael M Naydan *is Professor and Director of the Program in Slavic and East European Languages at The Pennsylvania State University, where he teaches Russian and Ukrainian Literature. He has published several collections of translations, notably from Tsvetaeva and from Skovoroda, and his translations have won many prizes.*

Tess Gallagher *is a poet and short-story writer; her published work includes* Moon Crossing Bridge, Portable Kisses, *and many other books of poems, essays and short stories.*

from An Island Where Evening Never Comes: A Cycle

An Island Where Evening Never Comes
> *"Look, the sky is within you if you are pure of heart."*
> *from one of the Fathers of the desert, 3rd century*

I left the town behind me, trusting
the road would keep its mystery
perpetually.

It is a tender, familiar spring.
The apple trees beside me voice their beauty.
Their blossoms gaze into themselves
like young brides staring
into vast green mirrors
of sky. Their passionless confidence
calls to us.

Unreal green. Pure sky.
Peace runs to greet you

heralding the walls of a Monastery
surrounded, uplifted by trees
doubled in water.

At the centre of the disconsolate roar
within us – the blackbird –
that immaculate prayer.

The River Mouth

My open mouth fills up with stars
although it's only mid-day
in July.

I pass near a river or picture it,
and suddenly the air is bountiful
with wild strawberries.
A strange symbiosis
of light
        mountain
                and sea.
Then an eagle flies through
my heart of sand.
In the grip of its claws –
                    an oasis.

An Offering

First a path made of clay,
then a path made of grass,
then a path of forget-me-nots
that runs straight
to the sea.

My heart of shells.
My heart of flesh and blood.
My heart – a bruised star torn from your sky –
this is the one I bring to you, God,
as an offering.

Trinity

Sunbeams – ethereal paths
emerging from the sea.
The path of the Holy Spirit
takes a rest while flying inside
a tiny earthly pigeon.

Unclouded light, words
that don't begin, that will never be uttered,
tears not made of water:
                a Trinity
                etched
                on the walls of a cloister
                in the middle of the sea.

Flight

A yellow parrot screams
in a black cage.
He keeps striking his body
against the bars and flies
and flies
and flies
till the bars turn red –
a flame of blood floating out, a contrail of pain
wafting into the night.

Tired bird,
dreaming of liberty, you
can hardly breathe
practicing flight between the bars.
Even the grass screams
beneath its scattered feathers
suddenly gone white.

My unshelterable heart gets lost
from its body
in the rigorous liberty of a prayer.

The Decor of Luxury

A small square of grass
enlivened by sunbeams – firs and birches above –
from their branches odd lavish cages dangle:
dry and white, filled with the shadowy despair
of green and blue parrots.

Closer and closer I move toward
the sea that tastes like the red core of a watermelon.
Farther and farther away
my heart drifts
with its voracious
but serene scream, my heart
that tastes like pomegranates –
more and more luminous. Yet quieter.
                              Almost a pilgrim.

Paul Valéry
France

Translated by James Kirkup

Our readers may remember that *MPT* 16 (*German and French Poetry*) included James Kirkup's translation into two *tanka* of a prose passage from Valéry, quoted in *Télérama*. Neither he nor we could trace the origin of the quotation at the time, but Kirkup now writes to say that he has remembered the source (leaving us feeling rather foolish). The jellyfish appear in the chapter of Valéry's *Degas Danse Dessin* entitled 'De la Danse'; they are offered as the epitome of dance, 'La plus libre, la plus souple, la plus voluptueuse des danses possibles'. (We would add that the television critic who quoted Valéry in fact misquoted him: the poet wrote 'chairs de verre follement irritables', not 'instables' – though in the context the meaning is little affected by the change.) Kirkup has now translated the whole passage into *tanka*:

Jellyfish

Not girls – but beings
of matter beyond compare –
   lucent, sensitive,
flesh of crystal, absurdly
unstable, domes of drifting

   silks, with hyaline
tiaras, long lianas
   shivered all over
in racing ripples, fringes
and flounces they furl,

   unfurl, overturn,
change shape, take flight, as fluid
   as the massed fluid
that compresses them, weds them,
uplifts them in all their parts,

   gives way to them at
the slightest inflection and
   restores them to shape.
In the incompressible
plenitude of water that

seems to offer them
no resistance, these creatures
  benefit from some
ideal motility –
relax within it, recover

  all their radiant
symmetries. There is no ground,
  nothing solid for
dancers of the absolute;
no flooring – but a theatre

  that can be leaned on
at every point, that gives
  way in whatever
direction they choose to
take. – Nor in their crystalline

  elasticities
do there exist any bones,
  articulations,
invariable jointings,
countable segments . . .

  Never did human
dancer, woman aroused and
  drunkenly mobile,
racked by the poisons of her
overextended powers,

  the ardent presence
of gazings charged with desires,
  express her sex's
imperious offerings,
the mimed invitation to

  prostitution's calls
as does the Grand Medusa
  whose undulations
thrust through the flood of festooned
skirts she flourished and flaunts

    again and again
with a weirdly shameless and
    depraved insistence,
transforming herself thereby
into a dream of Eros;

    and then, suddenly,
casting aside all her vibrant
    flouncing finery,
her crinoline's scalloped hems,
sinks back, exposing herself

    furiously wide
open – but all at once pulls
    herself together,
quivers, dispersing herself
within her own element,

    her montgolfière
ascending with her into
    luminous regions
of forbidden space, domain
of the day-star, and mortal air.

Aleksander Wat

Translated by Frank L Vigoda

Frank L Vigoda *lives in Boston, MA and is a translator of Polish poetry and prose. He has translated* Hanged Man's Lover, *a volume of poetry by Rafal Wojaczek, as well as poems by Arnold Sucki, Jerzy Ficowski, Janusz Stycze, Anna Janko and others. His translations have appeared recently in* Chicago Review *and* Przekladaniec (Krakw). *He is currently preparing a volume of essays and poetry by Aleksander Wat.*

Midrash Cain: A Pastoral Poem

Aleksander Wat's *Pastoral Poem* is hardly bucolic; its title is obviously ironic. This monologue by Cain, who from a heap of rotting leaves ponders God, creation and history, is a first-class *midrash*, a reading into the Scripture from the perspective of our experience and knowledge.

It is a piece, several pages long, of rather nebulous literary form; it mixes free verse of irregular length and rhythmic patterns with essayistic and narrative prose. *Pastoral Poem* derives from and comments upon the well-known Biblical story, the few verses from the book of Genesis, chapter 4 about the arch-brothers whose offerings did not find equal favour in God's eyes, here quoted from the Revised Standard Version:

> [2] Now Abel was a keeper of sheep, and Cain a tiller of the ground. [3] In the course of time Cain brought to the LORD an offering of the fruit of the ground, [4] and Abel brought of the firstlings of his flock and of their fat portions. And the LORD had regard for Abel and his offering, [5] but for Cain and his offering he had no regard. So Cain was very angry, and his countenance fell. [6] The LORD said to Cain, "Why are you angry, and why has your countenance fallen? [7] If you do well, will you not be accepted? And if you do not do well, sin is crouching at the door; its desire is for you, but you must master it." [8] Cain said to Abel his brother, "Let us go out to the field." And when they were in the field, Cain rose up against his brother Abel, and killed him. [9] Then the LORD said to Cain, "Where is Abel your brother?" He said, "I do not know; am I my brother's keeper?" [10] And the LORD said, "What have you done? The voice of your brother's blood is crying to me from the ground. [11] And now you are cursed from the ground, which has opened its mouth to receive your brother's blood from your hand. [12] When you till the ground, it shall no longer yield to you its strength; you shall be a fugitive and a wanderer on the earth." [13] Cain said to the

LORD, "My punishment is greater than I can bear. [14] Behold, thou hast driven me this day away from the ground; and from thy face I shall be hidden; and I shall be a fugitive and a wanderer on the earth, and whoever finds me will slay me." [15] Then the LORD said to him, "Not so! If any one slays Cain, vengeance shall be taken on him sevenfold." And the LORD put a mark on Cain, lest any who came upon him should kill him. (Gen. 4:2-15.)

Like Job from among the ashes, Wat's Cain asks God from his heap of leaves, why? Who is responsible? Like a romantic rebel he challenges God, scorns Him, hurls accusations and demands an answer. And like a child trying to deflect responsibility, he puts the blame squarely on God, lies and concocts lame excuses.

The originality and importance of Wat's *midrash* consist in presenting Cain's story as the defining moment for humankind, equally important as the creation itself, or perhaps even more so. According to Wat, Abel's killing by Cain, the first death ever, sets history in motion, creates civilization and determines the fate of humanity.

The poet boldly mixes times past, present and future; he blends history and fiction. Cain not only tries to make an argument in his defence from the *Akedah*, the binding of Isaac, but also evokes Dostoevski's hero Verkhovensky, Kierkegaard, Freud and Brigitte Bardot; he not only closely reads and comments on the Biblical narrative, but also inserts German quotations from Novalis and interprets a miniature from a medieval bestiarium. In Wat's poem the three idioms of Western civilization, Jewish, Christian and classical (Greco-Roman) are tightly interwoven.

Born in 1900 in Warsaw to a Jewish family that was drifting away from religion, in his early twenties Aleksander Wat became an avant-garde poet. In the 1930s he was close to Polish communists and edited their front journal in Poland, *The Literary Monthly*. Arrested by the Soviets in Lwów at the beginning of WWII, he spent 6 years imprisoned and in exile in Kazakhstan. This radically cured him of his communist leanings. In Saratov prison he had a mystical illumination and converted to Catholicism. He returned to Poland in 1946 and was briefly active in Polish literary life, but was soon silenced because of his outspoken anticommunism. In 1953 he suffered a brain hemorrhage that resulted in recurring excruciating pains. Because of his ill health he was allowed to travel abroad and eventually settled in France. Invited by the University of California Berkeley, he spent a year in San Francisco where *A Pastoral Poem* was probably written. His pains did not allow him to work consistently and to alleviate his anxiety Czesław Miłosz arranged a series of recorded conversations with Wat; they resulted in *Mój wiek*, a two-volume "spoken memoir" published after Wat's death, one of the most fascinating and important testimonies about 20th-century Eastern Europe (English translation by Richard Lourie, *My Century*, University of California Press, 1988).

In addition to *My Century*, some of Wat's writings have appeared in English including a volume of poetry *With the Skin* (translated by Czesław Miłosz and Leonard Nathan) and a collection of prewar short stories, *Lucifer Unemployed* (translated by Lillian Vallee). A monograph of Wat by Tomas Venclova, *Aleksander Wat, Life and Art of an Iconoclast* was published in 1996. Still, much remains to be done to secure Wat the place he deserves in the pantheon of 20th-century literature.

Wat left behind some 250 poems, many of them of amazing beauty and profound insight, and a sizable body of largely unfinished prose writings. They include part of a large-scale novel, *Lot's Flight*, intended as a response from a Jewish perspective to Thomas Mann's *Dr Faustus*, several literary and political essays (the most important of them, *9 Notes to a Portrait of Stalin*, is about two-thirds finished) and miscellaneous notes and memoirs.

Like most of his longer writings, *A Bucolic Poem*, Wat's "Midrash Cain," is unfinished, missing the author's final touch. Its editor Krzysztof Rutkowski compiled the present version from four sources, and we don't know how much editing he did. Rutkowski wrote ('Uwagi wydawcy', *Zeszyty Literackie* 9/1985):

> In Aleksander Wat's archive there are four components of this difficult piece. First consists of 20 typed pages of thin paper corrected and numbered by the author. They contain the latest and the largest version of the poem, the one he worked upon for the longest time (this is evident from many cross-outs, additions, and comments made at different times). On the first page, near the handwritten title *Poemat bukoliczny* there is the crossed-out original title: *Kain*. The second one consists of nine very thin leaves of white onionskin, typewritten and with a few hand corrections and additions by the poet. They contain a draft of the whole poem in a much shorter version . . . Three very thin and crumbling leaves of onionskin that is closer to grey than blue . . . are typed; they are corrected and numbered by the author. At the top of the first page . . . there is a note, "To Cain". It is the original title or, what is more likely, a kind of reference to different earlier fragments. It is impossible to establish which version (the "white" or the "grey") is earlier; besides, each of them corresponds to a different part of the poem's root version. The fourth and last element is a single typewritten page with corrections in the author's handwriting entitled (in translation): 'Introduction to the epic Cain & Co. (many years in progress)'.

Rutkowski also explained the symbols he introduced in the text: [. . .] means an illegible word/s; [?] an uncertain rendering; [also] a word or its part inserted by the editor. These markings were retained in the translation. The punctuation in the published version is the editor's; in this translation it has been further adjusted to conform with English usage.

A Pastoral Poem
> *Introduction to the epic Cain & Co.*
> *(in progress for many years)*

Once when wandering around the city N***,
in the USA, I was struck by a neon sign.[1] It was on
the mezzanine level, stretching above an entire rather broad
sidewalk: a circle, rhythmically pulsating, spectacular,
braided from small vipers, each in a different colour,
only their eyes were alike, piercingly ruby, the eyes of a Chinese
dragon. This was in Chinatown, with all its kitsch.
An inscription was in the centre: *KAIN & Ska.*, in Polish.
Don't get carried away by your imagination, I cautioned myself,
remember, you're in a city of sombre people! (In spite – or perhaps
        because of this? –
I love them. They've treated me better than anywhere else in the world.
Perhaps they thought me *an underdog*, if so,
they were wrong. I hate dogs, I'm a cat person
and cats come to me, even wild cats. Only once,
on Aventine . . . but that's a different story.)
Don't get carried away by your imagination! – I repeated to myself.
I did.
And . . .
(But what do this introduction and sign have to do with the epic
        (in progress?) Nothing,
absolutely nothing. Except the title, which is inappropriate for
        an epic anyway.)

A pastoral poem

I don't get it. I'm a clod, a boor,
what do I understand of the flowers of His thought?
An oaf so reeking of manure that animals in the woods
bump trustingly into me. I twist the legs of some,
for others, I clip wings; for birds, I mostly pluck the

eyes. One or the other: flying or looking.
If I were the Creator
I would assign one creature one
function, that's it. But for man I'd give them all, for the sake of
    the economy of wastefulness!
Real and imaginary ones. Natural and virtual, identical and
    contradictory, etc., etc.
Man is the crown of creation!
Universal man, as the French padre
Teilhard de Chardin will some day put it. The king of nature. Oh,
these digressions, will I ever learn to think, methodically reason,
build an argument?
But how? I never went to school. A farmer, that's what I am, an oaf.
    He made himself comfortable on the pile of rotting redwood
        leaves. They say the smell of rot
improves thinking. He yawned,
stretched. Rotting-brown colours; since the expulsion,
it's always autumn. People will call it winter, spring, summer and
    autumn, again and again,
but this won't be true, as with all human names.
Fine. Let's try to understand this, put it in order.
Since the expulsion it's always autumn, or more precisely, *Fall*;
a bit of psychoanalysis won't hurt, not too little,
not too much. Patiently – whispered Cain, shading his eyes
from the too strong sun. He made himself comfortable like on
    a therapist's
couch. That's because you already could have psychotherapy, dreams
    had come into being.
Before there were no dreams. The first dream of humanity, at night,
no, not at night,
at the closing of the day, *entre loup et chien*,[2]
just after my brother's killing which strangely
exhausted me. After a second a voice awoke me [...] How
much can you dream during a second? An entire life.
Now I must close my eyes, not resist the flow of thought,
memories, let the subconscious speak; my eyelids are so thick,
night is always under them. So this was the first dream of history,
when I killed my brother. Before this
there were no dreams. How could there be? My father was made of clay,
my mother from a rib.
Clay, rib – but dreams?
Dreams, I tell you, came
from blood, the first
spilled blood.

Yield to the flow of dreams,
close your eyes. So there was water in that dream.
and nothing but water. (Water, water, water,
if only one inch of land, as the Polish poet Wat
will write.) And I feel it
with my ears, and through my ears.
It envelops my ears.
As if there were no other senses.
Say it's as if I were under water.
Water was because of my ears,
and my ears were because of water.
My ears are ringing, fear rings into them.
So there was also fear? Of course.
I'd love to say
fear was always. But this isn't true, either. It wasn't before.
The angel's sword was, the expulsion was, and toiling in sweat, you know, all those childhood frights like your Father's stern look or punishing hand. But not Fear. Fear came to being in my dream, the first dream of humanity. [Was it] after I killed my brother Abel? *Nascitur ex sangue Ultor*,[3] or however the poet Virgil has it. Enough of quoting poets, I despise them. Why should they be respected? Back to the matter at hand. Back. To the river of my first memory. And to fear, the first fear that was born like a dream in a dream from the first blood spilled in history, back to the river of my first dream, the first – no joke! – dream of humanity. *Zurück*[4] to the river, to that river. And to fear. Nothing more, period. But there was something more. Something afterwards, but what? Something's missing, but what? Let's try Jung's test. Water – ace of hearts. Fear – smear... Bullshit, I have a hole in my stupid head. Let's breathe in, inhale the rotten air through the nose deep into the lungs, then breathe it out through the mouth. Let's fix a dead motionless stare at a shining point, for example this point of light glinting through the brown-green sequoia leaves (after all, it is eternal autumn). Let's breathe deeply, alternating one nostril with the other. That's easy, but darling, try to siphon 5 litres of water with your dick like any fakir! Oh, you can't even dream of the things future generations will perform. Enough of sidetracks, no more!

He turned over. Now he was lying on his side, like Goethe in his well-known portrait in Italy, an elegiac Malte [?],[5] a sage-shepherd-pantheist. Well he didn't resemble Goethe at all, knotted, all muscly, covered in mud, sweaty, with the eyes of a murderer. A triumphant bird sang above him, and a freckled ladybug got entangled in the gray fur of his dishevelled beard.

Shall we look at this in a different way? Let's get back to water. Did it have a colour? For instance red? There was no red before my brother

Abel's killing. Certainly there was lots of light. And lots of darkness. They weren't finished yet, hadn't separated completely. Though they were on the waters, and in the water, their substances didn't mix. Each had its own existence, they were neither mixed nor separated. Only water and fear. Oh how I wished for a clump of mud, a mouse, a plant, an echo. But nothing.

Of course, today I can make up something about that first dream of humanity, anything you'd like. For example a fish like a mountain with knives instead of fins, knives instead of a moustache, and two bulging unblinking eyes that saw everything and remembered nothing. These eyes confirmed the existence of everything they saw through the momentary act of seeing; they reified it, certified and legalized like chief witnesses. And through the act of immediate forgetting they turned it into nothing, nullified what they had certified, murdered particular beings, murdered Everything (murdered metaphorically, in the imagination, not to be confused with real murder). "681. Kein Akt ist gewöhnlicher in uns – als der Annihilisationsakt. Eben so gewöhnlich ist der Positionsakt ... Es ist eine Art von Zauberei, durch die wir die Welt umher nach unsrer Bequemlichkeit und Laune bestellen."[6] To continue for another second (my stupid *Lust zum fabulieren*).[7] For example sailors will land on the back of this Leviathan mistaking it for land, finally dry land, oh joy, fair spark of the gods, as the ridiculous poet Schiller sings in the ridiculous symphony by the ridiculous Beethoven. They're stupid, this will cause grave results, of course, but they won't know it for hundreds of thousands of years, the Leviathan is patient, only sometimes shakes off this or that one and [...] under its fins. *A propos*, I stole this image from an illuminated manuscript in the Bodleian Library (MS, Ashmole, 1511, fol. 86v. – God knows what this Ashmole means – perhaps Asmodeus?)[8] Damn it, this smell of rotting leaves makes me not think but babble. Stick to the subject, you old head. Back to water, to water (but not the Freudian one, the pre-natal symbol, etc., etc.)

He suddenly fell asleep. But a few seconds later he woke up refreshed saying, water, water that wants to turn into blood. Eureka! Water, whose essence from the very beginning wanted to turn into blood is a puzzle for man who is 90% made up of water. His forefathers came from water, and in the end he will float down to water again, flushed by underground waters. These are foolish rationalizations, and here we have a mystical meaning. As usual, it's all about my fascination with water. Though not with bloody water. As we said, the water was absolutely colourless, without even the colour of colourless objects. Light and darkness were there, of course, but they did not marry water, for instance they had nothing in common with the water that glimmers under the St Louis Bridge. Water that wants transfiguration into the dialectic of Nature; nothing in history will ever match the power of this

want [...] – (my language is ugly, pretentious, ridiculous and boring, the language of a civilized boor, because civilization began after Abel's killing, but more about this later). Beasts, they imagine blood is for nourishing their rotting flesh! As if pus, lymph, and other filth weren't enough. Blood is for spilling. That's Cain's message for future generations. Therefore, is the only thing that matters water-blood? For everything else: birds, pterodactyls, minerals, bodies of young girls, frogs, the young moon over Marina Piccola, the twinkling city lights on the Seine, blue dragonflies over the Ś'weder River, and the boring half-baked dough that one day my many panegyrists will concoct in moments of poor philosophizing – all these are ephiphenomena. God knows what they will make of it, if one of these fellows, a fool, having crawled on all fours onto the rock in Préalpes de Grasse, yells over the mistral, calls me from there over the millions of years between us, wanting to have a philosophical-moral exchange! With me, Cain! They've lost the sense of the ridiculous, those late offspring, so arrogant and outrageous. But all these are epiphenomena, ephemeral states of transformation of water into blood. The spilled blood. It soaks into the ground and reaches the underground waters, the sources, there exciting the limitless insatiable potentials of the will to transform into blood, the transfiguration, as they later will call it. For that purpose I Cain am Cain, so that it could come to pass in the first pre-figuration. That's why I got my brother Abel, that's why I loved him, oh, how much I loved him, deeply, more than myself, much more, since I never loved myself. It was quite the opposite, purely, not with an antagonistic feeling or resentment, not a *Liebe Hass* or whatever they call it, but with pure hatred that according to Empedocles was coupled at the beginning with Love. With Love that wasn't yet. (Fear was.) But *revenons à nos moutons*,[9] as Stepan Trofimovich Verchovensky will say.[10] So, Fear and water. And hatred, and water wanting to turn into blood. With this one can develop a cosmogony. And for this craving I was just an agent, nothing more.
At last a moral problem arises.
If at the beginning there was the will of water to turn into blood, spilled blood, naturally, and I just was the first agent of this will and nothing more, then, first off, why punish me? Comrades, you really should put up a monument to me. Secondly, how can you punish me for murder if the law "You shall not kill" did not exist yet, and as everybody knows, law is not retroactive – unless we accept the prosecutor Vyshinsky's[11] philosophy that time is an illusion, which indeed makes some sense. Okay, I can do without this argument. So, secondly, if we have Punishment, why is it so paradoxical? There are so many rational pragmatic punishments like Ixion's wheel, Procrustes' bed, Kolyma, Auschwitz, solitary confinement, etc., not mentioning the ones invented by poets. Or what Phorbas did, for example. He sat under an oak tree

and hung the cut-off heads of his adversaries from the branches, those who sinned against him. Imagine Him, sitting under the large arch-oak of knowledge with the heads of sinners dangling from each branch. True, there was no punishment by death yet, but death already existed, exactly from the moment I murdered my dear brother Abel.

    Because of Abel's killing,
    our chambers fill with Death.
    I cannot run from it.
    My life is agony.
    I will shake in agony
    with plague or leprosy,
    with tumour or thrombosis.
    Nobody gets just deserts
    save in Heaven, Hallelujah!
    Not even in Heaven!

Then secondly, if death came to being, it was for me, first of all and above all for me (I want it so badly!). An eye for an eye was for me, and the right of tally, so reason says, and not just reason, but the soul, the pneuma as well. Instead, what we have here is delays, schemes, endless postponement; from now on in every generation man will be tormented by the puzzle, and in every generation the tormented will ask over and over, "Why do the just suffer and the wicked prosper? *Unde* our *mala*?" – until crazy with madness.[12]

Thirdly, why exactly did I kill my brother whom I loved, oh how I loved him. Don't think there was even a bit of envy in me because of his beauty! On the contrary, precisely because of that I wholeheartedly accepted
    my homeliness, so that its contrast
    reaffirmed his beauty, so that Caliban's
    ugliness was a hymn to his beauty,
    the first human beauty, for I realize,
    needless to say, our parents weren't pretty,
    they were heavy, not completely formed,
    of clay clumsily hardened,
    rough,
    hairy, purulent, snotty, drooling.
I repeat, why was it I who had to kill?
Couldn't He wait a bit for my offspring?
He had just created man, and immediately pushed him
first to sin and punishment, and then in the very next generation,
to murder. Was it me because I was
the first disadvantaged one? Yes, I was the first
of these disadvantaged people who will be making
your futile revolutions.

Nor did I kill from envy,
a cluster of suppressed feelings, as the philosopher
Max Scheller will call it. For there was no envy between me
and my brother; it came to being only when He stood among us
        and between us.
When He accepted Abel's offering, and rejected mine.
So didn't envy come from Him and not from me? Only
after the killing did I become the patriarch
of the disadvantaged, disillusioned, all the frustrations; the whip against
the chosen children of fortune, gods, or history.
It was a frustrating situation of one intrinsic frustration.
We all know this: the oppressed disadvantaged one becomes
        the oppressor himself,
and *da capo*.[13] That's how History got started. For history
also started with me, i.e. with the act of killing, before that
there was no history.
Let's move on. I was the first farmer,
my brother Abel was the first herdsman (psychologically speaking
it should be the other way around, *passons*.)[14] He did not accept
        my offering
though/because it was the innocent fruit
of the soil, instead he accepted the offering of my little brother
Abel though/because it was the blood of the firstborn
of his flock. It's clear (in the boorish mind
He gave me) that He principally
accepts only blood offerings. I, Cain,
was a farmer, so whose blood could I offer Him?
My brother's, of course. You can't expect me to steal
a calf from my brother, or a he-goat, or a cow. I'm a killer, not a thief.
        Killing Abel was
my offering, the offering I gave to Him, that's how I understood it;
        I could have been
wrong, but the reasoning was correct. Whatever I had. That my
        reasoning wasn't
completely wrong, see Abraham's offering on
Mount Moriah!
Sure, sure, in the last second He turned it into a joke,
but Abraham, while walking up Mount Moriah
with his promised son and an offering knife did not
even suspect that a miracle would occur, he took it
seriously. Which means the custom of presenting God with offerings
of people was *chose courante*[15] even among the chosen people
for so many years – half a million, after me. Not to mention other nations.
Even humanitarian Greek playwrights have many hints of it, even Hesiod,

even the socialist-realist Homer; Pausanias will write about it quite openly.
Not to mention primitive civilizations. A hell of a lot.
    He turned again on the heap of rotten leaves. Did he fall asleep?
He woke up, the night was moonless. Now, where did I stop?
        Oh, I know, the
incredible
bizarreness of my punishment. I don't get it at all.
Let's see, "What have you done? Do you hear the voice of
    your brother's blood
crying to me from the ground? (I heard nothing, it did not cry,
    this was just a figure of
speech.) And now you are cursed
from the earth which opened her mouth to receive your brother's blood"
(again rhetoric, 'the earth's mouth', the first bad poetry!)
"You will be a fugitive and a vagabond on the earth of the settled."
(They're so eager to banish you! While
a settled man has a great itch
to wander in order to affirm himself
in his settled state; if so, how much of a punishment is it?)
A dialogue ensued, "My punishment is greater
than I can bear (you're supposed to say stuff like this). You drive me
from Your face, and I shall hide from You,
(could we wish for anything more?) and be a fugitive on the earth
of the settled; and whoever finds me can raise his hand on me
and slay me." Here the most unexpected thing happened, the mystery of
mysteries,"Whoever slay Cain, vengeance shall be sevenfold (?!)
taken on him." And He put a mark on my forehead, a sign so that
    no one would lift his
hand against me. How should one understand this? Maybe He
    thought, like Nietzsche,
like Seneca (see *Consolatio a Marcia*, XXII, 3) or like Kohelet, life is
    the worst of
punishments and it would be better
not to be born, or, being born,
to die at once? Would the act of Creation be an act of punishment [?]
Of punishing? But at the beginning He liked
everything. And He saw it was good, the Holy
Bible says, well before Cain had emerged from nothingness,
right after *bereishis; reishis* alone would do, what's this *be-* about?[16]
I don't get it with my boorish
brains, obviously. A punishment combined with immunity, a taboo?
The killer's the only person in history protected
from being killed. How many people would dream of such punishment!
Maybe to get this punishment they will kill their

brothers over and over. Not to kill, but to not be killed
they will race to see who gets whom first, watch each others' hands,
movements, look each other in the eye, they won't have a moment
of peace, a moment without fear, everyone will be scared of
                       everyone, a father
of his son, until they erect a monument to Pavlik Morozov
in their neighbourhoods, a thoughtful monument to fearing
                       your neighbour.[17]
This monument will restore for them the sense of higher dignity.
Let's go back to the beginning, a crime should be either met
                     with punishment
or not. Either I Cain am guilty, even if without
guilt, and after a brief attempt at cheating (more about
this later), convinced about my guilt.
In this case, punish me equal to the extent and
degree of my guilt – and my crime was indeed monstrous,
with no extenuating circumstances, considering the beauty,
charm, naïveté, and innocence of the victim, such charm
that, if I hadn't killed him I would have surely raped him, therefore
committing two stains hideous to His eyes, homicide
and incest. So charming that in fact,
he Abel, provoked me to one and the other.
So it was in fact an extenuating circumstance. Back to the matter
                     at hand, the river
of my first dream. Back to it, I felt better there,
                                     I had more space.
    What was I talking about again? So it was punishment-not-punishment. Why? As a prevention programme, socialist pedagogy. May the dishevelled slob with hungry eyes wander around, a vagabond, *reiser, clochard, urke, bezprizornyi*, with a mark burning on his low forehead, "Untouchable". So that others can see where disobedience and indecency lead, so that they won't slay each other like praying mantises, bucks, dogs fighting over a bone. Of course they do it in mating or from hunger, whereas the king of creation is always prone to murder. But at the end what difference does it make if they slay each other? Let them be. Is there anything more simple than to take another clump of clay and breathe on it? Since when don't we like experiments? Sorry, I'm a clod, I don't do irony well. Idiots, they think blood is for feeding their flesh. Idiots, pus would be enough, or snot, or dung that fertilizes your potatoes. You were given blood so that you would spill it. Not slyly, but openly so that "the earth's mouth" (what a crude image!) can drink it and cry upon the heavens. It doesn't even think of crying. (Nothing cries. There's nothing but silence, the most real thing on earth.) And it will be like this until he will come who will be the Cain for his Abel and the Abel for his Cain, and

he will be killed not at once, but will die from dusk to night before giving up Abel's ghost. Then that which had been will be again. But this is still far away from now, this singular moment when guilt and punishment, death and history will cease to exist, distant, suspended; and afterwards there will be again so distant, so eternally distant. Although this moment, this only moment, [...] results, will never ever cease to exist.

Grosso modo,[18] boorishly – he said after a pause and turned again on his back, staring at the stars – all of history will occur between those who kill and those who are killed. The struggle for survival, for territory, class struggle, or whatever they will call it. But since affirmation precedes negation there must have been a "You shall kill" before "You shall not kill." By the way, note that seven of the ten commandments are negative. Again, I'm leading to the fact that history began with Cain's crime. Before that we had the kingdom of Nature. *Natura naturans*, still not *naturata*.[19] Good, some smartass can say, Cain killed Abel who/because he killed an ox that/because it killed (drank) water, that/because it killed fire, that/because it swallowed the cane, that/because with it Cain killed Abel, to paraphrase the old Jewish Haggadah.[20] Smartasses are fond of little loops of snakes swallowing their tails, *corsi ricorsi*, etc.[21] But firstly, Abel did not kill the ox, he brought it as an offering; it's a semantic error, the original flaw of human language that is ill suited for precise thought. Secondly, he did not kill, I was the first who did, and be what it may, I'm not giving up my rights to the original killing. Secondly, [sic] I killed not with a cane but a chopped flint since there were no other tools yet; as I said, civilization has started with me. It was said that killing Abel gave birth to civilization, and to history, and to death, and to dreams, and to fear. Besides, as everyone knows, a transition or leap from one Kingdom of things and states to another not always and not fully depends on the changes in them, but on the place, meaning, and value they acquire in the new general configuration of things and states. Thus Abel's killing of the ox wasn't murder; it did not have the value and meaning of murder, though if we consider only the factual side, it was undeniably murder. This is what language is for, despite its lack of precision, for establishing this distinction. And by establishing and expressing this distinction, to endow it with the quality of essentiality; hence the offering by killing an ox was the ox's sanctification, not murder. Wasn't it a natural and necessary act in the design of universal harmony and balance between God, man, and the well-balanced world of flora and fauna? Certainly, there were all these little games, original sin, my father's stupidity, my mother's greed, the tree of knowledge (by the way, Zeus dealt better with this knowledge: he swallowed Métis, Athena's mother – Μητις is advice or wisdom – so that she got stuck in him and told him good from bad), the deception, the snakes. I can't deny it, but they were for the sake of harmony. They added energy and drama, inspiration and diversity, without them everything would have grown sluggish, drowned in eternal boredom. Harmony burst when I, Cain killed my brother Abel, i.e. when not only a change of meaning occurred, but a new fact [. . .] revolutionary. "Where is Abel your brother?" I was squatting in the brushwood, not because of fear yet, though it already existed even though it had only just appeared in my dream, but because I was simply scared of the father's punishing hand (bourgeois semanticists, learn to distinguish these!). I understood He didn't like what I did. Firstly, Abel was His protégé; secondly, He had warned me – in obscure words, but unambiguously, as it came out afterwards, "Why are you so upset?" He asked me shortly before the killing, "Why are you pouting? If you were *blagonadiozhnyi*[22] you wouldn't lower your head but walk with your head up." I swear, I wasn't angry at all, and if I walked around with my head down, who didn't since the ground was full of snakes, amphibians, huge insects, and all kinds of creepy-crawlies. It's the same way as when you ask a calm person like your wife, why are you angry? Even if she's not, you drive her crazy with this. What a vulgar example.

So He warned me, but why? He could have prevented it altogether, not let it happen. Maybe it was supposed to be like, "Do what you want. I'm not interfering, I gave you free will, but if you do this you will regret your free will." Or maybe – if not for this warning, "I want to try you like I will try Abraham later " – maybe I would never have to kill my brother? It's a kind of *smerdyakovshina*.[23] "Am I my brother's keeper?" I answered from the ferns, still squatting and not getting up. Note this "Am I". I did not say I'm not, etc. but I dodged it even if I knew He knew, etc., etc. That was the beginning of the endless history with the police and *doprosy*.[24] From then on the *arme Menschenkinder*[25] will always be in some interrogation. That's how lies start, initially shyly. "Where?" "Am I?" I know but pretend I don't, and He knows but still asks, and then you swim in pure lies like fish in water, with lovely splashes and squeals. Thus as you see, lies and police, which is history, started the moment when Cain killed Abel.

Death and the earthquake in Messina, and Brigitte Bardot, and growing corn, and beautiful dragonflies screwing upon the Ś'weder River – all of this started with the megalomaniac Cain? – a smartass would ask. You see, yes, my dear; and he was a megalomaniac, you're right about that too. Only you're wrong about this screwing, but more about this later. A megalomaniac, simply because then everything was mega-, tigers had not yet shrunk into cats, dinosaurs into the lizard that you scared with your careless glance from the marble balustrade in your villa in Settignano when it lazily basked in the sun. Look how it scampers off under the vine leaves while you, dizzy with the fragrance of the grapes ripening in the sun, catch in your thin nostrils [. . .] a whiff

of roses from the garden as you look now at your refined fingers on the
Neapolitan tufa and then at the golden shade of the mist over Arezzo,
everything in the hot vibration of happiness. Oh give me a break. Well
I am an aesthete too, don't forget, darling; aesthetics also started with
me. My expelled parents saw their awkward nakedness and covered it
out of moral, not aesthetic shame. It was only when I saw Abel's beauty
turning in an instant into greenish meat, I immediately recognized
ugliness and beauty, my own hideousness and the beauty of the
landscape; that explains my stupid remark about Settignano.
As for the screwing dragonflies,
oh, then everything
was screwing, everywhere, in the air and
on the land and in the water. One big
pan-screwing. This wasn't
like making love quite yet, but a frantic
dance of procreation, one unceasing ecstasy
common for all, for if they
stopped, it was just
to start
again, that
makes sense.
The endless
hymn of praise to the glory of Creation.
First they humped without producing offspring,
but after original sin, it toook off . . . !
The *libido procreandi*[26] and the proliferation took off,
you shall screw and endlessly multiply
at a hyper-geometric rate. Maybe,
maybe Cain's unleashing the chain
of killing was to be the antidote, because soon there would be no room
left for people, spiders, mammoths, infusoria, etc.
Wasn't killing Abel a hygienic act,
population control? But why? Didn't He accomplish the same thing
later in a simpler way, with the flood? That's it! Well,
the first attempt didn't work, the tribe of Cain
was too lazy to murder, so he invented
a more effective means, the deluge. But the swarms of mantises,
              locusts and ants will
come again
and will make the defiled earth home.
If this was so, it would explain much, including the mild
punishment. But why all these complications? Making people believe,
arme Menschenkinder, that having offspring is the greatest
happiness while the best is not to be born at all, and being

born, etc ...,
and graft this onto eternal nostalgia for the lost
delights of screwing forever? What about Your disgraceful attitude,
                for instance,
towards that good old man who was just scared
to leave this world without offspring, well? You deceived him,
                provided him with a
descendant in his old age,
and then sent him to the summit of a mountain with a cord, a knife,
and a bunch of wood. In fear and trembling Abraham raises his knife
over his only son – enough. Søren
Churchyard will describe this better. Though most certainly he was
wrong, because the *Allmacht der Ideen*[27] is not in fear and trembling,
but in trusting, in Stalinist obedience.
But in my time ideas weren't around yet,
honestly speaking there were no such things. There were
                concrete individual
beings not conceptualized yet: a dinosaur, a spring,
a redwood, a piece of gneiss. Only after Abel's killing – ideas, symbols,
for example after Abel's death making love became a symbol
                (or an imago,
if you prefer) of killing, but that's beside the point.

He felt refreshed, rested after sleep, energetic. He looked at the stars, and all of a sudden, without even realizing it, started talking to them, "The egotist's megalomania, yes my dear, this too appeared after Abel's killing. Before, there was Cain, Abel and the two old folks. But not I-you because there was no mine-yours. Only, "where is your brother?" First your, then mine, then one's own – that's how it started, personalities and the cults of personalities and nations. Then I – personally [...] – anti [...] – you. And so it started. *Paashlo*...[28]

What started? Everything everything everything. Our dearest escape from nothing nothing nothing. That so neatly swallowed my brother Abel. Let's go back to making love. Everybody screwed everybody else unceasingly, almost bodilessly, just like dragonflies but more transparently, and dragonflies were still large and so transparent on the very edge of bodilessness, with only the faintest coloration providing them bodies, merely a beginning, a sketch of the later universe of colours. Upon the face of the waters. Everything got baser and smaller when it proliferated, a simple economy of living space, but that wasn't enough to stop this procreation volcano. But fixing it with killing when it would be so easy to introduce birth control? True, that's the economy of wastefulness. Still, from His vast closet of imagination He could have picked up a hundred better things! For example something finite, no birth and no death. Such and such number of you, and that's it. True, without death everything would become sluggish, that's right. So what about starting the whole thing again before the sea annihilated everything? Can't complain about the shortage of invention. Can't complain about the shortage of clay. Breathe once and a new *kadmos*[29] stands before us, better done, more obedient. Death is tied with birth. *Salome interfectrix*, as the apocrypha will say.[30] He was neither a foreman nor an economist but an artist, and death was a means against the boredom of existence and entropy of desire. But the killing... not to mention the fact that He could wait, there was an abundance of reptiles and flies, but only four people. Why would He [...] kill at the beginning of history. Yet even that killing didn't work, and He had to resort to a flood. If ambition didn't allow You to admit the product wasn't good enough since it was said "And saw it was good", then perhaps a simple burning breath would have done, as if by accident, and then just breathe again; no big deal. But maybe the number of breaths was limited by fate to say 9999^{99} times, and He already had breathed these billions of times, and the results were worse and worse, or horrors, always the same. Adam always ate from the tree of knowledge, Cain always killed Abel, and for the billionth time in a row Abraham dragged himself on the same donkey to the top of the same (even the name was the same, God!) Mount Moriah, horrors, enough, have mercy! Or else every subsequent breath was more teratologic, more and more degenerate, and finally He gave up, let it be as it was. The lesser evil. And He appointed me, Cain, as the garbage collector for his failed opus? Why not the other way around, why not Abel? Abel was his favourite. To let the favourite be killed, and *laufen* His disliked son *lassen*?[31] What a perversity of feelings, this smacks of Marquis de Sade or Sacher Masoch. The whole vast world without His only favourite, what a horror! (For He hated my parents too.) Did He want to punish Himself, perhaps because of His flawed product? This doesn't hold up either. Not wanting someone dear to your heart in the whole vast universe? Just like a mother fed up with family life drowning her kids?

Is it that I'm an instrument of His loathing towards His work? You're by definition unfailingly perfect, and is everything You do rubbish You despise? Is this simply a botched job that needs constant fixing, improvements and then desperate removal of these improvements, over and over again? Retracting your always failed attempts? Did You entangle yourself in this dialectic – from thesis to antithesis to worse? Don't You have enough power to create better? Nonsense. Are you so perfect that all you create has to be less perfect in order to make the perfect perfect by the fact of its very imperfection? But if this is so, whence loathing? It is an imperfect feeling of someone imperfect towards something less perfect but cannot be a feeling of the Perfect.

Because it casts phlegm on perfection and deperfects it. Or maybe You are a perfection that always and [...] longing for degradation, a fall; then this whole affair with me is just a distasteful staging of Your sick desire. Let's go back to the beginning. Why are You punishing me anyway if in this case, as much as any other, I was just Your instrument, and why this crap about free will? Unbecoming to both of us. I'm not complaining, maybe I have even become fond of this game, but I want to know everything, understand everything. The religion you demand of me is not the beginning but the end of knowledge. As the poet Novalis will say, "448. Alle historische Wissenschaft strebt mathematisch zu werden. Die mathematische Kraft ist die ordnende Kraft. Jede mathematische Wissenschaft strebt wieder philosophisch zu werden, animiert oder rationalisiert zu werden – dann poetisch, endlich moralisch, zulezt religiös" (*Philosophische Fragmente*).[32] I want to know even if I will suffer from this knowledge more than I suffer now; because I suffer, oh, I do.
The cries of my offspring
reach even here, to my rock.
They wake up to their day
full of cries and whims.
The offspring, but whom do they come from?
The Holy Scripture speaks of three of us,
my parents and I, and much later
Seth. Then where did I find a wife?
Not incest. The rabbis will explain,
from a she-devil. Not true. Simply,
I too took a clump of clay and breathed on it.
And it worked, beyond expectation! The eon's echo was still in me,
and I was the first sculptor, oh yes, believe me my dear.
Only your sculptors can't breathe life.
And what I breathed out! Read the description
in Machiavelli's letter to
Guicciardini, of that beauty with whom he had intercourse in
pitch darkness; compared to mine she was
an Egyptian beauty. What could I do, my breath was already
bad, after the killing my teeth
started rotting, my stomach
was ruined, I had constant hiccups; that's because the process
of aging had already come into being, death had already come
    into being, death was already
in me, and my massive bone frame
was already but a skeleton.
So my wife wasn't beautiful even if I am an aesthete.
Passons, she was the mother of my sons Menoch, Irad, and Mechuil.
  Suddenly he felt drawn to people. But he suppressed it quickly. He

convinced himself that he felt loathing towards them, towards his ugly children, grandchildren, and great-grandchildren who built huts, smithies, and in the evenings danced to a lute, fought, squealed, cried and laughed. But the truth is he doesn't like to show the mark on his forehead, while it's not safe to cover it in his offspring's settlements with so many good-for-nothings around. Still it's good to look at them from above, in the end they're my children, bone of my bone and blood of my blood. Also, *per procura*,[33] of Abel, my brother whom I murdered out of envy that the Lord accepted his offering and not mine. Some of them practise throwing spears, others make baskets, throw pots, trade in the market, and shoe horses. Their women dance at the bonfire, mothers feed babies, quarrel, and their squealing, their unbearable squealing reaches all the way up here, youngsters run from an angry old man, captains order trumpeters to play the wake-up call, soldiers go plunder and rape farmers' daughters, and the king's daughter with her maids approaches the well, fishermen throw their nets into the sea with swarming proliferating fish, a cup circles among the guests, and also a knife, a blacksmith sharpens a blade in his smithy, boon flies from the spinning wheel in a mother's hands, a stranger is crucified on a hill, a cleric slays a lamb on a sacred stone, naked children and dogs run around in the crowd, a prostitute with big eyes stands like a tower at the crossroads, her great hair rises, her combs made of tortoiseshell and mother of pearl, behind the wall a farmer leads a fat ox with the plough, on a tower an astrologer composes a horoscope, it is pleasant, the earth is tended in a human way, the earth of the settled. But I am an eternal exile on the earth of the settled.
He dozed off. When he woke up
an earthworm stood before him. It shook as if doing the twist.
It was slender and pretended to be a snake.
It was all flesh, naked, unprotected
(except for hair), pinkish-yellowish, defenceless.
A drop of moisture
was on the slimy surface, between the hairs.
It was scared, obviously, uncertain if before it lay
a beam, a strange stone, a carnivorous body
or a worm sick with bloat,
or a Mystery; all its cartilage
crunched, this probably woke
Cain . . . All eyes, it stared
at that unknown thing not knowing
if edible, safe. To crawl up the unknown, to taste it with a tooth
               would be an exhilarating
pleasure, a dangerous life
for the earthworm. I don't murder, it used to say with pride to its
               children,

I feed on what others
have murdered. Poor thing, what went on in it
when Cain lifted his heavy eyelids and it saw
(with all its length, and it was long, 3 metres and 28 centimetres)
his eyes. It froze. Suddenly it fell
to the ground which never before seemed
so motherly, mother earth, *mat'
zemla syraia*,³⁴ this bizarre phrase
travelled from it to people, from the earthworm of the dawn of
history.
Cain felt very tired,
he carelessly shook off the grass and ants, took his stick and started
walking.
It was well into the day.
In the distance the cries of his offspring faded.

Notes

1 San Francisco.
2 In the dusk of the evening.
3 "The Avenger was born of blood", (a paraphrase of *Aeneid*, IV, 626).
4 Back.
5 Square brackets indicate Polish editor's intrusions: [. . .], a word/s illegible; [?], a possible reading; [and], or an[d] a word or its part inserted.
6 "No act is so common to us as the act of annihilating. Equally common is the act of building . . . It is a kind of magic through which we arrange the world around us according to our whim and convenience." Novalis, *Neue Fragmente*, 681
7 Delight in making up stories.
8 "Boat with three sailors lands on whale", *Ashmole Bestiary*, circa 1210 AD, MS Ashmole, Bodleian Library, Oxford, Folio 86 verso. Sir Elias Ashmole (1617-1692) donated his collection of books and artifacts to Oxford University.
9 "Back to our sheep", a quotation from *La Farce de Maistre Pathelin*.
10 Stepan Trofimovich Verchovensky, the hero of *The Devils* by Dostoevsky.
11 Andrei Vyshinsky (1883-1954), famous Soviet attorney-general under Stalin; his penal code did not contain a provision for innocence.
12 *Unde malum* – where does evil come from?
13 Over and over.
14 Never mind.
15 An everyday thing.
16 "In the beginning" (Gen. 1.1)
17 Pavlik Morozov, the young pioneer who informed on his parents and caused their execution, and then was killed by his grandfather.
18 Roughly speaking.
19 *Natura naturans*, creative nature, *Natura naturata*, nature created.

20 A paraphrase of the *Had Gadya* song from the Passover Haggadah.
21 Ital. *corsi e ricorsi della storia*, history repeating itself in cycles; from the philosophy of Gianbattista Vico.
22 Law-abiding.
23 An appalling combination of physical and moral degeneration, cowardice and savagery; from the name of Smerdyakov, a hero of Dostoevski's *Brothers Karamazov*.
24 Interrogations.
25 Poor human beings.
26 The procreative urge.
27 The omnipotence of ideas.
28 It took off.
29 Adam Kadmon, Kabbalistic primordial man.
30 "Salome the murderess". The reference is confusing since several women named Salome appear in different apocrypha, however none of them in an adverse role. On the other hand, the young dancer who demanded the head of John the Baptist, traditionally identified as Salome, appears, albeit without a name but as "the daughter of Herodias", in the canonical Gospels: Mark 6:22-26, Matt. 14:6-11.
31 *Laufen lasssen* – allow to escape.
32 "All historical sciences strive to become mathematical. The power of the mathematics is in organizing. All mathematical sciences strive in turn to become philosophical, to become live sciences, or rationalistic – then poetic, then moral, and finally religious."
33 Substituting for.
34 The earth, a moist mother.

Mehmet Yashin
Turkey/Cyprus

Translated by Taner Baybars

Mehmet Yashin (Yaşin) *is considered one of the leading poets and writers in contemporary Turkish literature. He lives between Nicosia, Istanbul and London. His prize-winning poems and other literary works have been well known to Cypriots as well as mainland Turks and Greeks since the early 1980s. He studied at the universities of Ankara, Istanbul, Birmingham and Middlesex. His books of poetry are:* My Love The Dead Soldier *(1984),* Ladder of Light *(1986),* Pathos *(1990),* The ChairMan *(1993),* To Repair a Daydream *(1998). He has published a novel,* Your Kinsman Pisces *(1994), and a collection of essays* Poeturka *(1995). He is also the editor and translator of* Anthology of Early Cypriot Poetry: 9th century BC to 18th century AD *(1999) and* Anthology of Turkish-Cypriot Poetry: 18th to 20th centuries *(1994) and* Step-Mothertongue – From Nationalism to Multiculturalism: Literatures of Cyprus, Greece and Turkey *(2000). His most recent publication is a volume of selected poems in English,* Don't Go Back To Kyrenia, *(Middlesex University Press, 2001).*

Taner Baybars *is a British poet and translator of Turkish-Cypriot origin. He worked for the British Council from the 1950s until his early retirement in 1988. He now lives in France and acts as Corresponding Editor for the avant-garde London magazine,* Ambit. *He is also recognized as the English translator of Nazim Hikmet. His translations of other Turkish poets have appeared in various magazines and anthologies on both sides of the Atlantic. Apart from his very first poetry collection (1954), his output has been entirely in English. His works include:* To Catch a Falling Man *(London, 1963),* Susila in Autumn Woods *(London, 1974),* Narcissus in a Dry Pool *(London, 1978),* Pregnant Shadows *(London, 1998). He has also written a novel,* A Trap for the Burglar *(London, 1965), and an autobiographical work,* Plucked in a Far-Off Land: Images in Self-Biography *(London, 1970).*

> *"If you should come to Kyrenia*
> *Don't enter the walls.*
> *If you should enter the walls*
> *Don't stay long.*
> *If you should stay long*
> *Don't get married.*
> *If you should get married*
> *Don't have children."*
>
> From an old Ottoman-Turkish song of Cyprus
> Translated by Lawrence Durrell

Don't go to Kyrenia

'Don't go to Kyrenia', they said,
but if you do, have no children.
hundreds of times they said it,
your fault if you paid no attention.

It was the same boat that docked,
you thought the sail was satin, it was a shroud.
They unloaded the songs to the port
but they were not the songs of our love
the amphoras were filled with sea-blood
and those who drank from them were poisoned,
but if they didn't drink, they'd die of the plague,
and if they didn't die, they'd go to war.

The lights at the discotheque daze,
let them daze whether we die or not
we spin in slices of multicolour shadows,
let the lights daze, daze . . .

I don't know what tremor of war
has petrified Kyrenia but left her eyes wide open,
in a confusion of who's gone away
who's come back,
the loved ones who have sailed away,
and the dead
and the dead have sent back.
Kyrenia will be machine-gunned if she moves,
and if she doesn't, she will still be bombed by planes.

Love will move, even if we won't
don't water the garden they said

but if you do, don't dig,
there'll soon be a war, anyway.

If we'll strip down to soldiers in the Fort,
whether the geraniums burst open or not, in a tumult of noises,
or not bloom at all, around the Loveterranean, our sea.
If we light a fire and dance,
if we dance in the submarine-caves
with LSD and videos and revolvers, we'll dance,
whoever doesn't dance will lose his mind
and who doesn't lose his mind will drown in salt.

Don't go to Kyrenia they said,
the lights at the discotheque, let them daze
there'll soon be a war, anyway,
let the lights daze, daze...

Album
to Mehmet Yashin

Like underwear, your shorts and shirts,
the negatives are clipped on the drying line,
beginning a new album of your life.
Tearing apart the twelve years '83 – '95,
as the scattered pages of an empty photobook . . .
Perhaps the apocalypse of your first love,
the death of a mother, and the endless
uprootings of yourself, old as Exodus,
in fact, the result of what you wrote by hand!
Not yours, the medieval history of your fate
when violent times turned you into a poet
in foreign lands! And those state-run societies
which force you to role-play . . . Like a 36-exposure film
half-finished in a camera, I'm taking your pictures,
my life, for my new album.

The Door!
Let them knock. Let them.

You can count yourself safe inside, never revealing,
yourself to yourself, totally sealed.
The telly is your single-eye window to external time,

colour by colour, channel by channel, zap zap zap . . .
The door! Let them knock.
Who can it be anyway, a lover? . . .
Men or women, lovers *could* be windows,
each one opening to a different adventure
serial after serial, zap zap. The door!
Is it worth answering who ever it may be
just now? Freedom is a prison of sorts . . .

Janus has two faces, bright door and murky
    door!
No, let it remain shut.

A Ghost

> *Phoenician inscribers of epitaphs were killed by*
> *Phoenician warriors themselves,*
> *because they advocated an end to the*
> *war with the Greeks, and those who*
> *remained, continued to live like ghosts under*
> *threat of death*
>
>   From a tombstone in Idalion, Cyprus, 8c BC

Only as a ghost can I now return to my own home,
emerging from blurred mirrors. I haven't much time.
I throw the windows open, in utter dark, starlight
floods the rooms. I shake the dust off the curtains,
off the linen draped over bookshelves. I must also clean,
with my moist breath, the family pictures in frames.
The avenging angels of this polyglot house, now silenced,
make every one who enters it promise to write
against wars, against everything jingoist, even tongues.
Sprinkle the antkiller around like enchanted words,
the mothballs. I've wiped the floors clean. I lock the doors,
and I'm off again, no one has even seen me.
    I'm a phantom . . . they can't have me killed.

Andrea Zanzotto
Italy

Translated by Andrew Fitzsimons

Andrea Zanzotto, *born in 1921, has published an important body of work, including thirteen volumes of poetry, a collection of short stories and many critical essays. In later life he experimented increasingly with the poetic use of the dialect of his native region; some of his dialect poetry, translated by John P Welle and Ruth Feldman, appeared in* MPT 3.

Spring

Here the primrose and the warmth
at your feet and the wisdom of the world

the uncovered carpets
the verandahs stirred by the wind and the sun
the worm quiet in the thorny wood;
my distant pain, the sharp thirst
like another life in the breast

Here there's nothing to do but wrap
the landscape round you
and turn your back.

Distance

Now all your distance surrounds me
and I stand disarmed inside the evening

the honey smells sweet upon the table
and there is thunder in the valley

I am a lived-in space
deserted by your sun
Come ask me where
shout at me solitude

This blue streaked with despair
and mountain lights
has known me forever inside and out.

Ten poems from The Greek Anthology

Translated by John Wareham

John Wareham's *translations of Classical Greek poems have appeared in* MPT *13 and 15. He is a poet, born in Hampshire, who now lives in Essex.*

Praise for the Thracians

The Thracians have a way: they mourn
Their sons as soon as they are born,
And those on whom Death lays a hand,
Unforseen drudge of Fates, they commend.
For the span of the living is desolate;
Only the death have found an antidote.

  [Archias of Mitylene, from Book IX, No 111]

*

You are all words, man, but soon your mouth
Is filled with earth.
Stay quiet while you still can breathe
And think on death.

  [Palladas, from Book XI, No 300]

*

For self, children and wife
Androtion built me. As yet
I'm no one's tomb, long may this remain;
But if the time comes let
Me greet earlier the earlier born.

  [Anonymous, from Book VII, No 228]

Niketas Returns to Stay

Why bury me close to the sea, sailors?
The crashing of waves makes me shudder;
They destroyed me. A shipwrecked man's tomb
Should be inland. Yet at least you pitied Niketas.

   [Posidippos, from Book VII, No 267]

*

My tomb is surrounded by thorns and stakes
And you will wound your feet if you approach.
Timon the misanthrope lives within;
But pass on, curse me if you will, but pass.

   [Hegesippos, from Book VII, No 320]

*

Heliodoros died before her,
Diogenia followed within the hour:
Both content to share a tomb
As, before, a room.

   [Apollonides, from Book VII, No 378]

*

While he lived the miller owned me,
A loud-growling, rotating millstone
Grinding fertile Demeter's wheat.
When he died he placed me on his tomb,
As symbol of his calling. I was heavy in his work,
Now I rest heavy on his bones.

   [Philippos of Thessalonika, from Book VII, no 394]

*

Tread softly by Hipponax's grave,
Don't wake that malicious wasp
Only just now laid to rest:
His sharp words stung even his parents,
His red-hot lines can sear you even in Hell.

    [Leonidas, from Book VII, No 408]

*

Ploughman, is no more earth left?
Must your oxen now stumble on tomb-roofs,
Your ploughshare cut the bones of the dead?
How much wheat will ashes yield?
Your time will come, and someone will plough you
Who broke ground in evil tillage.

    [Antiphilos, from Book VII, No 175]

*

Hand me the sweet cup made of the clay
I came from and shall return to one day.

    [Zonas, from Book XI, No 43]

Three Polish Poets

Translated by Ryszard Reisner

Ludwika Amber *was born in Kowary, Poland, in 1948, and arrived in Australia in 1982. She has published many books of poetry, in both Polish and English, and edited* Green Winter, *an anthology of Polish poetry and prose from Australia. Recently, in Poland, she has published a collection of her poems,* Delfiny, *and an anthology of Australian poetry,* Billabong.

Marek Baterowicz, *who was born in 1944 and migrated to Australia in 1987, holds a PhD in Romance Languages and has published work in Polish, French and English. He won the Italian Circe Sabadia Prize for Poetry in 1985. A selection of his poems written over two decades,* Z tamtej Strony Drzewa, *appeared in Melbourne in 1992, followed by* Na Wydmach Czasu *(Sydney, 1993) and* Miejsce w Atlasie *(Sydney, 1996). He has also published prose works, many books of poetry, and translations into Polish of Romance literature and of English poetry by Polish-born writers.*

Marius Rosiak *was born in 1958 and graduated with an MA in Cultural Studies at Mickiewicz University, Poznan. His poems have appeared in many Polish literary journals, and he has published several books of poetry and numerous articles on literature and contemporary art. He has been Director of the Poznan City Art Gallery and currently runs his own gallery of contemporary art, Gallery 'R'.*

Ryszard Reisner, *born in Lodz, Poland, in 1954, arrived in Australia with his parents in 1960. He has edited and translated the work of other Polish poets resident in Australia, and organised publications and readings with the support of the Australian Literature Board, some of which were featured on national Australian radio. He was on the Executive Committee of the Polish Studies Foundation at Monash University, and also on that of the Australian Literary Translators Association. He returned to Poland in 1997, and is lecturing at the School of Translation, Adam Mickiewicz Univeristy, Poznan. At present he is working on a number of translation projects embracing contemporary Polish prose and poetry.*

Ludwika Amber

The Unlocking of Borders

we were returning through the continents
of tongues rituals altars colours
and the music of gestures

slowly we were opening doors
of new scents of the bush
we were learning
the fingers of our own hands
the Esperanto of lips
distances between bodies
faith in the feathers of parrots
hues of the earth the air
the trace of a stream

we were coming by water and landstretch
we outsped clouds
we crossed the river of childhood helplessness

Terra Australis – we shouted at the border
and set first foot
our imprint on the shore

Sandglass of the First Generations in Australia

the glass doors of childhood
I leave ajar
through the narrow chink
autumns and winters are turning
when I'm falling asleep
a dream is passing to the north
and before dawn returns
here where it scatters my paths
written in goose quill
on the map
of south pole memory

The Hired Warrior

is deft
does not trust anyone
draws his sword in an instant
before him
and with ease dissects a butterfly
which flew so childishly
out of the chrysalis of his heart

Marek Baterowicz

Under the Sun's Divine Eye

Gazelle clouds soar
    over the immense ocean discus
rotating without change
shaken by the planet's mortal fever
although the waves bring the essence of existence,
and far away change into steel and silver
    like snake skin
drowning under the sun's divine eye.
Oh, my beloved and never met,
the sea effaces your footsteps
and the choir of cicadas wakes to a crescendo
commenting with passion
on our present tragedy,
the drama of this century,
in which the voices of Solon and Sophocles have stilled,
and righteous debaters in columns' shadow,
at the time when the Gods do not hesitate
to come amongst mortals,
worship the beauty of earthly women,
create demi-gods and heroes.
Now Satan has taken their place,
hatching his sons
under the sun's divine eye.

Prophecy

This isn't a mighty angel
    with a flamecopper trumpet –
proclaiming us the end of an era,
    no cracking of broken seals
opens the book of judgement

This is a small defenceless girl –
    without a blazing sword
playing tremolo on the flute
    announcing prophecy to the world
pregnant like the sands of Sinai

Sinai – where the wind is born olive –
    has so much sun and skyblue
for churches out of chaliced bones
    for synagogues full of seagulls
and for mosques out of melaphyre

It has so much sun and skyblue
    but the seals still crumble
and the books glow in the ashes.
    The flame copper wind blinded the angel,
the flute glistens like a sword over the century

Mariusz Rosiak

In My Country on the Corner of Europe

In my country on the corner of Europe
where the hand of God still reaches
where faces of children in windows flutter like heralds
where people are more ebullient than rivers
where winds blow and clash together
where birds still return in winter
where love is spoken of even earnestly

In my country on the corner of Europe
where we live out of one crock
out of one shaft of air
words again have their meaning

Poem Brought from Australia

It is painful to be unable to return to your own country
curse rivers, trees and streets
which as shards engraved themselves in the memory of flesh.
To be a branch broken off cruelly from a tree,
feed on sap not from your own roots
and continually wait. The way death awaits the newly born.

It is appalling to be unable to return to your own country.
Even more appalling not to want to return there.

Three Russian Poets

Translated by Stephen Capus

Stephen Capus *studied Russian literature at the Universities of Birmingham and London. He has published poems and translations in various magazines, including* Acumen *and* Thumbscrew. *He currently works as an administrator at University College London.*

Anna Akhmatova (1889-1966)

Mayakovsky in 1913

I never knew you in the days of your glory,
Your turbulent dawn in all I know;
But perhaps I'm qualified to tell your story
At last of that day from long ago.
The lines of your powerful verse were filled with
Strange new voices we'd never heard . . .
And your youthful hands were never still as
You raised up a terrible scaffold of words.
Whatever you touched was no longer the same as
The thing it had been before that time,
All that you censured and covered in shame was
Condemned to death in your thunderous lines.
So often alone and disaffected,
You impatiently tried to seep up fate,
For already you freely, gladly accepted
That soon you muct go and take part in the great
Struggle. And as you read an answer
Of rumbling dissent could be heard all round
And the angry rain eyed you askance as
You debated at length with the outraged town.
And now a name, unknown, obscure,
Was flashing around the stuffy hall,
And all through the land today it endures,
Reverberates still like a warrior's call.

Vladimir Mayakovsky (1893-1930)

To Comrade Nette – The Steamship and the Man*

I had cause to shudder – it wasn't a spectre.
Into port, gleaming in the molten light,
Entered Comrage 'Theodore Nette'.
Yes, it was him alright.
I knew him from the lifebelt-glasses he was wearing,
Just like in the old days. Nette, how are you?
I'm so glad you're stil with us, alive and sharing
In the smokey confusion of cables and cargoes.
Come closer – if it's not too shallow for you here
After steaming from Batum throught the open seas.
Nette, d'you recall how in your previous career
As a man you once drank tea on a train with me?
The others were all snoring like dormice by you
Ttayed awake and talked about Romka Jakobson
And poetry all night – yet your eyes stayed glued
To the diplomatic bags – till finally around dawn
You nodded off to sleep with your hand still clamped
So tightly round your gun you must have had cramp
In your finger... You're welcome to come and have a go,
If you've got the never! At the time did you dream the
Moment would arrive in year or so
When we'd meet again – and that you'd be a steamer?
The moon glows like a conflagration.
And now it's declined, dividing the flood.
As though you trail behind you form that confrontation
On the train a heroic stream of blood.
Communism from books is never quite real.
'Any kind of nonsence can find support
In books'. But the act which you performed reveals
The essence and soul of communist thought.
We live, united by a common conviction;
For its sake we'll encure all manner of afflication:
To live in a unified world, made happier
By the absence of divisions like Russia and Latvia.
Blood, not water, flows through our veins.
Marching through a storm of bullets, we try
To ensure that one day we'll be born again
In steamships, in words – in things that never die.

*

I'd like to live, careering through the years.
And yet I can think of nothing better
Than to face my death without regrets or fears
The way it was faced by Comrade Nette.

* At readings, Mayakovsky often introduced this poem with the folloiwng anecdote: 'Nette was one of our diplomatic couriers . . . I knew Comrade Nette well . . . In Rostov I heard the newspaper-vendors shouting in my street: "Attack on Soviet couriers Nette and Makhmastl". I was stunned. This was my first meeting with Nette after his death. Soon the initial grief abated. I found myself in Odessa. I boarded a steamship for Yalta. As our ship was leaving harbour, it was met by another, bearing the name, written in golden letters gleaming in the sun: "Theodore Nette". This was my second meeting with Nette; but by now he was no longer a man, but a steamship.

Maria Tsvetaeva (1892-1941)

The Poet

The poet acquires his speech from afar.
Speech carries the poet beyond the stars.

The obliquities of parables and portents – those
Are the way of the poet . . . Between *yes* and *no*
Leaping headlong from the dizzy top
Of a tower, he still contrives to stop
And make a detour . . . Because the poet travels

The way of comets. Causality unravelled,
It's links dispersed – that's the law which guides
the poets eclipses. Look up at the sky
And despair, astronomer! For the poet's path
Can't be plotted by the curve of a graph.

He's the one no granite Bastille can hold,
The one whose tracks have always gone cold.
He defies the laws of number and weight,
He's the train for which everyone is always late.

He asks the questions even Kant doesn't know
The answer to . . .

>   Because the poet goes
The wasy of coments, he doesn't warm,
he burns, he doesn't nurture – he's violence and storm –
Poet, the trajectory of your fiery path
Can't be plotted by the curve of a graph!

Peter Viereck
by Daniel Weissbort

I first met the American poet, historian, teacher, translator Peter Viereck in 1974, when Joseph Brodsky, Michael Hamburger, Viereck and myself had lunch at an Indian restaurant in London. In 1975, some of Viereck's translations of Stefan George were published in *MPT*, First Series, 21 (this selection including 'Knights Templars', reprinted here in a substantially revised later version).

We corresponded for a while and then lost touch. However, I would hear about Viereck from time to time from Brodsky, who was a close friend and admirer of his and who co-taught courses with him at Mount Holyoke College in South Hadley, Massachusetts, where Viereck was Professor of History. He taught there from 1948 beyond his retirement in 1987 until 1996-7. It was Viereck who brought Brodsky to Mount Holyoke. They had met in Leningrad in 1962 and renewed their friendship when Brodsky came to the US, in 1972. Perhaps the last letter Brodsky wrote before his death in 1996 was to Viereck. He was looking forward to again teaching their seminar, officially called "Poets under Stalin and Hitler", for which their secret name was "Rime and Punishment". Viereck adds, in a letter to me: "Or shd I say: 'Punnishness'?"

Born in New York City in 1916, Peter Viereck, who in 1949 was awarded the Pulitzer Prize for Poetry for his first book of poems, *Terror and Decorum*, is also among the most creative and original translators of poetry. His approach can perhaps be characterized as holistic, surrendering neither to the sense nor the sound, but trying to render both. Here is Viereck's own characterization of his translations (to be found in his 'Background Note on Stefan George', partially reproduced below): "[The translator] prefers to call the result a transplanting, not a translation: because the commentaries and sometimes non-literal renderings try to reproduce the original soil (context, music, intent, connotations) rather than the dictionary-meaning denotations." In the present climate (among translators, at any rate) of post-colonial foreignization, this might make some uneasy. But Viereck has earned the right ("The translator has worked on this 'impossible' translation attempt for some sixty years, starting 1936.") to be taken at his word. He is, it seems to me, describing a kind of translation that derives not from political conviction but from an interior knowledge of the source texts. Perhaps this is the "real" foreignization, or perhaps great translators, of whatever persuasion, converge.

The late Katherine Washburn, herself a noted translator of Paul

Celan, among other German poets, and editor of the huge Norton anthology *World Poetry: An Anthology of Verse from Antiquity to Our Time* (1998), said of Viereck: "no one has ever translated Goethe as well into English". She included more of his translations (Heym, George) in the anthology than of anyone else's.

Among Viereck's many collections of poetry is *Archer in the Marrow: The Applewood Cycles 1967-1987*, published in 1987. Frederick Turner writes of it: "One reads *Archer in the Marrow* with the same amazement and trembling that *The Wasteland* must have inspired in its first readers. The language blazes out as if it had never been used before." Joseph Brodsky again – and this returns us, in a way, to our translational theme – wrote of this volume:

> *Applewood* is the major event in American poetry of today, on a par with Williams' Paterson or Pound's Cantos (although Mr Viereck would resent such a comparison). It would be considered a major event in any literature. Had *Applewood* been written in French or German, it would be no doubt a lot luckier: by now we'd have had it translated into English several times, hailed, imitated, parodied.

Tide and Continuities, Last and First Poems (1995-1938) was published by the University of Arkansas Press, which with some justification refers to Viereck's poetry as "an ongoing experiment in the symbiosis of poetry and history". The book includes an argumentative verse preface by Brodsky, from which I have extracted these stanzas:

> He's in his seventies. He saw
> more of humanity's seesaw
> than you who will peruse these pages,
> heart-rending, gorgeous, outrageous,
> thus spanning roughly five decades
> – the Nazis, the Cold War, and AIDS,
> the ogres turning mediogres –
> such is the nature of our progress. [. . .]
>
> Unlike the bulk of current stuff,
> rough-hewn, minimalist, and tough,
> this book, left to its own devices,
> is an homage to Dionysos:
> it is a growth. In its design,
> by turns malignant and benign,
> it tends to leap, digress, meander;
> in short, its target is its grandeur. [. . .]

The "punnish" invention or neologism "mediogres", in the first of these stanzas, is recycled from a free self-translation of one of Brodsky's own poems, in English titled 'In Memoriam' where it also rhymes with "progress". The relationship between these two poets, having as much to do with prosody, a regard for metre and rhyme, as with philosophy or political beliefs, is worth exploring, but I have no space to do so here. However, I should like to quote Viereck's unpublished memorial to Brodsky. Professor Viereck sent this to me, remarking that he had heard that *MPT* had had a Brodsky issue (in fact a Special Feature on Brodsky, in *MPT* 10 (*Russia*), in 1996, the year of Brodsky's death) and that perhaps this would be acceptable as a late contribution.

Not Works
(For Brodsky)

The night the poet died his metaphors
Gloated in liberation round his corpse.
Now rouged clichés, disguised as muse,
Ignite a bombing bombast's purple fuse.
Cant sneaks its Trojan Pegasus
Into Parnassus. Hoarse refugees race to warn us
That exclamation marks are running wild
And prowling half-truths carried off a child.
Fixed stars his vision etched into the skies
Now gouge – as falling stars – his too-wide eyes.
    Yet he throbs on in form to shatter
    This formless mutiny of matter.
    His dust is dead, his pulse a frightening thunder.
    Bell, book, and test tube can't exorcise its gong,
    Pulsing us into shapes of gargoyle wonder.
    In vain we drive our stakes through such a haunter.
    Are we but split iambics of his song?
    Are hearts feet lungs and couplings strummed
    By two-way thump,
    Scanning our outraged flesh with metric flow?
Yet some sereneness in our rage has guessed
That we are being blest and blest and blest
When least we know it and when coldest art
Seems hostile, useless, or apart.
Not worms, not worms in such a skull
But rhythms, rhythms writhe and sting and crawl.
They spin the seasons round from bud to snow.
And all things are because he tuned them so.

[revised March 2000]

Metapolitics: From the Romantics to Hitler was hailed by Thomas Mann for its indictment of the Nazi menace. Other historical/political works by Viereck include *Conservatism Revisited: The Revolt Against Revolt, 1815-1949*, which proposes a political and cultural programme for the West based on a new interpretation of modern history. *Shame and Glory of the Intellectuals: Babbitt Jr vs the Rediscovery of Values* and *Dream and Responsibility: Four Test Cases of the Tension Between Poetry and Society* appeared in 1953, and in 1956 Viereck published two volumes defending the Western heritage of individual freedom against communism and fascism: *The Unadjusted Man: A New Hero for Americans: Reflections on the Distinction Between Conforming and Conserving* (1956, 1962) and *Conservatism: From John Adams to Churchill* (1956). In *Conservatism Revisited and the New Conservatism: What Went Wrong?* (1962) Viereck describes the degeneration into thought control and material greed of some aspects of the "new conservative" movement which his earlier work in 1949 had helped to found.

Peter Viereck is among our few genuinely independent literary and scholarly illuminati and has, to some extent, paid the price for his originality. Michael Lind, author of *Up from Conservatism: why the Right is Wrong for America*, wrote: "Peter Viereck is one of the most accomplished and unjustly neglected thinkers of the twentieth century". He aligns himself neither with the right nor the left. The tactics of the neo-conservative right wing of contemporary politics, he calls "mean-spirited and petty". But he is clear in one respect: "I never distinguished between Fascism and Communism [. . .] They are based on dry, cold, abstract slogans felt in the head, but not in the heart."

Arthur Schlessinger, commenting on Viereck's *Metapolitics* in his memoirs, *A Life* (2000), quotes Thomas Mann: "Peter published Metapolitics, an important and original work tracing the historical roots of Nazi racism and messianism to the excesses of German romanticism . . . Wagner was darkly prominent in Peter's analysis, and Thomas Mann, though a fan of Wagner, approved Peter's account and praised him for going back to 'the sources of German Nationalism which is the most dangerous in existence, because it is mechanized mysticism.'" Schlessinger, recalling that Viereck, amazingly enough, was the great-grandson of Kaiser Wilhelm I, through the Kaiser's mistress, the actress Edwina Viereck, calls him "a romantic classicist, a poetic constitutionalist, an immoderate moderate, a Bohemian who argues for propriety and restraint". Viereck himself put it this way: "progress is achieved in zigzags, by constant readiness to readjust to reality. A straight line is the longest distance between two points. And the bloodiest."

Viereck is the only Guggenheim recipient to have received a Fellowship in two categories: poetry and history, repeating his much earlier performance at Harvard when he received the Garrison prize for the best undergraduate verse and the Bowdoin medal for the best prose. It is not hard to understand what drew Brodsky to him. "Ideas must dance", he wrote, "and metre is Time in leotards". In a recent letter to me, Peter Viereck commented on his own fascination with Brodsky's "technically 'incorrect'" self-translations: "They give me a better, newer understanding of my own language. As if Eng [sic] were a prism suddenly turned to a new angle." A master of the language and of its prosody, Viereck is among the few with enough generosity of spirit and freedom from dogma to be able to make this claim.

It is impossible to encapsulate Peter Viereck's career and creative personality in so brief a piece. Last year at my request, he sent me, among other writings, the manuscript of his 65-year project, 'Transplantings'. About half of this consists of translations: Goethe, in particular a number of "turning points" from *Faust*, which cannot be excerpted and so are not represented here; Stefan George (1868-1933); Georg Heym (1987-1912); and related poets like Hofmannsthal. The other half is short essays on the translation of each poem and on its cultural context. This prompted me to re-start *MPT*'s 'Translators of Poetry' series, which has included Michael Bullock (No 3, Summer 1993), Robert Friend (No 4, Winter 1993/4), James Kirkup (No 11, Summer 1997). We can do no more, however, than taste or dip into these allusive texts, which cross-reference one another and in a sense form a single entity. It is to be hoped that the complete work will find a publisher in due course and that other works by this remarkable poet-thinker will be brought back into print.

Transplanter Credo

by Peter Viereck

Be bilingual, of course, but also bicultural, steeped in both histories, both nightmares. Always bear in mind that the same words may have different cultural contexts in different languages. The soil must suit the root. Synonyms may not be synonymous. Given its history, "Volk" means more than "folk", being more sentimental and more sinister. Not dictionary but context is all. The four seasons have different connotations in different languages and geographies (ancient Greek having basically only three) and translate differently. German seasons are more directly symbolic of man's life than in English. Transplant simultaneously for ear, for eye, for cultural memory. Boycott any prose trot. No matter how accurate, a trot sacrifices connotation to denotation. Be faithful to the original's form and metrics, whether feminine rhyme, masculine rhyme, or free verse. But English (more monosyllables, few declensions) is shorter than German. So occasionally a German five-beat line requires an English four-beat line. Thou shalt not pad a line with deadwood filler to achieve five beats.

Don't choose between a word's sound and a word's meaning; render both. Example: the first word in Heym's line "Aber die Tiere". Literal translation of "Aber" is "But". "But" loses the sonorus vowel sound of the "A" in "Aber". My suggestion: "Ah but the creatures." This is what I mean by distinguishing between transplanting and literal translating. The aim: colloquial *English* poems in their own right, not pedantic translationese. Having shed declension endings because of 1066, English has fewer feminine rhymes than other languages. So keep inventing new feminine rhymes, even if slightly off. To work out the right mix of sound and meaning has often taken me (as with "Aber") three years. This is not at all long, considering that my book [PV's *Complete Translations*, as yet unpublished] took me over 65 years, ever since in 1934 I first read its poets: Hölderlin, Goethe, Hofmannsthal, George, Heym. Often the meaning is better clarified, less distorted when you substitute an equivalent for an equal. Example: to translate from Latin the phrase "in the Greek kalends" (meaning "never"), I simply invented "on February 30".

from **A Goethe Sampler**

Wanderer's Night Song

To every hill crest
Comes rest.
In every tree crest
the forest
scarcely draws breath.
Each bird-nest is hushed on the heath.
Wait a bit; soon you
will find rest too.

Wandrers Nachtlied

Über allen Gipfeln
ist Ruh.
Über allen Wipfeln
spürest du
kaum einen Hauch:
die Vögelein schweigen im Walde.

Warte nur, balde
ruhest du auch.

Translator's comment on Goethe's 'Wanderer's Night Song'
In 1780 young Goethe pencilled these eight lines on the wooden wall of a mountain lodge. Along with Pushkin's 'On the Hills of Georgia', this is the *simplest* great poem in history. So naïve-sounding a rhythm, diction, and feeling can only be the product of the most sophisticated craftsmanship. As with the Pushkin poem, translators have either betrayed Goethe's simplicity by cleverness or cloyed it by banality.

To substitute for the resonance of feminine rhyme in German (uninflected English having more masculine rhymes), I've increased the number of rhymes with the key word "rest". And to prevent this increase from becoming monotonous, I've used one rhyme with accent not on "rest" but on the penultimate syllable: "forest" in line four.

To enhance the hushed mood by echo, Goethe on line six alliterates the "w" of "schweigen" with the "w" of "Wald". Analogously in line six of the English, "hushed" and "heath" alliterate. This is achieved at the cost of using an eye rhyme (heath, breath) instead of a "perfect" ear rhyme. In denotation, "heath" is not a proper translation of "Wald". The former has mere thickets; the latter is arboreal. But the emotional connotations are partly similar: rustic, unpruned, unmapped, a wilderness for wanderers at night. I don't want to repeat the earlier-used concept of forest and woods. The reader's ear needs the couplet ending in "eath" to escape for just a moment the restless "rest" rhymes.

Blessed Longing

What I tell you, better censor.
Bruit it only to the wiser.
I celebrate what lives intenser:
Life that yearns for death-by-fire.

Nights of loving, nights of cooling,
Where you're begot, where you're begetting,
Seize you with what eerie feeling
When hushed candle-rays are jetting.

Shadows of the dark no longer
Bind you down to be night's plaything.
Now you're launched by newer longing
Up to ever higher mating.

Now no distance is too distant.
Wafted spirit, spellbound flesh.
Moth compelled by flame's insistent
Magnet, you must burn to ash.

And till you confront this test,
This dying-and-becoming,
You'll only be a dismal guest
at the earth's dim gloaming.

Selige Sehnsucht

Sagt es niemand, nur den Weisen,
Weil die Menge gleich verhöhnet,
Das Lebendge will ich preisen
Das nach Flammentod sich sehnet.

In der Liebesnachte Kühlung,
Die dich zeugte, wo du zeugtest,
Überfällt dich fremde Fühlung
Wenn die stille Kerze leuchtet.

Nicht mehr bleibest du umfangen
In der Finsternis Beschattung,
Und dich reisset neu Verlangen
Auf zu höherer Begattung.

Keine Ferne macht dich schwierig,
Kommst geflogen und gebannt,
Und zuletzt, des Lichts begierig,
Bist du Schmetterling verbrannt.

Und solang du das nich hast,
Dieses: Stirb und werde!
Bist du nur ein trüber Gast
Auf der dunklen Erde.

Translator's comment on Goethe's 'Blessed Longing'
Goethe wrote these stanzas on July 31, 1814, during his flight toward inwardness from that time's outward wars and politics. The poem was included in his *Westöstlicher Divan*, 1819. Only later did he append the last quatrain, with the unexpected irregularity of its two trimeter lines.

The original had appeared earlier and separately under the title 'Vollendung' ('Fulfilment'), perhaps a better title, in *Taschenbuch für Damen*. It was inspired by a German translation of the Persian poet Hafiz, whose version likewise has a burned butterfly (actually moth) and the line "the soul burns like the candle".

The German critic von Loeper called Goethe's lyric "the profoundest of all German poems". Usually labelled "mystical", it also merits the adjective "magical" (in the sense of Keats' "magic casements opening on the foam / Of perilous seas in fairylands forlorn".) The critical debates about its "meaning" obscure its distinguished achievement in sheer aesthetic craftsmanship. By concentrating almost exclusively on its undoubted spirituality, most critics unduly subordinate its powerful sexual carnality. Starting with Eckermann, Goethe's compatriots have been trying to gentrify his true greatness, a conspiracy he himself in the end joined.

This lyric has been called "untranslatable". Certainly this is true of line six. Furthermore, the total effect in English depends on keeping, throughout, as many as feasible of the feminine rhymes, always a challenge in monosyllabic English.

Stefan George
(1868-1933)

A Nietzschean despiser of mass-men, mechanization and modernity, Stefan George was a Rhineland-rooted admirer of French and Hellenic culture. As such, he was morally opposed to the growing Germanic anti-Semitism around him. In 1933, George rejected brusquely the Presidency of the Writers Academy offered him by the Nazis – and left Germany to die in Switzerland. Earlier, his extremely ill-considered use of words like "Führer", intended mostly for his private group of disciples, was often misunderstood as public and political: cf. 'The Anti-Christ' below (from *Der Siebente Ring*, Berlin, 1907). This poem, warning against the holocaust of a false "Reich" and a false Führer, helped inspire the famous assassination attempt against Hitler by George's disciple Claus von Stauffenberg.

George broadened the limits of German diction in two ways: by creating a new poetry that was sometimes as musical as Italian and sometimes as monosyllabic and rugged as English. He also achieved greatness by his translations of Baudelaire, Dante, and Shakespeare. Today his prophet-robes have faded into an art-nouveau period piece, and his cult of master and disciple would strike the Anglo-American sense of humour as preposterous, yet his is the marvellous achievement of almost single-handedly restoring authenticity, austerity, and the dignity of form to German poetry at a time when it fell between the two evils of a slack epigone-romanticism and an arid unimaginative naturalism. Not his cult but his lyricism will appeal to readers today.

I have included, as indicated in the Introduction to this feature, Peter Viereck's translation of 'Templars', also from George's Der Siebente Ring. *Interested readers may like to dig out this translator's earlier version, published in* MPT, *First Series, 21. I have been obliged, for reasons of space, to excerpt drastically from the 'Translator's comment on "Templars"'. This is regrettable since much of the joy of reading Viereck's essays (as with his friend Joseph Brodsky) comes from following where a richly stocked mind leads. [DW]*

The Anti-Christ

"He comes from the mountain, he stands in the grove!
Our own eyes have seen it: the wine that he wove
From water, the corpses he wakens."

O could you but hear it, at midnight my laugh:
My hour is striking; come step in my trap;
Now into my net stream the fishes.

The masses mass madder, both numbskull and sage;
They root up the arbours, they trample the grain;
Make way for the new Resurrected.

I'll do for you everything heaven can do.
A hair-breadth is lacking – your gape too confused
To sense that your senses are stricken.

I make it all facile, the rare and the earned;
Here's something like gold (I create it from dirt)
And something like scent, sap, and spices –

And what the great prophet himself never dared:
The art without sowing to reap out of air
The powers still lying fallow.

The Lord of the Flies is expanding his Reich;
All treasures, all blessings are swelling his might . . .
Down, down with the handful who doubt him!

Cheer louder, you dupes of the ambush of hell;
What's left of life-essence, you squander its spells
And only on doomsday feel paupered.

You'll hang out your tongues, but the trough has been drained;
You'll panic like cattle whose farm is ablaze . . .
And dreadful the blast of the trumpet.

Der Widerchrist

'*Dort kommt er vom berge · dort steht er im hain!*
Wir sahen es selber · er wandelt in wein
Das wasser und spricht mit den toten.'

O könntet ihr hören mein lachen bei nacht:
Nun schlug meine stunde · nun füllt sich das garn ·
Nun strömen die fische zum hamen.

Die weisen die toren – toll wältzt sich das volk ·
Entwurzelt die bäume · zerklittert das korn ·
Macht bahn fur den zug des Erstandnen.

Kein werk ist des himmels das ich euch nicht tu.
Ein haarbreit nur fehlt · und ihr merkt nicht den trug
Mit euren geschlagenen sinnen.

Ich schaff euch für alles was selten und schwer
Das Leichte · ein ding das wie gold ist aus lehm ·
Wie duft ist und saft ist und würze –

Und was sich der grosse profet nicht getraut:
Die kunst ohne roden und säen und baun
Zu saugen gespeicherte kräfte.

Der Fürst des Geziefers verbreitet sein reich
Kein schatz der ihm mangelt · kein gluck das ihm weicht . .
Zu grund mit dem rest der empörer!

Ihr jauchzet · entzückt von dem teuflischen schein ·
Verprasset was blieb von dem früheren seim
Und fühlt erst die not vor dem ende.

Dan hängt ihr die zunge am trocknenden trog ·
Irrt ratlos wie vieh durch den brennenden hof . .
Und schrecklich erschallt die posaune.

Note:
Lines 1 and 2: hain/wein, the only true rhyme; the rest is spoken by Anti-Christ and has false rhymes [PV]

George invented his own typography for his printed works: no capitals for nouns, commas and semicolons replaced by a raised dot.

Translator's comment on 'The Anti-Christ'

Though published in 1907, George's 'Anti-Christ' today seems amazingly prophetic as a warning against Hitler and the flaming end of that twelve-year "thousand-year Reich". George's disciple, Claus von Stauffenberg, leader of the unsuccessful military plot to assassinate Hitler on July 20, 1944, recited this poem to friends before setting off the bomb that wounded the Führer.

A brief word on form. The original metre and rhyme have been retained in my English translation. The meaning here *is* the form (proof that the form is organic, not, as too often, mechanic). The first two lines rhyme, being spoken by the admiring and deceived multitude, to which false and true seem to "rhyme", that is, to coincide. All other opening couplets of all remaining tercets, being spoken not by the multitude but by the Anti-Christ, have a false rhyme (vowel-echo yes, consonant rhyme no); in other words, the Anti-Christ knows what he knows. The author's purpose (not explicit but unmistakably implied): to show that this Führer, ruling what the poem calls his "Reich", is an impostor, separated by what the poem calls "a hair-breadth" from the true redeemer. Without retaining this tacit pervasive rhyme-consciousness (and the onomatopoeia of the accompanying metre, which imitates an almost demagogic breathlessness), the main point of the poem would be lost. So would the main beauty: the treacherous enticing lure (aesthetic Satanism) of richly-vowelled half-rhymes. So much for critics who ask our translations to omit rhyme as "outdated".

Templars

Once merged with all mankind in golden idyll,
For eons now we orbit exile's cycle.
We live two fevers in the same proud fashion:
The rose's passion, and the cross's Passion.

In dark's bleak hush, we tame the weaving talons
Of Norns and tilt the cataclysmic balance.
Our weapons, flagellating crowd and crown,
Thunder a twittering generation down.

Take back your tome of rules, that cardboard anchor.
We shrug your side-glance off, its trustless rancour,
Its hate that turns to panic as it crashes
Against love's exorcizing lightning flashes.

Our gold? – with slash and catapult we plunder
Established trash for our contempt to squander.
Our justice? – while men flee its white-hot anger,
We kneel before an infant in a manger.

That unslicked hair, that arson of the eyes
Which once revealed the lord in rags' disguise
We're veiling from the rabble's pushy homage;
Our shade, not us they deck with showy plumage.

The lap that mothered us was not our mother's.
The loins our heirs will spurt from are another's.
Such stock – adopted sons, adopted sires –
Outlasts, outglows mere copulated fires.

And every brazen deed and every fated
Crossroads is ours alone who consummate it.
"Save us", men beg. We save them. Our reward:
They stone us, shouting "Curse what you have wrought".

When Magna Mater deserts from nurturing
And thirsts exhausted for life's buried spring
In universal night, then only one
Who always fought her and her law of spawn

Can grab her braids, can grip her fingers tight
Until she re-enacts her age-old rite
Where freely she – look quick, where two worlds mesh,
What flesh writhes up from god, what god from flesh?

Templer

Wir eins mit allen nur in goldnem laufe –
Undenkbar lang schied unsre schar der haufe
Wir Rose: innre jugendliche brunst ·
Wir Kreuz: der stolz ertragnen leiden kunst.

Auf unbenannter bahn in karger stille
Drehn wir den speer und drehn die dunkle spille.
In feiger zeit schreckt unsrer waffen loh'n
Wir geisseln volk und schlagen lärm am thron.

Wir folgen nicht den sitten und den spielen
Der andren die voll argwahn nach uns schielen
Und grauen wenn ihr hass nich übermannt
Was unser wilder sturm der liebe bannt.

Was uns als beute fiel von schwert und schleuder
Rinnt achtlos aus den händen der vergeuder
Und deren wut verheerend urteil spie
Vor einem kinde sinken sie ins knie ·

Der augen sprühen und die freie locke
Die einst den herrn verriet im bettelrocke
Verschleiern wir dem dreisten schwarm verschämt
Der unsre schatten erst mit glanz verbrämt.

Wie wir gediehn im schoosse fremder amme:
Ist unser nachwuchs nie aus unsrem stamme –
Nie alternd nie entkräftet nie versprengt
Da ungeborne glut in ihm sich mengt.

Und jede eherne tat und nötige wende:
Nur unser-einer ist der sie vollende –
Zu der man uns in arger wirrsal ruft
Und dann uns steinigt: fluch dem was ihr schuf't!

Und wenn die grosse Nährerin im zorne
Nicht mehr sich mischend neigt am untern borne ·
In einer weltnacht starr und müde pocht:
So kenn nur einer der sie stets befocht

Und zwang und nie verfuhr nach ihrem rechte
Die hand ihr pressen · packen ihre flechte ·

Dass sie ihr werk willfährig wieder treibt:
Den leib vergottet und den gott verleibt.

from **Translator's Comment on 'Templars'**
The Knights Templars, a crusading religious order, were founded 1118-1119 in Jerusalem: to protect pilgrims to the Holy Land. In 1312 Pope Clement suppressed their entire order. They were exterminated by mass killings and burnings at the stake by King Philip lV of France, 1314. Motive: to seize their wealth. He accused them of heresies, conspiracies, Satanic abominations, and sexual perversions (all mostly unproved). Rather than marry and have children, they carried on their secret society via adopted sons, as noted in stanza six. As armed priests, shunning women and bonded to their male Grand Master, their resemblance – hieratic, psychological, erotic – to the George circle is almost embarrassingly self-evident. But the poem triumphantly universalizes the merely personal and quirky. It makes the élitism one of idealistic service, not mere selfish arrogance.

*

The role of the needed outsider, the redeeming outlaw, was always the author's obsession but never so successfully universalized as here. Here the outsider forces the exhausted earth mother to renew her insider role: to heal the body-spirit split. Critics have argued about what kind of outsider George is summoning. Let each reader choose his own outsider archetype . . . [. . .] It enhances the magic of the lines that you can read all or none of these figures into it.

Though it smacks of reductive pop psychology, you can view 'Templars' as an outburst of its author's megalomania. Young George once boasted, "Had I only had a few hundred loyal followers, I would have overthrown every throne in Europe". Reversing Napoleon's "I love power as an artist" ("j'aime le pouvoir comme artiste"), George remarked: "I love art as power" ("j'aime l'art comme pouvoir"). He identified with defeated emperors, not only Napoleon but Heliogabalus. His combination of seeing himself as hated outlaw and beloved saviour shows how personally he meant the "we" of this poem. He might have said of it, like Louis XlV, "l'état c'est moi". But what matters most is what he created out of his Yeatsian "rag-and-bone shop of the heart". Aesthetically supreme is the sheer propulsiveness of its torrential rhythms and the vigour of its images. This may be the greatest as well as most offensive poem in modern German literature.

*

[...] The last line reconciles the sundered halves. "Polarities", in William Blake's phrase, "are positive". And this through the organic growth of life itself, not through a merely mechanical Hegelian logic of thesis-antithesis-synthesis. Life and logic, both indispensable, grow in very different yet parallel ways. Life is biology: a rambling English-style garden. Logic is geometry: a symmetric garden of Le Nôtre at Versailles. At least this is how I see both life and this poem.

How, then, to translate the reconciling last line? Essential: to preserve the unifying repetition of "gott" and "leib" (god and flesh). Literally: to deify the body and embody the *deus* (or embody the divine). But "deus" isn't English, and "divine" is a weak, gushy, arty adjective. Needed instead: a strong monosyllabic noun of exciting physical action. So I have recast the line to make it strong and immediate.

In the third line from the end, "freely" ("willfährig", voluntarily) is an important qualification: the coercion of earth is not violating her nature, her ancient rite, but renewing it: a qualification that may or may not convince the reader. A poem must be read in the context of its time and culture. Modern feminism versus macho coercion, these belong to a valid but later context. Or shall the coercive Templars be a second time burnt at the stake six centuries later, this time the stake of political correctness? [. . .]

*

Though the real Templars were, in their own odd way, Christians, the poem not only distorts and idealizes them; it mixes them with very different religions. The Christ-child reference of stanza four is, to be sure, Christian. But the "dunkle Spille" (dark spool) of line 5 can only refer to the thread of life spun by the three Norns (Fates) of Scandinavian myth. The actual word "Norn" is not used except in my clarifying translation; myth-conscious German readers did not need it. The "spring" of the next to last stanza refers to the Icelandic "Edda" epic. [. . .]

*

Particularly un-Christian is the concluding god embodiment. It is George's interpretation of the Hellenic heritage. By writing "god", not "God", he signalled that he preferred the Greek gods to the monotheistic "God" of his Catholic childhood. Here, as in all his work, the Nietzsche influence is obvious.

*

How relevant is intelligence to poetry? Auden called Tennyson "the stupidest of the great poets". Lyricism makes poetry beautiful; intelligence makes it interesting. Are they compatible? The book *The Seventh Ring* (1907) proves they are. The whole volume, 'Templars' in particular, shows an inventive, form-shaping and idea-spewing intellect, a pinnacle of IQ, whether or not you agree with the ideas (I often don't). Combining traditional forms with daringly unconventional contents, George was one of the most intelligent and also well-educated autodidacts in literature. Hence ever interesting, ever fascinating.

Georg Heym
(1887-1912)

An aesthetically and politically radical co-founder of the German "expressionist" movement, Heym died by drowning in a skating accident at the age of 24. His early poems are mostly worthless, being imitative juvenilia. The poems written in the very few months before his early death are among the most original in the twentieth century and today surprisingly "modern". First forgotten, then rediscovered (after World War II seemed to justify his desperate predictions of doom), Heym has become a leading influence on German literature today.

The younger poet, Heym, was always circling around the older one (George); it was an oscillating orbit because Heym simultaneously imitated George to the point of near-plagiarism and detested him, a classic instance of a love-hate relationship to one's literary father. While denouncing George at literary cafés as a reactionary "corpse", Heym secretly (as I discovered) tried to get acceptance into the élitist George circle.

Both poets incarnate the moment of transition from French-influenced "symbolism" to revolutionary German "expressionism", although George is usually classified only as a symbolist and Heym only as an expressionist.

In Germany the post-war Heym cult has produced more studies than anyone would want or need to read. Mostly they overstress his supposed "prophecy" (which may have been coincidence and is irrelevant to his aesthetic genius) of World War I.

After which it seems problematical to be presenting Peter Viereck's translation of Heym's poem 'War' (September, 1911), a posthumously found draft, rather than some other poem! I take responsibility for so doing. [DW]

War

Risen is the sleeper from the vaulted past,
Risen from deep under and returned at last.
Huge and strange he looms there, in the twilight mist,
And he snuffs the moon out with a coal-black fist.

Cities teem with hubbub of the thickening dusk,
Frost and shadow swaddled in an alien husk;
Street-sounds of the markets halt their rounds and freeze.
Silence now. And no man knows, yet each man sees.

People in the alleys feel him on their trail.
Questions. And no answers. Faces turning pale.
Swinging in the distance, bells are whining thin.
Every beard is trembling on its pointed chin.

He's begun his *danse macabre* where the hilltops arch,
And he's screaming: "All you soldiers, forward march."
Listen to the pounding of his swart brow's pulse;
That jangling is his necklace of a thousand skulls.

Tower-tall he lumbers from the sun's last ray;
Bloody torrents follow on the heels of day.
Countless are the corpses that the swamp has spilt;
Droppings of the death-bird are their last white quilt.

> [Here three first-draft stanzas, partly in illegible handwriting and partly repetitious in effect, have been omitted. PV]

Forest after forest feeds the flaming jaws;
Yellow bats of arson flex their zigzag claws.
Like a furnace helot, he hacks his poker deep,
Stoking up the embers to their wildest leap.

Hurtling without outcry into nightmare's gut,
Metropolis is choking on its own pale soot.
Over glowing rubble he gives a giant lurch;
Through frantic skies he three times waves his torch, –

Mirrored in the hurricane of mangled clouds,
In the dead cold desert of the midnight shrouds.
Night itself dries up beneath his farflung fire;
Sodom has collapsed upon its funeral pyre.

Der Krieg I

Aufgestanden ist er, welcher lange schlief,
Aufgestanden unten aus Gewölben tief.
In der Dämmrung steht er, gross und unerkannt,
Und den Mond zerdrückt er in der schwarzen Hand.

In den Abendlarm der Städte fällt es weit,
Frost und Schatten einer fremden Dunkelheit,
Und der Märkte runder Wirbel stockt zu Eis.
Es wird still. Sie sehn sich um. Und keiner weiss.

In den Gassen fasst es ihre Schulter leicht.
Eine Frage. Keine Antwort. Ein Gesicht erbleicht.
In der Ferne (wimmert) ein Geläute dünn
Und die Bärte zittern um ihr spitzes Kinn.

Auf den Bergen hebt er schon zu tanzen an
Und er schreit: Ihr Krieger alle, auf und an.
Und es schallet, wenn das schwarze Haupt er schwenkt,
Drum von tausend Schädeln laute Kette hängt.

Einem Turm gleich tritt er aus die letzte Glut,
Wo der Tag flieht, sind die Ströme schon voll Blut.
Zahllos sind die Leichen schon im Schilf gestreckt,
Von des Todes starken Vögeln weiss bedeckt.

[...]

Und die Flammen fressen brennend Wald um Wald,
Gelbe Fledermäuse zackig in das Laub gekrallt.
Seine Stange haut er wie ein Köhlerknecht
In die Bäume, dass das Feuer brause recht.

Eine grosse Stadt versank in gelbem Rauch,
Warf sich lautlos in des Abgrunds Bauch.
Aber riesig über glühnden Trümmern steht
Der in wilde Himmel dreimal seine Fackel dreht,

Über sturmzerfetzter Wolken Widerschein,
In des toten Dunkels kalte Wüstenein,
Dass er mit dem Brande weit die Nacht verdorr,
Pech und Feuer träufet unten auf Gomorrh.

Translator's comment on 'War'

How odd, and what a lesson to "realists", that the most truly realistic description of World War II – say, of the destruction of Coventry, Rotterdam, Dresden – was written not at the time but back in 1911. The slow caesura'd rhythm of Heym's embodied "War", lumbering along as if it were not a human but a Frankenstein robot walking, is suited perfectly to its macabre subject, namely to the impersonality of the mass-killing Heym foresaw, just as George – also during 1911-1913 – foresaw it in his 'Cleansing Doom' poem; in both cases, with the same hypnotized fascination.

Here the duplication in English of Heym's rhythms has been the transplanter's main endeavour, if only because nothing is so challenging as the impossible. In these four months before his death at 24, Heym became the greatest master since Hölderlin of rhythm orchestration (exceeding even his secret model, Stefan George). Of all Heym's poems, 'War' was the hardest to translate. This is because most of its lines can be simultaneously scanned as six-beat and four-beat. Of the six accents in each line, the second and fourth are usually so much fainter than the other accents that they can be slurred over so as to make it a four-beat line. The result – no other poem in all literature is quite like it – is that the six-beat foreground is gradually overwhelmed by an ominous four-beat droning in the background, which by its very monotony produces not boredom but cumulative horror. This ambiguity of rhythm is (if the poem is seen aesthetically rather than prophetically) the whole point of the German original; accordingly the transplanter has tried to retain the same ambiguity of four-beat versus six-beat in English, with the same slurred faintness of accents 2 and 4 and the same hammering stress upon accents 1, 3, 5, 6, with every opening foot an aggressive trochee.

Final Vigil

How dark the veins of your temples;
Heavy, heavy your hands.
Deaf to my voice, already
In sealed-off lands?

Under the light that flickers
You are so mournful and old;
And your lips are talons
Clenched in a cruel mould.

Silence is coming tomorrow
And possibly underway

The last rustle of garlands,
The first air of decay.

Later the nights will follow
Emptier year by year.
Here where your head lay, and gently
Ever your breathing was near.

Letzte Wache

Wie dunkel sind deine Schläfen
Und deine Hände so schwer,
Bist du schon weit von dannen
Und hörst mich nicht mehr?

Unter dem flackenden Lichte
Bist du so traurig und alt,
Und deine Lippen sind grausam
In ewiger Starre gekrallt.

Morgen schon ist hier das Schweigen
Und vielleicht in der Luft
Noch das Rascheln von Kränzen
Und ein verwesender Duft.

Aber die Nächte werden
Leerer nun, Jahr um Jahr.
Hier, wo dein Haupt lag, und leise
Immer dein Atem war.

Here follow some excerpts from Peter Viereck's major essay, 'Ogling through Ice: the Sullen Lyricism of Georg Heym', published in Books Abroad, *April 1971. 'Final Vigil' is included in this essay. The version of the translation printed above is a revision of that originally printed in* Books Abroad. *It is followed by a Translator's Note, with a subtle analysis of the translational decisions taken. I have, perhaps mistakenly, excerpted from the first rather than the last, more technical part of this essay . . . [DW]*

Though typical of Heym in craftsmanship, 'Final Vigil' is untypical in subject matter. Its subject is an individual death. His other poems more often deal with mass doom. They parade a veritable menagerie of morgues, suicides, madmen, hanged criminals, deaf men, blind women, and some choice somnambulists worthy of Dr Caligari. Heym records his doomed parades not through direct observation but through a shimmer of sinister "Fun House" reflections. It was still a cosy warm world in 1912, but he photographed it through a cold blue lens, as if already ogling up from under the ice that drowned him.

Heym's treatment of death is often delicate and hushed. For example, his Ophelia elegy, not to mention 'Final Vigil'. Yet even more frequent is what we must call the lurid Heym. His more lurid poems of death teeter on the edge of silliness. They include, depending upon which way they teeter, his best and worst writing.

*

We believe that Heym's rhythmic originality (which our translation endeavours partly to convey) is so considerable that no other German or English poet can, on that score, be compared with him . . . [. . .] However, in his never static, always propulsive metaphors Heym does have one equivalent in American letters and one in British letters: Hart Crane [. . .] and the South African Roy Campbell. As an epitaph for the breakneck gallop of Heym's imagery, we may cite a line from Campbell: "stunned by his own expenditure of force." In all three poets, metaphor loses autonomy and becomes a subtopic under the category "rhythm". In all three, the rhythms are emphatically preferable to their surface message (meaning by "surface" their mere ideological rather than emotional insights). By such a preference are we falling into the formalist trap of selling content short? Such is certainly not the intention. The intention is simply to keep content in perspective. This seems a needed corrective in the special case of Heym, whose lurid surface-content has been disproportionately emphasized by both his followers and detractors.

Sometimes one oversimplifies for clarity. Some oversimplifications seems justified, some not. In the oversimplified distinction above, between form and content, it must not be forgotten that content is able to form and that form is able to contain. The oversimplified distinction does seem at least partly justified in the exceptional case of Heym's way of coping with more emotion than words can bear. No hermetic aestheticism: we are not saying, "Look only at his form, look only at his rhythms". We are saying, his rhythms are relatively unoriginal and unilluminating – though valuable in other ways: namely intellectually exciting, metaphorically dynamic, stimulating to the nerve ends but not to the core. [. . .]

*

[...] It is worth learning German just in order to savour Heym's swollen, magical two-syllable rhymes – and then forgetting German again so as to savour a music unencumbered by message. He wrote more feebly as he became fastidious and mature; the "Old Wordsworth" disaster waited just around the corner and waited in vain.

This selection concludes with Peter Viereck's transplantation of Pushkin's tiny poem 'On The Hills of Georgia', referred to by him, in his 'Translator's Comment on Goethe's "Wanderer's Night Song"', as, along with the Goethe poem, "the simplest great poem in history". It seems to me appropriate to end with a poem and also to recall Peter Viereck's dedication to Russian as well as German culture. We are, in any case, only two years past Pushkin's bicentenary, which was commemorated in MPT 15 with a 'Pushkin Portfolio'. As with Brodsky, Peter Viereck's contribution comes to us late but no less welcome! Having myself attempted a translation of this lyric, I appreciate in particular Viereck's manipulation of the rhyme scheme, allowing him to give the poem's aphoristic pathos, dare I say it, an additional charge. Pushkin's text alternates feminine and masculine rhymes, a/b/a/b/c/d/c/d. Here is a literal prose version of the poem: "On the hills of Georgia lies a nocturnal mist, / The Aragva roars/ stirs before me. / I am sad and easy/light: my sorrow is bright, / My sorrow is filled with you, / With you, with you alone... My dejection / Nothing torments, troubles, / and the heart again burns and loves – because / It cannot not love." Now Viereck. [DW]

After Pushkin's 'On the Hills of Georgia'

Night over Georgia; mist across the heights.
Before me, the Aragva ripples off.
Only my chained and prancing heart's distress
Remains intense, a pain so filled with you –
Totally you – that all its darkness lights.
How can I help, combustible anew,
But live in love, even a bitter love? –
Being powerless to live in lovelessness.

Review

Seamus Heaney, *Beowulf: A New Translation*
London: Faber and Faber, New York: Farrar, Straus & Giroux, 1999
Also in *The Norton Anthology of English Literature*,
New York: Norton, 2000.

RM Liuzza, *Beowulf: A New Verse Translation*
Peterborough, Ontario: Broadview Press, 2000.

Seamus Heaney has long displayed sympathy for the language and poetry of Anglo-Saxon times. He strips bare the layers in 'Bone Dreams' in his collection *North* (1975):

> Bone-house:
> a skeleton
> in the tongue's
> old dungeons.
>
> I push back
> through dictions,
> Elizabethan canopies.
> Norman devices,
>
> the erotic mayflowers
> of Provence
> and the ivied latins
> of churchmen
>
> to the scop's
> twang, the iron
> flash of consonants
> cleaving the line.
>
> In the coffered
> riches of grammar
> and declensions
> I found *ban-hus*,

its fire, benches,
wattle and rafters,
where the soul
fluttered a while

in the roofspace.

Here an Old English kenning for the body sparks new life, stirred by Bede's famous sparrow, while the whole collection brims with modern-day kennings, i.e. compound words containing a compressed image, like the *skull-ware* of the Bog Queen, or the *oak-bone, brain-firkin* of the garrotted bog woman, or Hercules as the *sky-born, snake-choker, dung-heaver*. In that collection, Heaney demonstrated how northern mythology and turbulent northern history could resonate with a contemporary landscape of violence. Throughout his poetry, a sparseness of line, a concrete quality, and a love of heavy-consonanted monosyllables ('the iron/ flash of consonants/ cleaving the line') have made Heaney's poems resonate with Anglo-Saxon poetic technique. In such ways, he has long been borrowing from the Old English tradition; now he returns the favour by translating the most famous of Old English poems, *Beowulf*, and the pay-back is handsome.

Heaney's sureness of touch is evident from the very opening:

So. The Spear-Danes in days gone by
and the kings who ruled them had courage and greatness.
We have heard of those princes' heroic campaigns.

There was Shield Sheafson, scourge of many tribes,
a wrecker of mead-benches, rampaging among foes.
This terror of the hall-troops had come far.
A foundling to start with, he would flourish later on
as his powers waxed and his worth was proved.
In the end each clan on the outlying coasts
beyond the whale-road had to yield to him
and begin to pay tribute. That was one good king.

Heaney's choice of a four-stress line unified through alliteration and with the hint of a caesura clearly conjures the form of the Old English verse line without holding closely to its stricter conventions. Such a choice is broadly characteristic of many *Beowulf* translations. What is most distinctive here is the freedom Heaney gives himself in tackling Old English syntax, which is so heavily accretive and appositional that it has led many translators to bog down in a mire of grammar words and dangling clauses as they chase the will o' the wisp of closeness to the original.

Take another recently published translation of the poem, this one by RM Liuzza. Liuzza is an academic Anglo-Saxonist with years of teaching *Beowulf* and numerous essays on the poem to his credit. His translation provides a perfect counter-example to Heaney's, even in this opening:

> Listen! We have heard of the glory in bygone days
> of the folk-kings of the spear-Danes,
> how those noble lords did lofty deeds.
>   Often Scyld Scefing seized the mead-benches
> from many tribes, troops of enemies,
> struck fear into earls. Though he first was
> found a waif, he awaited solace for that –
> he grew under heaven and prospered in honor
> until every one of the encircling nations
> over the whale's-riding had to obey him,
> grant him tribute. That was a good king!

Liuzza has adopted the same formal constraints as Heaney: a four-stress line, a caesura, and (mild) alliteration. His version is much closer to the Old English, particularly in syntax, but therein lies the problem. In the original, the first three lines read:

> Hwæt! We Gar-Dena   in geardagum
> þeodcyninga   þrym gefrunon,
> hu ða æþelingas   ellen fremedon.

As an inflected language, Old English signals clearly that *þrym*, 'glory', is the object of the opening verb, *gefrunon*, while *þeodcyninga* is a genitive dependent on *þrym*, and *Gar-dena* is either a further dependent noun in apposition or qualifies *þeodcyninga*. Liuzza's translation retains this perfectly, even replicating the mild ambiguity ('glory of the folk-kings from among the spear-Danes' or 'glory of both the folk-kings and the spear-Danes'). Yet the Old English does all this with economy and punch. Liuzza's repeated 'of the' sounds ponderous by comparison, no matter how accurate. His semantic closeness is also a problem: *fremedon* in the third line means *did*, but it probably did not sound as enervated as the modern verb does. And the things we have heard that they did, *þrym* and *ellen*, are reasonably glossed by Liuzza's 'glory' and 'lofty deeds', except that the Old English words packed a far heftier punch with none of the hint of embarrassment that accrues to 'glory' in the world of poetry after Wilfred Owen or the stiffness of 'lofty deeds'.

How, then, might that more forceful effect be conveyed? Heaney uses two words to do the work of *ellen* – 'courage and greatness' – which between them give a straightforward and unironized sense of assertiveness. *þrym* becomes 'heroic campaigns', again more assertive, this time because more specific. The *þeodcyninga* have become 'the kings who ruled them', a more comprehensible relation than the literal 'folk-kings'. Heaney switches round the verbs and alters the syntax, saving the 'we have heard' to act as main verb in a second sentence, thereby staying true to Modern English's imperative to signal relationships with a subject-verb-object word order. Liuzza translates the 14 words of the Old English sentence with 25 words, Heaney with 26, yet Heaney's two sentences and avoidance of a concatenation of grammatical words makes for the more vigorous and economical-sounding translation. Heaney's relative freedom produces something more powerfully compelling and therefore, paradoxically, closer to the effect of the Old English.

The same is true for the treatment of variation in the next lines. Again, Liuzza's version stays very close to the movement of the Old English: 'from many tribes, troops of enemies' reproduces precisely the Old English technique of variation in these lines (*sceaþena þreatum/ monegum mægþum*). Heaney reproduces the effect rather than the specifics, varying a sequence of parallel descriptive epithets which get across the idea of the Old English while remaining natural to a Modern English ear ('scourge of many tribes, a wrecker of mead-benches' was 'rampaging among foes'). Heaney stays close to the content of the lines but not so close to the wording as to falsify the voice of his own verse.

Of course, such choices reflect an age-old conundrum for translators, articulated in English as early as King Alfred (reigned 871-899), who claimed that his translations from Latin proceeded 'hwilum word be worde, hwilum andgit of andgiete', 'sometimes word for word, sometimes sense by sense'. It is surprising to what extent an attempt at word for word translation, i.e. closeness to syntax and to detail, has been the tradition in translations of *Beowulf* for most of the last century. Charles W Kennedy's translation from 1940, kept alive through its reproduction in the Oxford Anthology of English literature (*Medieval English Literature*, ed. JB Trapp), opens:

> Lo! we have listened to many a lay
> Of the Spear-Danes' fame, their splendor of old,
> Their mighty princes, and martial deeds!

Variation is in full play, encouraged by the single main verb, creating a listing effect that results in anticlimax. Michael Alexander (*Beowulf: A Verse Translation*, Penguin, 1973) begins:

> Attend!
> We have heard of the thriving of the throne of Denmark,

> how the folk-kings flourished in former days,
> how those royal athelings earned that glory,

for a translation that manages to take liberties, use archaisms and overly-close glosses ('folk-kings', 'athelings') and still sound tiresomely grammatical. SAJ Bradley's prose translation from 1982, common in Old English courses because of the scope of the volume in which it is published (Everyman's *Anglo-Saxon Poetry* contains almost the whole corpus in translation), opens:

> Listen! We have heard report of the majesty of the people's kings of the spear-wielding Danes in days of old: truly, those princes accomplished deeds of courage!

The turgid triple 'of the' phrases, with two more *of*s lurking later in the sentence, introduce immediately the slough of grammatical detail within which this translation will remain enmired.

Such close translations have been standard perhaps because of the apparent closeness of Old English to Modern English, although the differences in syntax and semantic resonance have already been suggested. The result, to my ear, has been a tradition of unreadable or of lame *Beowulf* translations that, for all their closeness to the poem, always fail to capture any of the excitement of the original or hint why it might be interesting to read the Old English version. This is a tradition I am delighted to see bucked in such style by Heaney.

Not that Heaney chooses to make his language entirely and straightforwardly accessible to the average reader. He eschews archaisms that spring from over-close translation, but includes a striking array of unfamiliar words: *bawn* (a fortified enclosure), *brehon* (judge), *bothies* (huts), and *wean* (*wee ane*, a young child) all derive from Celtic originals. Another cluster of unfamiliar words derive from Old English and became obsolete in standard English but survived in dialectal usage, particularly in the north, such as *tholed* (suffered), *graith* (war-gear), *reek* (smoke). Still others are dialect words of obscure origin, such as *stook* (bundle), *keshes* (crags?), and *hoked* (hollowed out). It is striking how many of these words are heavy-consonanted monosyllables ('the iron/ flash of consonants/ cleaving the line' again). The effect of such vocabulary on most readers, I suspect, is to keep the reader conscious that the work is, indeed, something old and strange. For a particular locality such words are apparently familiar: Heaney talks in his introduction about how his acquaintance with the verb *thole* in the Ulster dialect of his family gave him a point of entry to the language of the Anglo-Saxons (which might otherwise be thought Anglo-Saxon in the more restricted sense of White Anglo-Saxon Protestant). He also talks of how his own writing consciously broke away from seeing a clashing nationalist opposition between Irish and Anglo-Saxon into a more creative synthesis, 'into some unpartitioned linguistic country, a region where one's language would not be simply a badge of ethnicity or a matter of cultural preference or an official imposition, but an entry into further language'. His use of Ulster dialect words in an Anglo-Saxon epic is part of that rapprochement.

The opening word of the poem encapsulates the challenge of translation in miniature. *Hwæt!* is a traditional opening of Old English poems and a conjurer of attention in Old English prose. It is hard to translate because interjections have become so quaint in Modern English as to sound either farcical or maudlin (or both): Lo! Ah! Oh! Indeed! Liuzza's 'Listen!' is probably as close as uncolloquial English comes to the effect. Heaney's 'So' is so much more forceful because it conjures his story-telling voice, suggesting in his Ulster dialect that a story is about to begin so you'd better pay attention and that there'll be consequences in that story – all things implied by Old English *hwæt*. This particular translation choice is also discussed by Heaney in his introduction. He explains that he has adopted for the poem the 'big-voiced' language of his Ulster Catholic family: 'in that idiom "so" operates as an expression that obliterates all previous discourse and narrative, and at the same time functions as an exclamation calling for immediate attention. So, "so" it was.'

So, Heaney has a voice for translating the epic, but how does he do with the story? *Beowulf* is, at core, an account of action, of a hero fighting three monsters – a fact that any interpretation ignores at its peril ever since Tolkien's famous essay from 1936 – and Heaney is good with this action. The *Beowulf*-poet gives considerable space to each of the fights, describing them in attentive detail, as when the hero and the audience first view Grendel in action. The scene is translated closely by Liuzza:

> he seized at once at his first pass
> a sleeping man, slit him open suddenly,
> bit into his joints, drank the blood from his veins,
> gobbled his flesh in gobbets, and soon
> had completely devoured that dead man,
> feet and fingertips (740-45a).

This is a heightened moment of terror in the original (nicely and emphatically paced in Benjamin Bagby's oral performance of the poem), with the unusual use of rhyme ('slat unwearnum, / bat banlocan, blod edrum dranc', 741b-742) and that rapacious rhythm is captured by Liuzza's 'gobbled his flesh in gobbets'. Heaney maintains a more measured pace, albeit with an onomatopœically shaved-down penultimate line:

> he grabbed and mauled a man on his bench,
> bit into his bone-lappings, bolted down his blood
> and gorged on him in lumps, leaving the body
> utterly lifeless, eaten up
> hand and foot.

Here the vocabulary is appropriately revolting, with a particularly striking kenning for *banlocan* (glossed by Mitchell and Robinson as 'bone-lock, (i.e. joint)'), namely 'bone-lappings'. The heavily-consonanted monosyllables work to good purpose and join the strong alliteration to replicate the *Beowulf*-poet's *tour de force*. Characteristically, Heaney does not just achieve the occasional good phrase but maintains his effect consistently over the sentence.

Some of the lustre of Heaney's translation comes from his handling of weapons, where the Old English word-hoard was clearly more expansive than what is available to a modern translator. Heaney explicitly begs off close translation of terms for weapons or battles in his introduction, claiming that he cannot match the multitude of words in the poem: 'Old English abounds in vigorous, evocative and specifically poetic words for these things, but I have tended to follow modern usage and in the main have called a sword a sword'. Nevertheless, weapons are given the heft they deserve. Hrunting, the important sword given by Unferth which is not up to the business of Grendel's Mother, is a 'wave-patterned sword, / hard-edged, splendid' in Liuzza's close rendering, but a 'sharp-honed, wave-sheened wonderblade' in Heaney, which gets across the (sharpened) point. In the Finnsburh Episode, Heaney brings to life the word for the sword that at a crucial moment passes from the son of Hunlaf to Hengest, 'hildeleoman/ billa selest' (1143b-44a), 'a glinting sword, / the best of battle-flames' in Liuzza's perfectly reasonable translation, '*Dazzle-the-Duel, the best sword of all*' in Heaney's bold reanimation of the kenning as sword name.

In speaking of kennings in his introduction, Heaney remarks 'I try to match the poet's analogy-seeking habit at its most original' and he is predictably good at this throughout. The *fægne flæschoman* of Grendel's Mother (literally 'the doomed flesh-garment') becomes 'the doomed/ house of her flesh'. The *banhus* of Heaney's reflections in 'Bone Dreams' is rendered simply as 'bone-house', while *bancofa* (glossed by Mitchell and Robinson as 'bone chamber (i.e. body)') becomes 'the bone-cage of his body'.

But there is more to *Beowulf* than the series of fights undertaken by its hero. For a start, there is a lot more fighting beyond the central action, which helps create the dark tone that pervades most of the poem, a tone often called elegiac. For example, when Beowulf has disposed of Grendel and all would appear happy in Denmark, a poet tells a story at the celebratory feast about an earlier Danish engagement among the Frisians in which nobody looks very glorious. This story, known as the *Finnsburh Episode*, is introduced by the Old English poet through the doomed figure of Hildeburh, wife of the Frisian leader Finn and sister of the Danish visitor Hnæf, who cannot turn out a winner since both her brother and her son have died fighting, but on opposite sides. Heaney's verse becomes heightened here through a depressing spareness of line:

> Hildeburh
>   had little cause
> to credit the Jutes:
>   son and brother,
> she lost them both
>   on the battlefield.
> She, bereft
>   and blameless, they
> foredoomed, cut down
>   and spear-gored. She,
> the woman in shock,
>   waylaid by grief,
> Hoc's daughter –
>   how could she not
> lament her fate
>   when morning came
> and the light broke
>   on her murdered dears? (34-35)

The fractured lines emphasize the lament and pained non-understanding. Heaney's telling of the whole story matches the bleakness of the original.

This elegiac tone becomes particularly prominent in the last third of the poem. Two famous moments play such sadness to the full – the lament of the last survivor of his race who buries the treasure now useless to him that will become the dragon's hoard (2247-66) and the lament of a father for a dead son judicially hanged (2444-62a) – and both are *tours de force* in Heaney's translation. The last survivor laments the absence of the joys of the heroic life:

>   'No trembling harp,
> no tuned timber, no tumbling hawk
> swerving through the hall, no swift horse
> pawing the courtyard. Pillage and slaughter
> have emptied the earth of entire peoples.'

Here, unusually, Heaney makes his emotive point through a series of qualifiers – trembling, tuned, tumbling, swift – and through forceful verbs suggesting action now denied – the swerving of the hawk, the pawing of the horse. The right tone is established for the last survivor's demise ('death's flood/ brimmed up in his heart') and a bleakness is associated with that treasure hoard.

Even when things are going well in this poem there is a spirit of doom lurking. *Beowulf*'s most characteristic movement is an insistence on *edwenden*, 'reversal', usually figured as an awareness of impending doom that will undercut even the most celebratory moments of the narrative. So, when Hrothgar is on the rise and has the glorious hall Heorot built, the poet cannot resist inscribing within its building a hint of the hall's impending destruction:

> The hall towered,
> its gables wide and high and awaiting
> a barbarous burning. That doom abided,
> but in time it would come: the killer instinct
> unleashed among in-laws, the blood-lust rampant.

Blood-lust rampant is very much the point: even if the precise details of this encounter are murky (Beowulf predicts a conflict between Hrothgar and his son-in-law Ingeld in his report-back to Hygelac), the moral of the interruption lies in that killer instinct, the blood-lust rampant, an idea the Old English poet can convey with the compounds *ecghete*, '[sword-]edge hatred' and *wælniðe*, 'slaughter-hostility', more literally but less informatively translated in Liuzza's

> The hall towered
> high and horn-gabled – it awaited hostile fires,
> the surges of war; it was not yet long
> before the sword-hate of sworn in-laws
> should arise after ruthless violence. (82-85)

Liuzza's close translation of the temporal markers for the shift in fortunes makes for an awkwardness overcome by Heaney's explicit rearrangement: 'That doom abided,/ but in time it would come'.

The Old English poet is fond of expressing this pattern of reversal with an economy that can't be matched in Modern English. Heaney anticipates the ever-present doom, the suggestion that something is rotten in the state of Denmark, with pleasing simplicity in his use of adverbs.

> The Shielding nation
> was not yet familiar with feud and betrayal,

the poet observes, where the word *yet* does plentiful work; or, at a moment of Wealhtheow's exercise of *realpolitik*,

> and Wealhtheow came to sit
> in her gold crown betwen two good men,
> uncle and nephew, each one of whom
> still trusted the other,

in which that *still* hangs in the air over any accommodation the queen can suggest. Again, in Hrothgar's so-called sermon, Hrothgar holds up his own case as a moral for the young Beowulf, calling attention with that problematic *hwæt*:

> Hwæt, me þæs on eþle   edwenden cwom,
> gyrn æfter gomene (1774-75)

translated emphatically if not quite idiomatically by Liuzza:

> Look! Turnabout came in my own homeland,
> grief after gladness

and more quietly but effectively by Heaney:

> Still, what happened was a hard reversal
> from bliss to grief.

In *Beowulf*, the movement 'from bliss to grief' is very much the point.

While the poem may be doom-ridden in its implications, it is not consistently decorous in its bleak tone. Indeed, the original includes a strand of (mostly dark) humour, that is a challenge for the translator to match. For example, part of the horror of Grendel's ravaging of Heorot is his disregard of the feuding system and the poet grimly jokes on the retainers' inability to receive *wergild*, the appropriate compensation in place of revenge:

> nor did any of the counselors need to expect
> bright compensation from the killer's hands,

as Liuzza suggests, with a note about the *wergild* system. Heaney offers:

> No counsellor could ever expect
> fair reparation from those rabid hands,

where the shift from description of monstrous action to the counsellors' expectation for normalcy hints at the joke without needing a footnote, and where the decorum of *reparation* is clearly incongruous beside the lack of control suggested by *rabid*. Subsequently, as Beowulf makes his defiant speech in front of Hrothgar, he briefly engages the possibility of losing and being carried off by Grendel, an unsettling possibility that he allays through macabre humour nicely retained by Heaney:

> 'Then my face won't be there
> to be covered in death . . .
>   No need then
> to lament for long or lay out my body;'

no need, indeed, since the body won't be there.

> 'Fate goes ever as fate must'

concludes the hero with gnomic pithiness appropriately captured by Heaney and rather ducked by Liuzza's '*Wyrd* always goes as it must!'

Heaney does not rise to all the comic moments, though. In a particularly clear-cut case, when the retainers reach the terrible mere of the Grendels, one of the Geats kills a water-monster with an arrow. The Old English poet provides a laboured joke, captured by Liuzza:

> he was a slower swimmer
> on the waves, when death took him away. (1435-36)

An Old English tradition of understatement allows a listener no doubt what is at stake in such tardiness of motion, yet the literal sense creates a comic incongruity, a joke in keeping with the laboured death of a creature defined in a nearby kenning in relation to his motion as a *wægbora* (1440, Liuzza gives 'wave-roamer'). Heaney presumably finds the joke distracting and its underpinnings untranslatable and so gives a straight version:

> his freedom in the water
> got less and less. It was his last swim.

This spells out the point even as it refrains from attempting the tone of the original.

A more serious moment of comedy is also underplayed by Heaney.

When Grendel's Mother surprises the Danes with her revenge attack, Beowulf knows nothing of the calamity when he is summoned by a newly-grieving Hrothgar. As he breezes in, his enquiry about how Hrothgar slept is a *faux pas* in the newly-serious circumstances, picked up by a distraught Hrothgar. Beowulf

> asked him whether
> the night had been agreeable, after his urgent summons.
> Hrothgar spoke, protector of the Scyldings:
> 'Ask not of joys! Sorrow is renewed
> for the Danish people. Æschere is dead' (1318-23)

in Liuzza's translation. The humour depends on realizing the incongruity of *agreeable* beside *urgent summons*, as does the Old English in contrasting *getæse* with *neodlaðu*, a unique compound presumably coined for the occasion. Heaney makes the exchange more forceful by playing a single word across Beowulf's blunder and Hrothgar's grief. Beowulf enters:

> asking if he'd rested,
> since the urgent summons had come as a surprise.
>
> Then Hrothgar, the Shieldings' helmet, spoke:
> 'Rest? What is rest? Sorrow has returned.
> Alas for the Danes! Æschere is dead.' (44)

As often, Heaney provides more clarity than the original with that explanatory conjunction ('since') and makes explicit the echo across the speeches ('rested'/'rest'). The effect here is to make Beowulf sound a little more in control than the Old English poet allows him to be. Heaney's statement of the grief of Hrothgar (strikingly named 'the Shieldings' helmet' as in the Old English 'helm Scyldinga') is forceful in its pithiness and in that way matches the original. In other words, Heaney is being as effective as ever here in getting across the poet's main thrust but, since Old and Modern English have different ways, he is forced to sacrifice the comic nuances that the Old English poet can play even in a predominantly serious scene.

The balance within *Beowulf* of a celebratory but elegiac world is matched by the balance with which the poet places his characters in a pagan world viewed from a Christian perspective, an apparent dichotomy about which the poet seems to worry very little. In summing up the fate of Beowulf, the poet observes:

> Famous for his deeds
> a warrior may be, but it remains a mystery

where his life will end, when he may no longer
dwell in the mead-hall among his own,

suggesting a pagan viewpoint, which is kept in balance by Wiglaf's anachronistic-sounding memorial that Beowulf will lodge 'for a long time in the care of the Almighty'. Such a balance is retained in the famous final lines, which Heaney renders:

They said that of all the kings upon the earth
he was the man most gracious and fair-minded,
kindest to his people and keenest to win fame,

where public opinion mostly reflects neutral or Christian values (gracious, fair and kind) until that final word, *lofgeornost*, turns back to an economy of heroism where the lasting memorial depends upon the story-telling potential achieved through a life's reputation.

Beowulf himself makes a strong statement of heroic values earlier in the poem. After he has committed his little gaffe in asking about Hrothgar's night's sleep, and after Hrothgar has expressed his sorrow, Beowulf reestablishes verbal control with a strong assertion:

'Ne sorga, snotor guma.   Selre bið æghwæm
þæt he his freond wrece   þonne he fela murne',   (1383-4)

which is rendered by Liuzza:

'Sorrow not, wise one! It is always better
to avenge one's friend than to mourn overmuch.'

The Old English here is particularly forceful and concise. Part of the effect is achieved by the parallel yet contrasting verbs in the second line which are balanced through placement and through grammatical rhyme and yet are antithetical in content ('he... wrece/ he... murne'); part is achieved through the appeal to a gnomic voice expressed through an impersonal generalizing ('selre bið æghwæm') which, nevertheless, keeps an active agent in the following clause ('he... he') – literally 'Do not sorrow, wise man. It is better for each one that he avenge his friend than that he mourn much'. Heaney gives:

Wise sir, do not grieve. It is always better
to avenge dear ones than to indulge in mourning,

where the slight assonance of *avenge/indulge* matches the balanced grammatical rhyme of *wrece/murne*, and where the lexical choice 'dear ones' for 'his freond' avoids the pitfall of a false cognate and extends the generalized wisdom. Still the utterance is not as forceful as in Old English and the impersonal voice does not allow an active agent in the second line. Heaney continues building effects as the speech continues:

> For every one of us, living in this world
> means waiting for our end. Let whoever can
> win glory before death. When a warrior is gone,
> that will be his best and only bulwark.

'Glory before death' has much of the climactic weight of the forcefully straightforward original, 'domes ær deaþe'. On the other hand, 'bulwark' may represent a heavy-consonant too many, suggesting a solidity not apparent in the original.

So, Heaney's translation presents a dazzling success, yet even Heaney's version lacks some of the poetic force and misses some of the tone of the original – inevitably, of course, since Old English and Modern English have different ways. Heaney's is the best translation available and as such deserves its place in the Norton Anthology. Here is a translation that makes for a coherent and exciting reading in Modern English and that achieves a music of its own. If a reader is tempted to turn from this to the Old English poem itself, Liuzza's volume might serve well as a bridge. Heaney includes a judicious and very readable introduction to the poem (in the Faber volume), but this is inevitably quite brief. Liuzza provides a more extensive if still concise introduction, which will bring a reader up to speed on the major critical issues surrounding the poem. Liuzza also provides a number of useful appendices including, most valuably, a wonderful collection of analogues to the poem, many newly translated. Gathered together here are the remaining Old English heroic fragments, such as *The Fight at Finnsburg* and *Widsith*; the obvious Norse analogues for the major action of the poem, including the parallel monster fight from *Grettissaga*; and a number of Latin and Old English contexts for understanding the balance between Christianity and paganism or Old English attitudes towards Danes, including a generous selection from the leading churchmen of the time of the *Beowulf*-manuscript, Ælfric and Wulfstan. Liuzza's translation, if somewhat heavy-going as an independent work, would serve well as a crib to the original poem. And the serious student of the poem can now approach that original with relative ease in the newly-standard edition by Bruce Mitchell and Fred C Robinson, *Beowulf: An Edition* (Blackwell, 1998).

Still, while I may hope (as a professional Anglo-Saxonist) that Heaney's translation will bring enthusiasts flocking to read Old English in the original and to discover the rest of the Old English wordhoard, its most important function will be to give readers with no knowledge of Old English a taste of the vitality and complexity and music of the poem *Beowulf*. To do that, it was necessary to create a gripping epic that, while as true as possible to the original, works in the modern language to entertain, to challenge, and to amaze modern readers. Heaney has done that and it is an accomplishment well worthy of the Whitbread Prize. Once again, as is narrated once in the poem:

> a carrier of tales,
> a traditional singer deeply schooled
> in the lore of the past, linked a new theme
> to a strict metre. The man started
> to recite with skill, rehearsing Beowulf's
> triumphs and feats in well-fashioned lines,
> entwining his words.

Jonathan Wilcox

Review

Dionysios Solomos, *The Free Besieged and other poems*,
Translated by Peter Thompson, Roderick Beaton,
Peter Colaclides, Michael Green and David Ricks
Edited with an introduction by Peter Mackridge
Shoestring Press, 2000

The collection brings together a selection of poems by Greece's national poet, Dionysios Solomos (1798-1857). The study of European Romanticism may find in Solomos' case an exponent of German thought and a cultivated verse informed both by the Greek tradition of fifteen-syllable verse, folk songs, and by poets such as Novalis and Dante. Educated in Italy, he studied law and spent his mature years in Corfu. He was a contemporary of Manzoni, Hugo and Heine, and some parallels can be drawn between elements of his compositions and poetry by Coleridge. A number of his poems make reference to Missolonghi, the place where Byron died and which is connected to uprisings and resistance to Turkish sieges. He took the sufferings and afflictions of these people as his subject matter. His work, unlike that of other poets, remained incomplete and unpublished. The lyrical character of certain parts of his compositions suggests a remarkable expressivity – this is some of the best verse written in Greek. Nature and freedom, death and religion, love, anger and fascination structure the recurrent themes of Solomos' poems. His contact with German philosophy and poetry was by means of Italian translation. Bicultural and bilingual Solomos composed his first conception of each poem in Italian, and then proceeded to work the verses up in Greek. 'The Cretan' (translated by Roderick Beaton) appears to refer to a survivor from Crete who left the island having lost all his family in the uprisings against the Turks. The narrator of the poem deals with time and eternity, loss and memory. In the case of 'Free Besieged' (translated by Peter Thompson), Solomos worked on various versions between 1833 and 1847. The poem refers to events in Missolonghi and is set during the last days of the siege. It has been argued that the poem represents the triumph of the human spirit over physical adversity. 'The Woman of Zakynthos' (1826-1833; translated by Michael Green and Peter Colaclides) is here presented as a poem in numbered verses. The narrator is a certain Hieromonk (priest-monk) Dionysios. The work is considered an allegory, more of a satire *à clef*. The poem 'Shark' (translated by David Ricks) is based on a real event. In 1847 a young soldier from the British garrison in Corfu was killed by a shark. In the poem the swimmer experiences a mystical union with the universe followed by his own death. 'Carmen Saeculare' (translated by Roderick Beaton) was written in both Italian and Greek. Interpreters of this poem have associated it with theosophy and notions of art. The Greek poet's work was published by his friends who assisted the main editor Polylas in the first posthumous publication of Solomos' poetry. The present collection makes use of different editions of the poems. And the introduction by Peter Mackridge discusses Solomos' work in the context of European Romanticism, the practices followed by other editors of the poet's work (published in Greek) and instances of bilingualism. The selection brings together some established translations of poems by Solomos and could be very useful in discussing aspects of European Romanticism, in comparative contexts. In a broader context the volume could be of interest to those studying intellectual movements in the nineteenth century, because Solomos, like many of his contemporaries, showed an interest in the creative sciences of his time (including psychology) which is clearly reflected in the poems published in this volume. His choice of diction and the refined lyricism of the best of his poems that have reached us through single verses, together with various fragments indicative of the poet's attempts to restylize existing versions in Greek according to his preferred mode of composition, suggest that Solomos continued experimenting with his versification and rhythmical prose throughout his years of poetry writing. This constant process of finding a poetic language and a voice in Greek in a dialogue with other languages and poetry traditions may bring Solomos in line with our modern sensibilities in respect of intertexts and enigmatic narratives.

Marianna Spanaki
University of Birmingham

Books Received

We receive more books than we can adequately review. The alphabetical list below mentions those publications that we think will be of interest to our readers.

Abdullah al-Udhari, ed. *Classical Poems by Arab Women.*
Saqi Books, 1999. ISBN 0 86356 047 4 *(Bilingual ed.)*
(Poems by Andalusian women poets, translated by al-Udhari from Arabic and Hebrew, appeared in MPT *14 – Palestinian and Israeli Poets, which also featured Amichai.)*

Yehuda Amichai, *Selected Poems.*
Edited by Ted Hughes and Daniel Weissbort. Various translators.
Faber, 2000. ISBN 0 571 20457 0

Werner Aspenström, *The Wind Itself: Selected Poems.*
Translated by Robin Young.
Planet, 1999. ISBN 0 9505188 6 7

Tahar Bekri, *Unknown Seasons: Selected Poems.*
Translated by Patrick Williamson, Barbara Beck, George Ellenbogen and John Taylor.
L'Harmattan, 1999. ISBN 2 7384 8444 1 *(Bilingual ed.)*
(Three poems by Tahar Bekri translated by Williamson appeared in MPT *16.)*

Guillevic, *Carnac.*
Translated by John Montague. Introduction by Stephen Romer.
Bloodaxe, 1999. ISBN 01 85224 393 7 *(Bilingual ed.)*
(Readers may like to compare this version with Robert Chandler's, which appeared in MPT *8, 1995.)*

Edvard Kocbek, *Embers in the House of Night.*
Translated from the Slovene by Sonja Kravanja.
Lumen Books, 1999. ISBN 0 930829 42 5

Jules Laforgue, *Poems.*
Translated by Peter Dale.
Anvil Press, 2001. ISBN 0 85646 322 1 *(Revised bilingual ed.)*

Valerio Magrelli, *The Contagion of Matter.*
Translated by Anthony Molino.
Holmes and Meier, 2000. ISBN 0 8419 1400 1 *(Bilingual ed.)*

Eugenio Montale, *The Coastguard's House*.
English versions by Jeremy Reed.
Bloodaxe, 1990. ISBN 1 85224 100

Eugenio Montale, *Satura: 1962-1970*.
Translated by William Arrowsmith.
Norton, 2000. ISBN 0 393 04647 8

Evgeny Rein, *Selected Poems*.
Translated by Robert Reid, Daniel Weissbort, Carol Rumens/Yuri
Drobyshev, Paul Partington. Edited by Valentina Polukhina.
Foreword by Joseph Brodsky.
Bloodaxe, 2001. ISBN 1 85224 523 9 *(Bilingual ed.)*

The Poems of Sulpicia.
Translated by John Heath-Stubbs.
2nd. ed., 2000. ISBN 1 870841 75 1
(Available from Hearing Eye, 99 Torriano Avenue, London NW5 2RX, at £4.00 – a dozen pages of pure delight, and *the original Latin text.)*

Georg Trakl, *Poems and Prose*.
Translated by Alexander Stillmark.
Libris, 2001. ISBN 1 870352 718 *(Bilingual ed.)*
(Stillmark's versions of poems by Trakl appeared in MPT *8 and 16.)*

Tarjei Vesaas, *Through Naked Branches: Selected Poems*.
Translated by Roger Greenwald.
Princeton University Press, 2000. ISBN 0 691 00897 3
(Two poems from this collection appeared in MPT *16.)*

François Villon, *Poems*.
Translated by Peter Dale.
Anvil, 2001. ISBN 0 85646 323 X *(Revised bilingual ed.)*

Mountain River: Vietnamese Poetry from the Wars, 1948-1993.
Edited by Kevin Bowen, Nguyen Ba Chung and Bruce Weigl.
University of Massachusetts Press, 1998. ISBN 1 55849 141 4
(49 poets; bilingual ed.)

The Redbeck Anthology of British South Asian Poetry.
Edited by Debjani Chatterjee.
Redbeck Press, 2000. ISBN 0 946980 76 4
(74 poets, several of whom appeared in MPT *17, Mother Tongues.)*

In the Grip of Strange Thoughts: Russian Poetry in a New Era.
Edited by J Kates. Various translators.
Bloodaxe, 1999. ISBN 1 85224 478 X *(Bilingual ed.)*

Looking for the Cow: Modern Korean poems.
Edited and translated by Kevin O'Rourke.
Dedalus Press, 1999. ISBN 1 901233 51 0 *(72 poets.)*

New Swiss Romand Poets.
Translated by Patrick Williamson.
The Chariton Review, Vol 25, No 1 (Spring 1999). ISSN 0098-9452
(21 poets.)

Step-Mother Tongue: from nationalism to multiculturalism: Literatures of Cyprus, Greece and Turkey.
Ed. Mehmet Yashin.
Middlesex University Press, 2000. *(Essays, and an anthology of poems from the 9th to the 20th century.)*

Joseph P Clancy, *Other Words: Essays on Poetry and Translation.*
University of Wales Press, 1999. ISBN 0 7083 1554 2
(Includes many translations of Welsh poems, with discussion that deals with the general problems of translation much more extensively than was possible in Clancy's contribution to MPT*'s Welsh issue, No 7, 1995.)*

AN INTERNATIONAL MAGAZINE FOR LOVERS OF POETRY

Contemporary Poetry, Poets from the Past,
Guest Interviews, Poetry Related Articles,
Young Poets, Reviews

We publish quality poetry in English
or translated into English
with parallel text where appropriate.

We accept submissions of poetry, but no more than six, and it is advisable to see a copy of the magazine before sending your work. Back issues are available for £4 from the address below. We welcome ideas for articles, reviews and books to review. Please note we do not necessarily want poetry about Greece, although we welcome all submissions. Subscriptions for three issues per year are £16 in Europe (we accept sterling, dollars and drachmas).

More details of the magazine can be found on our website:
http://users.otenet.gr/~wendyhol/poetry_greece/

For further information contact:
Poetry Greece, Mitropolitou Athanasiou 10, 3rd Parodos,
Corfu 49100, Greece
Tel/Fax: 0030 661 47990
e-mail: poetrygreece@hotmail.com